CHAVASSE — DOUBLE VC

CHAVASSE
— DOUBLE VC

by
ANN CLAYTON

With a Foreword by the Bishop of Liverpool

LEO COOPER

London

For all those
who
grew not old

First published in Great Britain in 1992 by
LEO COOPER
190 Shaftesbury Avenue, London WC2H 8JL
an imprint of
Pen & Sword Books Ltd,
47 Church Street, Barnsley, South Yorkshire S70 2AS

Copyright © Ann Clayton, 1992

ISBN 0 85052 296 X

A CIP catalogue record for this book is available
from the British Library

Typeset by Yorkshire Web, Barnsley, South Yorkshire
in Plantin 10 point

Printed by
Redwood Press Limited
Melksham, Wiltshire

CONTENTS

ACKNOWLEDGEMENTS

Leafing through the annual magazine of Liverpool College one day in 1989, I realized for the first time that Noel Chavasse was one of the school's most famous Old Boys. A few days later, in Liverpool Cathedral, though I must have passed it hundreds of times, I noticed the carved memorial to Bishop Francis James Chavasse, founder of the building. The two facts came together in my mind in an instant that I can still recall. From that moment my search for Noel Chavasse's story and its realization in this book were inevitable.

From the very beginning of my research I have received the most generous and unstinting help, from individuals and from organizations, that any author could wish for.

Firstly, I owe an enormous debt to the Chavasse family; to Edgar Chavasse, whose enthusiastic response to my early tentative enquiries about his uncle Noel was the means of opening many doors. He first pointed me in the direction of the archive of Noel's letters and other family papers held in the Bodleian Library in Oxford; he read the typescript and made many valuable suggestions, and allowed me to peruse and quote from his father Bernard's papers. He and his wife Helen entertained me at their home, responding with a keen interest to my questions. A similar welcome was accorded me by Mr and Mrs John Chavasse in Oxford, where I was allowed access to many of his father Christopher's volumes of family photographs and boxes of papers, and to the papers of his aunts May and Marjorie, and by Miss Lois Foster-Carter in Yorkshire, who lent me documents and photographs relating to her mother, Noel's sister Dorothea.

In Birmingham, the Reverend Paul Chavasse's great interest in his family's history produced for me a family tree and several further contacts, as well as clearing up some of those little mysteries that appear in every family's background. His suggestions led to an important and hitherto untapped family archive in Worcestershire, and my thanks are especially due to Jeremy Quinney and his wife for their hospitality and for allowing me to borrow some of the most poignant material that any biographer could hope to find.

Other members of the Chavasse family who gave willingly of their time to answer my questions included Mrs M. Holder and Mrs G. McCracken; a distant relative by marriage is Captain Charles Upham, VC and Bar, and his wife Molly was kind enough to respond from New Zealand to my enquiry.

Librarians, archivists and curators deserve particular acknowledgement for their sympathetic and ungrudging assistance at every stage of the groundwork, and my thanks are due to the following individuals and institutions for their help and for allowing me to quote from manuscript and other material in their possession: the Master of St Peter's College, Oxford; Clare Hopkins, archivist at Trinity College, Oxford; Stephen Tomlinson of the Department of Western Manuscripts, Bodleian Library, Oxford; Magdalen College School, Oxford; the Liverpool Scottish Archive and Museum, Forbes House, Liverpool, the Commanding Officer, curators Denis Reeves and David Evans, and Mr A. Vick of the Regimental Association; Derek Crook of the Liverpool Medical Institution; the Headmaster and Board of Governors of Liverpool College; Adrian Allan, Archivist at the University of Liverpool; Janet Smith and her staff at the Local Record Office, Liverpool; Colonel Hibkin and Major Tanner of 208 General Hospital (V), RAMC, Chavasse House, Liverpool; Staff at RAMC, Millbank; Lieutenant-Colonel R. Eyeions of the RAMC Museum, Ash Vale; Regimental Secretary, the King's Regiment, Liverpool; Shirley Taylor of the Wellcome Institute for the History of Medicine; Peter Liddle, Keeper of the Liddle Collection at the University of Leeds; staffs of the Departments of Documents and of Photographs at the Imperial War Museum; the Commonwealth War Graves Commission, especially Stuart Walker; the Dean and Chapter of Liverpool Cathedral, and Peter Kennerley, Custos and Education Officer; Howard Lovell, Parish Clerk at St John's, Bromsgrove; staff at Bromsgrove Public Library; Birmingham City Libraries; Liverpool City Libraries; Librarians of the University of Liverpool, especially those of the School of Education, housed at No.19 Abercromby Square; staff at the Liverpool Polytechnic Library, especially at my own School in the Trueman Street Building; Peter Gray of the King's Regiment Archive at National Museums and Galleries on Merseyside, and Chris Lawlor of Liverpool Town Hall.

The encouragement and support of a large number of individuals has been much appreciated. They include Peter Stott of Liverpool College, who has always had a special interest in Noel Chavasse; Commander Ray Grist, Major Walter Clarke, Curtis Robb, Mr H. L. Lomax and Alex Service; also, many colleagues at the Liverpool Polytechnic, especially Jack Williams and Paul Hodgkinson, and Steve Lawler, to whom I am much indebted for his photographic and reprographic expertise. I have been equally sustained by the continuing interest of students of the Liverpool Polytechnic, both past and present.

I must mention specially two men who both knew and remembered Noel

Chavasse: the late Mr. H. S. Taylor, a Great War veteran of the Liverpool Scottish, who served with the 'Doc', and Robert Eager, who remembers as a child being operated upon by Noel Chavasse. It was a pleasure and a privilege to learn about Noel from their first-hand experience.

Someone who knew Bishop Christopher M. Chavasse and Mrs Gladys Colquhoun (née Chavasse) personally was Canon Selwyn Gummer, author of *The Chavasse Twins*, and I am grateful for his kindness in answering my queries.

Many readers of the *Liverpool Echo* responded to my appeals for information, and I thank them for their interest: George Powell, Mr Humphreys, Mr Hayes, Miss Margaret Chalmers, Mr Elder, Mr R. Roberts, Mr E. Hardisty, Arthur Thomas, Mr Parr, Mr I. McFadzean, Mr James, Mrs F. Albu, Mrs M. McKee and Mr and Mrs P. Taylor.

Last but by no means least, the contribution made by fellow members of the Western Front Association was of such importance that without it this book would probably not have seen the light of day. They include Ray Westlake, who was always ready to encourage my efforts and answer my questions and who helped enormously with the photographs; also Gerald Glidden, Terry Cave, Dave Ashwin, Bob Wyatt, Aleks Desayne, Graham Parker and his daughter Joanna, Bertie Whitmore, Graham Maddocks, Fraser Williams, Teddy and Tony Noyes, Frank Bond, Chris Everitt, Steve Wall, Colin Kilgour, Colin McIntyre, Ken Williams, John Bailey and many others.

Naturally my greatest debt is to my husband Peter, who always believed in the book and contributed many ideas for its development, and to my children Diane and David, who must have thought at times that their mother had taken root at her Amstrad. This book is for them, and for *my* mother, who would have loved to read it.

FOREWORD
By The Rt Rev. David Sheppard
The Bishop of Liverpool

The Roll of Honour at the Cenotaph in Liverpool Cathedral lists the names of nearly forty thousand servicemen from Merseyside who lost their lives in the First World War. One entry above all others attracts the attention of visitors and that is the name of Noel Chavasse, VC and Bar, MC. The extraordinary devotion and gallantry of this man, one of the twin sons of Francis James Chavasse, Bishop of Liverpool, has caught the attention of thousands of people though they may have known little about him apart from the brief account of the last days of his life as recorded in the official citation.

Many books have been written about the gallantry of men at the front in the Great War but Ann Clayton's work has a unique quality because she has been able to draw upon the extensive archives of the remarkable Chavasse family. Painstakingly she has examined the boxes of letters in the Bodleian Library; she has had access to family photographs and she has spoken with many members of the family. With sensitivity she has presented her account of the life and death of a great man and his remarkable family.

The resulting book is more than a vivid account of slaughter in Flanders. Though Noel's life is central to the work, it is also a revelation of the responses of his family to the horrors of war and their personal loss. Ann Clayton has marshalled her materials with meticulous scholarship and human sensitivity; the result is a memorable book which cannot fail to make a powerful impact on the thoughtful reader.

David Liverpool.

January 1992

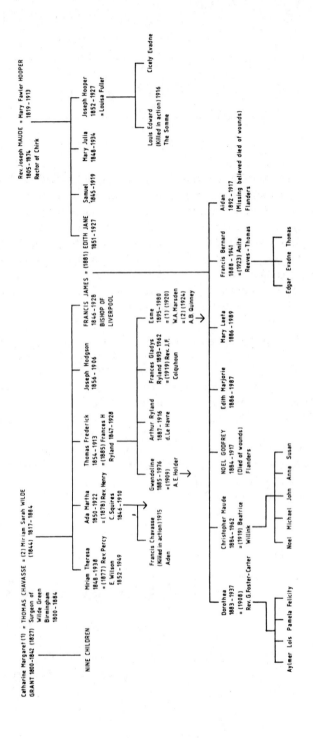

CHAVASSE and MAUDE FAMILY TREES

CHAPTER 1

Beginnings

Sunday 9 November, 1884, was a dark and dismal day in Oxford; as the trees dripped and bells summoned worshippers to morning prayer, there was feverish activity in the three-storeyed house at the end of a terrace in New Inn Hall Street. At last, just as the belfry of the church opposite fell silent to signal the start of matins, life began for the twin sons of the Reverend Francis James Chavasse and his wife Edith. While his wife rested, Mr Chavasse hurried across to church and sat in his pew in the chancel with a bemused smile on his face, a smile that broadened when Psalm 45 was announced:

> Instead of thy fathers shall be thy children, whom thou mayest make princes in all the earth.[1]

In church on the following Wednesday, the text of the sermon was from Ecclesiastes, chapter 4, verses 9 and 10:

> Two are better than one; because they have a good reward for their labour. For if they fall, the one will lift up his fellow: but woe to him that is alone when he falleth; for he hath not another to help him up.[2]

These most appropriate sentences were to follow the twins throughout their lives.

Born at Wylde Green House, Sutton Coldfield, on 27 September, 1846, Francis James Chavasse was descended from a French Roman Catholic who had arrived in England during the early years of the eighteenth century and had involved himself in the 1715 Jacobite Rebellion. Within two generations the family had been converted to Protestantism. Both his grandfather, Nicholas Willett Chavasse (1763-1818), and his father, Thomas Chavasse (1800-1884), were surgeons, and most other male members of the family entered the Church, the Army or the Inns of Court. So it was no surprise to the family that Francis James, despite early thoughts of medicine or a military career, chose to be ordained in the Church of England after finishing his education at Corpus Christi College, Oxford. Ordained in 1870, his first clerical post was as curate of St Paul's, Preston. Three and a half years later he became Vicar of the Church of St Paul, Upper Holloway, London, from 1873 to 1878. He then occupied the position of Rector of St Peter-le-Bailey in Oxford, having already been offered two other livings in the town.[3]

Delighted to be back in Oxford, he took up residence at Number 36 New Inn Hall Street, only a stone's throw from the little church of St Peter-le-Bailey opposite. The house was bought for him by his father and the household consisted of himself, his sister Miriam in the role of housekeeper and a couple of servants. As in every position he held during his life, he gave his full attention to his work; he was hardly ever absent from Oxford, except to visit his favourite brother Thomas Frederick, who was eight years his junior and was practising medicine in London. Francis James ('Frank' to the family) worked so hard that his flock sent him a gift of money with a letter expressing concern about 'how visibly your health is failing':

> [We] most affectionately beg of you to accept the accompanying and to use it in recruiting your strength... Only let your people know that you intend taking a holiday of at least 6 weeks, somewhere that perfect rest and quiet may be obtained. Might we venture to suggest the Continent?[4]

Thus it was that he made his first and last excursion outside the confines of the British Isles — to Switzerland with Thomas, in July 1880. They were both still bachelors.

Frank held Low Church views, perhaps better described as evangelical. He was always utterly convinced that his views were the right ones, and that he was given the strength and eloquence to persuade others to his way of thinking by a God who could likewise never make a mistake. If others managed through argument to change his mind, that must be God's will. Consequently, while he was a devoted pastor and much loved teacher, he was never slow to criticise clerics whose opinions clashed with his. This conviction that the right path lay clearly before him and that all he had to do was listen to his conscience and obey, was to be passed on to his seven children, and to the hundreds of young clerics who came to him to be prepared for ordination.

Small of stature, no more than five feet three inches tall, and hunchbacked due to complications following an attack of measles when he was a child at boarding school,[5] he was easily hurt by remarks about his physique. He nevertheless had a genuine sense of humour, his face lit up when he laughed and he could play a joke as well as anyone. In his youth he often went dancing, once falling down with his partner and vowing never to dance again. He tried skating, rowing and shooting, but strongly disapproved of the theatre and smoking. Two things offended him above all others: excessive indulgence in alcohol (he had himself become a total abstainer in 1871[6]) and anything that might reduce the respect due to women as wives and mothers.

Frank thought he would never marry. As he pointed out on more than one occasion, there were three things against him: not only was he a hunchback but he stammered and he was poor.[7] However, in 1880 he met Edith Jane Maude, daughter of the late Joseph Maude, Vicar of Chirk in Denbighshire. Since her father's death in 1874, Edith had lived with her mother and her sister in a rambling old house, Pen Dyffryn at Overton-on-Dee near Wrexham. A God-fearing and compassionate woman, Edith took a great interest in missionary work, and came to Oxford to seek Mr Chavasse's advice about the education of a Chirk missionary's daughter who had been left behind in England while her parents were in India.

On 27 September, 1881, his thirty-fifth birthday, Frank married Edith at her parish church in Overton. She was thirty years old. Solemn and thoughtful, with looks that some might call plain, and possessed of only a modicum of humour, she took her duties as the Rector's wife very seriously, even though parish occasions that thrust her into the public gaze were burdensome to someone of her retiring nature. However, she ran her household with great efficiency, and also with great kindness towards both servants and visitors, which was long remembered by any who crossed her path. She held the post of deputy organist at St Peter's and ran girls' Bible classes and mothers' meetings.

Soon the house in New Inn Hall Street began to fill with children. The first arrival was Dorothea, born on 13 February, 1883. The following year was one of great sadness for Frank because both of his parents died within months of each other, but on 9 November two more children were born to his wife. They were twin sons, christened Christopher Maude (the elder by twenty minutes) and Noel Godfrey.

So small and weak were they that their christening was delayed until 29 December, when they were baptized in the font at St Peter-le-Bailey by their father. It was believed at the time that they were named after two Oxford clerics, the Low Church Canon Christopher of St Aldate's and the Anglo-Catholic Father Noel, but it seems just as likely that the names were chosen due to the proximity of Christmas. Within the next year, the twins barely lived through an attack of typhoid, and their parents had them photographed in case they did not recover — the illness cost their father almost all of his savings of ninety pounds.[8] But survive they did, as alike as two peas in a pod and dressed in identical clothes (skirts for their first few years, as was the custom of the times) to be joined on 29 August, 1886, by twin girls, Edith Marjorie and Mary Laeta, known to the family as Marjorie and May. Unlike Noel and Christopher, the girls were not identical. The troop of nursemaids taking five children under the age of four for walks in the Oxford Parks in their perambulators caused no little local comment and amusement.

Frank's brother Thomas became Senior Surgeon at Birmingham General Hospital, and after his marriage to Frances Hannah Ryland in 1885 he moved into her parents' house, The Linthurst Hill at Barnt Green near Bromsgrove. Frank, with his wife and family, was a frequent visitor from Oxford.

During his years as Rector, the church and parish of St Peter-le-Bailey welcomed many young ordinands who came to sit at the feet of Frank Chavasse, now achieving a modest fame for his teaching and worship. With a growing family too, the Rectory was becoming overcrowded and the top floor was extended into the house next door which had formerly been inhabited by the churchwarden. But soon shortage of space ceased to be a problem. In 1889 Frank was promoted, in recognition of his pedagogic skills, to be Principal of Wycliffe Hall. He generously gave the house at 36 New Inn Hall Street, free of rent, for use as the St Peter-le-Bailey Children's Home.[9]

Situated at numbers 52 and 54 Banbury Road, close to the famous Parks, Wycliffe Hall consisted of two substantial houses, one for the students who were resident at the college to prepare for ordination in the Church of England, and one for the Principal's residence. The space and freedom available for the Chavasse children in the large gardens and adjoining Parks were put to good use. For sheer inventiveness the schemes and games of the young Chavasses would be hard to surpass, from waging a war against the student body, complete with strategic plans and diplomatic communications, to writing books and poetry, illustrated and circulated by themselves.[10]

Soon after the move to Wycliffe Hall, two more children were added to the family. Francis Bernard was born on 2 December, 1889, and Aidan arrived on 26 July, 1891. Returning to St Peter-le-Bailey for their baptisms, the family of seven children was now complete.

There is no doubt that Frank Chavasse's time at Wycliffe Hall was enormously successful. From the twelve or so students who were there when he arrived, the number grew to thirty-six before he left, with a corresponding expansion in accommodation taking place in 1896, when a new kitchen and bedroom wing was opened.[11]

Within a year of arriving at Wycliffe Hall, Frank Chavasse was invited to become Suffragan Bishop of Exeter, with the title of Bishop of Crediton,[12] and in 1891 the Marquess of Salisbury offered him the Deanery of Chichester,[13] but both proposals were refused. The Principal of the Hall had much work still to do in Oxford, and he was only forty-five years old.

The education of the children was placed in the hands of a governess and a tutor until Noel and Christopher were twelve years old. Then, while the three girls and the two youngest boys stayed at home, the twins became day boys at the famous Magdalen College School. Founded in 1480, the school accommodated about a hundred boys, half of them boarders, and was noted for its musical and choir training (the young Ivor Novello gained a place there in 1903). Noel and Christopher travelled the mile and a half to school each day on bicycles, passing along St Giles, the Broad, Turl Street and the High, where the illustrious old college buildings of Balliol, Brasenose, Trinity and Magdalen became day by day more familiar. Oxford was always the place they loved best on earth, and in the trenches during the Great War they were to remember with longing its tranquil streets and spires.

Neither of the boys was particularly receptive to academic work at first, but they excelled on the sports field and the athletics track. This showed in Noel's school reports:

Summer Term, 1897
English: Good except spelling.
Form Master: Rather an imp of mischief. When he settles down to his work he can do quite well.

Autumn Term, 1897
French: Naturally weak as a beginner, but I think he might have tried more.
Form Master: Has lost ground naturally through interrupted work, but more so through inattention and carelessness. He is far too much interested in other boys' mischief. I hope that next term he will steady down and try to take his proper place in the form.[14]

The form master writing these reports was Mr W. E. Sherwood, who became a much-respected friend and kept in touch with Noel and Christopher for many years after they had left the School.

As they neared the end of their time at MCS, however, their academic standing improved. As Noel wrote to his grandmother:

I am writing this letter on the last day of the holidays, and on next (black) Monday I begin the 'trials and troubles of this wicked life'. Next term is the Mathematical term and as Chris and I are the best boys in the form for Euclid and Algebra we hope that one of us may get a prize. Contrary to our expectations Chris and I have had good reports and I have got a prize for Science, besides having a 'most excellent' in my report for the same subject.[15]

Noel frequently lost time at school due to illness, as his reports indicated, but he was still able, together with his brother, to win a good number of athletics 'pots' or trophies. His special ability was in distance running, and he won the half-mile; Chris was not far behind but also performed well in athletics events, especially the long jump.[16] They appear to have done no training, simply turning out on sports days and doing their best. Neither boy was at all striking in physique, being below average height for their age and social class and tending to carry more weight than an athlete would today.

During the long school holidays, at least one extended visit would be made each year to Grannie Maude at Pen Dyffryn. From the age of five, Noel wrote to her describing their adventures at home, illustrating his letters with little drawings and paintings. These letters unwittingly portray the happy family life that gave all of the Chavasse children an extraordinary emotional strength upon which to draw in their adult years. After Christmas 1891, for instance, he wrote to his grandmother thanking her for 'all the nise presents' (sic) and adding this lively depiction of the family festivities:

> On Christmas day we had stockings and all went to Church in the morning, and after dinner we went into the drawing-room to have dessert. After tea we had Snapdragon. Little Bernard came down and was very pleased with the 'pretty fire'. We could not have Christingles for there was not time, but we are going to have them before the New Year. I made a little pair of cuffs for Bernard, and Christie knitted a little jacket for Aidan to wear when he goes out. On Bank Holiday, Father took us down to have a slide on the ice in the Park Meadow because the floods were out — if there comes some more frost, we are to have some skates.[17]

One of Noel's letters leaves no doubt as to his inventiveness and determination, as remarkable at the age of seven as it was in the Great War at the age of thirty:

> We are building a hothouse but not a real one for we could not do it; first we said we would put hot water pipes but Mother said that would not do for in real hothouses people have a fire in a stove so I thought we would make a fireplace and in summer we would have some hot water pipes and no fire and we are not going

6

to do it for it is not big enough, and we are going to make a windmill.[18]

Mrs Mary Fawler Maude was their only living grandparent; consequently, they became very close to her. Strongly Christian and Anglican, she was the celebrated author of several hymns, the best-known being *Thine for ever, God of love*. She was a delightful companion and correspondent herself and the children loved their holidays with her. Living in the heart of the Welsh border country, she and her daughter, Aunt Mary, had a pony and trap in which excursions were taken for picnics or sightseeing, and their house was surrounded by acres of fields and woods, with streams to dam and rivers to fish. On one of these visits, in 1897, Noel's difficulties with spelling are obvious. He wrote home to his mother in Oxford:

> We are having very nice times here indeed. Yesterday being wet we went and had a picnic tea at the Cocoa House and afterwards played bagatelle with Auntie, and now Grannie and Auntie have paid 4d. so that we can go and play whenever we want to. Christie and I made a little sledge and harnessed Warick [sic; a pony] to it and he trotted all over the place, we were going to harness Don [another pony] too only Grannie thought that he would not like it, and might get fearce [sic]. Today we went and got some hay with Roberts and have been raging about the whole afternoon in the loft and with the football or dogs. (We might not go into the woods as the keepers were shooting.) Please remember to send the cammerer [sic] and hamper.[19]

The spelling capabilities of 'Christie' were no better but the twins both grew up able to write an excellent letter, full of interesting detail and thoughtful judgements. Noel's ready wit, which could amuse his reader even in the dark days of the Great War, was already in evidence:

> We went to Church yesterday. There was no organ and Mr Unwin started a hymn. The hymn was a decided failure, except that we were enchanted by a duet sung by Mr Unwin and Auntie... In the valley, I practised bleating like the lambs and to my gratification was answered by some of the sheep (those who had not their children by then).[20]

Other holidays were taken on the North Wales coast near Harlech. Here Noel had a close encounter with death when one of their daredevil games went awry and he was nearly buried alive in the sand.[21]

More excitement could be found on visits to their father's brother, Uncle Tom, and his wife Aunt Frances at Barnt Green. Aunt Frances's parents were now dead, and she and her husband had The Linthurst Hill to themselves, together with their four children. The eldest was Gwendolen, born in 1885, then in 1887 came the only son and heir, Arthur Ryland; after a five-year gap Gladys was born in 1893 and Esme in 1896. At Barnt Green, where the house stood in extensive grounds adjacent to farmland, the cousins could play tennis, go haymaking or ride, for Uncle Tom was a keen huntsman and kept a large stable of horses and ponies. Not that the children had any structured riding lessons — Noel had to be taught to ride properly, as befitted an officer, by a cooperative sergeant during the early days of war in 1914.

As the twins grew into their teens they seemed to become more and more alike and even those who knew them best found it hard to tell them apart. Noel had a slightly longer chin, but schoolmasters and others outside the family found this of little help. They were ordered to wear ties of different colours at school, but as they habitually swapped clothes this was of no use either. In addition, they were developing that close spiritual affinity for which twins are renowned, suffering pain at the same time as each other, and even once being accused of cheating in a test because they had made identical mistakes.[22] This closeness was to increase during their lives, much more so than in the case of their non-identical twin sisters, Marjorie and May. In games such as tennis, May and Noel would line up opposite to Marjorie and Chris, but in most family activities all seven children were equally involved. Indeed, the family was to a large extent self-sufficient and had no need of external attachments. This may help to account for the absence of friends of the opposite sex in the lives of both Chris and Noel; their closest female friends, until death in Noel's case, were in fact their cousins from Barnt Green. May and Marjorie, while leading active lives with many social contacts, never married.

Relationships between the children and their parents were close, particularly as the young Chavasses grew old enough to converse and argue with their father. Their mother doted upon them, especially on the youngest, Aidan. Many years later Marjorie Chavasse remembered her father as 'a personage far beyond criticism':

> What he said must be right. This may have been partly from the respect my mother always felt for him and her deep love — while he had the same respect and love for her. Looking back I can never remember any sort of cross word between them and there was an atmosphere of calm and integrity in the house, which we took as a matter of course. He rarely took us to task, and if he

did it was devastating. While we lived in Oxford we did not see a great deal of him in term time as he breakfasted and dined in the Hall, but in the vacations he would read aloud to us after lunch. He was a lover of Kipling and particularly enjoyed 'The Jungle Books'.... I always thought of my father as a very brave man, for on two occasions when we had intruders in our garden he seized a stick and sallied into the garden to send them off.[23]

It was a sad day for the younger members of the Chavasse family when they realized that their idyllic years in Oxford must come to an end. On 3 March, 1900, their father received an offer of such preferment within the Church of England that he could hardly refuse it, though he apparently doubted his suitability for the post. A letter arrived from the Prime Minister, Lord Salisbury:

> The Queen has given me her permission to ask you whether you will accept a nomination to the See of Liverpool which is vacant on the resignation of Bishop Ryle. I have strong reasons to believe that your nomination will be satisfactory to the people of Liverpool as well as valuable to the Church, and I do not doubt that the field of action will be sympathetic to yourself.[24]

Having talked it over with his wife, who supported him absolutely in whatever he wished to undertake, and with several friends, Frank Chavasse called a family conference at Wycliffe Lodge to discuss the momentous move. He had visited Liverpool only once before, as a young man of nineteen on his way to the Isle of Man for a holiday in 1865, when he wrote in his diary:

> Liverpool itself, at least what we saw of it, seemed a nice town. The Mersey rather disappointed me. It is certainly a noble estuary, but I did not see so much shipping as I expected. The porters at the pier chiselled us out of a shilling simply for carrying our luggage down a few steps.[25]

He was not deterred by these first impressions, however, and replied to Lord Salisbury on 7 March:

> I have consulted nine of my friends, and yesterday and today have received their answers. They tell me, with one accord,

that I ought not to shrink from the responsibility, even of such
a Bishopric as Liverpool. There is, therefore, no course open to
me but to accept your Lordship's offer. I do so with a very heavy
heart, and with many strong misgivings. I can only try, by God's
help, to do my duty.[26]

The decision was to prove crucial for the whole Chavasse family. Frank
Chavasse, while sad to contemplate leaving Oxford, felt he had a mission to
fulfil in Liverpool, a city of paramount importance at that time in the affairs
of Great Britain, with its thriving port and busy waterway, its teeming
population and, as far as the future Bishop was concerned, social problems
on a gargantuan scale. Poverty, unemployment, poor housing, deprivation
of all kinds, presented a challenge that he could not ignore. On top of that,
Liverpool was a centre of seething controversy within the Church of England
on questions of extreme Protestantism, intemperance and Unitarianism.
Marjorie recalled that Liverpool was known in the Church as

'the black spot on the Mersey', because of the bitter rancour
between the different branches of the church and also the laxity
of many of the clergy.[27]

For Edith Chavasse the proposed move was something that she viewed with
dread. She was never at ease in 'society', and large formal gatherings were
anathema to her. She saw her role simply as that of dutiful wife and loving
mother and had no aspirations to fill a public role as wife of a bishop.
However, she kept her fears to herself. As always, her husband could rely
upon her complete loyalty.

The children were a different matter. Noel and Christopher especially felt
themselves to be part of Oxford life; they had made many friends at school
and had fully expected to complete their schooldays there and then proceed
to one of the Oxford colleges. The point of view of these two fifteen-year-olds
was listened to by their parents, but the boys' plea that they might be left
behind in Oxford to attend Magdalen College School as boarders while the
family moved to Liverpool fell upon deaf ears. Frank Chavasse would not
contemplate his sons being brought up elsewhere than in a loving home.
Many years later, when opening a War Memorial Appeal at Liverpool
College, he explained:

I kept all my boys at home for the reason that I believed that, if
a boy had a good home, it was best to keep him at home during
the most impressionable time of his life, so that parental influence
could be strongly brought to bear upon him, so that a lad could

learn, by mixing with his sisters, to honour and reverence womankind. And I am bound to say that, so far as I am concerned, the experiment has proved successful.[28]

So the decision was taken. Within weeks, Wycliffe Lodge was vacated. Frank Chavasse's books were packed into innumerable crates and, together with the children's toys and all the other impedimenta of a large family, sent up to Liverpool by cart and train. So sad were the twins to be leaving Oxford that they went out and purchased a large quantity of picture postcards of the town and pasted them into an album, a constant reminder of what they had left behind.[29] Christopher cherished that album to the end of his life.

Despite the reluctance of the whole family, Liverpool in 1900 cannot have failed to make a strong impression. Compared to their home town with its slow-moving traffic and genteel populace, this northern city was brash, noisy and smelly, its streets jostling with men, women and children whose speech, as well as being loud, was practically incomprehensible to ears attuned to the clipped accents of clerical and academic Oxford. The visible evidence of urban poverty was appalling, from the rags worn by street urchins to the squalid houses crowding near the river.

But the Chavasses found that their own new abode was situated in far more elegant and elevated surroundings than this. Their carriage took them from the station along Lime Street and turned left up the optimistically named Mount Pleasant, finally coming to a halt outside Number 19 Abercromby Square. This was to be home to the new Bishop and his family for the next twenty-three years.

CHAPTER TWO

Liverpool

> [Abercromby Square] is free from the rough rush of life by the
> riverside: it has not the hurry of Lime Street, nor the fevered
> pulses that stir near the Exchange: but it is comparatively quiet,
> it is retired, dignified, and decorous: the very place for the
> residence of a Bishop.[1]

Thus the site of the Bishop's Palace in Liverpool was described in 1888.
Built in 1863, the house was originally occupied by an American
businessman, Charles Kuhn Prioleau, whose firm in Liverpool staunchly
supported the Southern States in the American Civil War. The first Bishop
of Liverpool, Dr John Charles Ryle, had lived in the Palace since 1881, but
when the Chavasses arrived there was still a marked American influence in
the decor of the building. For example, a 'Lone Star' in the plaster above
the central first-floor window signified the Confederate State of Texas, and
inside the porch in front of the main entrance was a ceiling painting of the
palmetto tree from South Carolina.[2]

Inside were spacious entertaining rooms, their ceilings bearing exquisite
paintings on classical and philosophical themes. From the circular central
hall a magnificent staircase led upwards through two further storeys and a
series of attics to a spectacular dome. The children's rooms were on the
second floor, while the new Bishop set up his study in the same room as had
his predecessor, on the first floor overlooking the square. Mrs Chavasse had
a sitting-room or 'boudoir' on the same floor, while entertaining of a formal
nature took place on the ground floor. Here a number of handsome reception
rooms and the family's dining-room, as well as a room used as a chapel,
were all situated.

Naturally, a residence of this size required a large staff. The basement
housed a cavernous kitchen and associated domestic rooms, as well as a
substantial servants' hall presided over by a 'lady housekeeper' and a butler.[3]
The butler originally lived in the house next door, Number Twenty, but
very soon after his arrival in Liverpool, Bishop Chavasse arranged for it to
be taken over for use as a residence for the many young clergymen who came
to him to be prepared for ordination.[4] Also in the basement was a billiards

room, a left-over from the days of the Prioleaux; as a games room for the younger Chavasses this was an unexpected bonus. At the back was a garden which, while not really large enough for boisterous games, was nevertheless an oasis of peace in the increasingly busy square, through which trams ran every few minutes. From time to time, the Chavasses would gather here for the ceremonial taking of a family photograph. A coach-house was the main out-building of the Bishop's Palace, but this was converted into a garage well before the First World War.

After the family's arrival in Liverpool, events moved quickly. At an impressive ceremony at York Minster on 25 April, 1900, Francis James Chavasse was consecrated Bishop by the Archbishop of York, in the presence of trainloads of clerics brought over from Liverpool and Southport. His episcopal robes were a gift from his brother Thomas.[5] There being at that time no cathedral in Liverpool, he was enthroned as Bishop at St Peter's Church, the Pro-Cathedral, on 31 May. Immediately afterwards, a civic luncheon and reception were held for the Bishop and his wife at the Town Hall; Dorothea, being the eldest at seventeen, was an invited guest, but the younger members of the family stayed at the Palace. A grand procession to and from the Town Hall brought out thousands of onlookers, and Mrs Chavasse had the honour of accompanying the Lady Mayoress in the state carriage.

Local opinion about Liverpool's new church leader was favourable, and it was thought that his first sermons and other public utterances struck just the right note. The *Liverpool Daily Post and Mercury* commented:

> The civic welcome extended by the Lord Mayor was admittedly also the expression of the universal good feeling which has followed a wise appointment.[6]

The Bishop and Mrs Chavasse, however, were extremely sensitive to any hints that they were less than welcome, and this led to one misunderstanding that remained to haunt the Bishop until the end of his life. As his daughter Marjorie recalled:

> During his last illness he told me of a rebuff he had had at the very outset... He was not supposed to know, but if he made a good impression at the reception he was to be taken out to the (Corn) Exchange and to speak and be introduced to the members. But he was not taken and he knew they felt him to be too small and unassuming.[7]

The newspaper report of what happened was quite different:

At one o'clock, a large crowd of commercial gentlemen assembled on the Exchange Flags in the expectation that the Lord Mayor would introduce the new Bishop of Liverpool to them from the balcony overlooking the flags. On account of the workmen being engaged in the structural alterations to this part of the building, the Lord Mayor found it impossible to introduce the Bishop from the balcony, and the idea was abandoned.[8]

Sadly, however, this imagined slight caused much unnecessary distress at the Palace. No wonder that the children thought longingly of their beloved Oxford, where the family were accepted and highly thought of. That the children turned to each other for company, at least to start with, is hardly surprising. And for Mrs Chavasse this was only the first of many occasions when she had to stifle her feelings and face throngs of people who, she often imagined, were hostile. She had no small talk; even entertaining at the Palace, where at least she was on home ground, continued to be an ordeal for as long as she lived there. Thankfully, her elder daughter Dorothea had by 1900 been allowed to put her hair up, signifying womanhood, and was able to take some of the burden from her mother's shoulders.[9] The twins, May and Marjorie, aged fourteen, and the boys, Bernard and Aidan, aged eleven and eight respectively, continued their education in the care of a governess and a tutor in the school room up on the top floor. The question of the older boys' education was now addressed urgently, but in reality there was only one possible destination for them.

Liverpool College was a school for Liverpool's 'young gentlemen', charging fees of twenty-five pounds per annum with reductions for sons of the clergy and for second and subsequent sons.[10] The Upper School, which prepared its pupils for university entrance and for the professions, was situated in Sefton Park Road, on the edge of the then fashionable residential district of Toxteth. There were some 250 boys in the school and an Upper Sixth form of twenty-one. Here Noel and Christopher began their studies in the summer term of 1900, after a few weeks spent in getting used to their new quarters at the Palace.

The school was only a short walk from their home but they usually cycled there and back, meeting up with other boys on the way. They soon settled in, becoming known to fellow pupils and staff alike for their sporting prowess. But now there was a further movement in a direction that pleased their parents enormously: they were also being noticed for their involvement in other school activities, and were keeping up their academic standards very adequately. As an 'inky new boy', Chris deserved credit on 16 October, 1900, for leading the Proposers' side in a debate, 'that the recent Government in failing to make vaccination compulsory, has merited the severest censure"[11].

A turning point for Liverpool College and for the Chavasse boys was the arrival in January, 1901, of a new Principal, the Reverend John Bennett Lancelot, from the King's School, Rochester, Kent. He soon became a close associate of the Bishop. Indeed, Bishop Chavasse was invited by him to become Visitor to the College, thus sitting on its governing body and being closely involved with its development. Very soon the college magazine was able to speak of Prize Day in 1902 being graced by 'a few words from the Bishop, without whose presence a school function would now seem incomplete'.[12]

Lancelot was a man of the highest moral standards and a robust sense of duty founded upon an unshakable Christianity. Under his leadership the school blossomed, and so did Noel Chavasse; his parents were immensely proud when he was awarded the Earl of Derby's History Prize in 1901, and the Routhwaite Prize for Reading and Recitation in 1902.[13]

Meanwhile, there were more debates to speak in, Noel and Chris sometimes taking opposite sides to each other. One such occasion was in October, 1901, when the motion was 'Vivisection is a cruel and unnecessary practice'. The school magazine reported:

C. Chavasse, in an eloquent and amusing speech, vigorously attacked vivisection, stating that no great medical discoveries had been affected by its means. He mentioned that consumption had not decreased, and that the Pasteur cure for hydrophobia had killed half its patients. The action of medicines on the human system could not be reliably tested by vivisection, as men and animals differed very much in their organisms...

N. Chavasse very boldly took up the opposite side to his brother; in the course of his remarks he mentioned a discovery by which people's brains had been benefited by previous performances on monkeys.[14]

However, it was in the sports field and in the swimming pool that Noel and Christopher made their impact upon the school. Within weeks of their arrival in the summer of 1900 Noel won first place in 'Neat Diving For Beginners', and Chris gained a place on the 2nd Rugby XV and had scored against Birkenhead School. From this point on, the pages of the college magazine dealing with sporting achievement rarely went to print without at least one Chavasse success to record. In 1902, both boys played in the Cricket 2nd XI, and found themselves described in the magazine thus:

CHARACTERS OF THE 2ND XI

C. Chavasse (Captain): Has made an excellent captain and is

always keen on his team. As a bat plays steadily, but cannot be relied upon to last long. Fields the ball well and smartly and is a very fair wicket keeper. Should practise throwing.

N. Chavasse: Has scored well, though he plays too stiffly to be very successful. Fields very smartly at point.[15]

By the spring of 1904 they had both won places on the rugby team:

CHARACTERS OF THE IST XV

C. Chavasse (9st 10lb) — Right wing three-quarter. A neat player. An accident to his knee has prevented him playing since Christmas. In spite of his keen efforts he has given few signs of improvement. It is a pity his pace cannot be turned to better advantage.

N. Chavasse (9st 11lb) — Has worked hard to gain his place and consequently improved. An awkward player and poor kick, but he is strong and plays well on the loose. Seldom tackles low, but seldom fails to bring his man down. Played particularly well against Giggleswick and had hard lines in not scoring.[16]

A highlight of each of the four years they spent at Liverpool College was the annual 'Athletic Sports Day' held in June. In 1901 Noel's talent as a distance runner was apparent when he came second in the Half Mile Open. Chris, meanwhile, won the 220 yards and the sack race. In the next year, Chris came third in the Quarter Mile and again won the sack race; Noel was nursing an injury and did not compete, but now younger brother Bernard was at the school to keep the Chavasse flag flying and won the Quarter Mile race for under-thirteens.

In 1903 the three Chavasses swept the board. The next year, the twins' last at school, Noel broke school records to win the Hundred Yards, the Quarter Mile and the Mile races, and Chris came in second for the Quarter Mile and third in the Hundred Yards. Bernard was placed in three events. One imagines the sighs of relief breathed by all when the Chavasse domination of school sports began to diminish after this — but rivals could not rest for long: the youngest Chavasse, Aidan, was now at Liverpool College as well, and his name began to figure in the lists of winners from 1905.

Religion was never far from Noel's mind, but on occasion he was able to poke gentle fun at it, so that he never seemed to be a pious goody-goody. For example, on Dorothea's twenty-first birthday in 1904 he sent her the following:

My dear Dot,

I cannot moralize on this most solemn occasion, as I
have not time, so refer you to *Job Chap. III*. Read it over, and
then think for ten minutes, 'What have I done with my life?
Why was I born?' Review past sins. *Lamentations Chap. 1*.
Think for fifteen minutes on the sorrows of the world. *Psalms
88, 66, 137*. Think for 30 minutes, 'I have had no trouble so
far, how shall I be able to bear it when it comes?' Sing '*A Few
More Years Shall Roll*', '*Brief Life Is Here*'. Think for one
hour, 'I have passed another milestone on my road to the
tomb', 'I shall die sooner than I did twenty-one years ago', 'I
may die any moment'. May these special portions and verses
help to give you a truly joyous and happy birthday.
(Many happy returns of the day).
Amen.
Noel.[17]

Schooldays at Liverpool saw two turning-points in Noel Chavasse's life.
The first was at the sports day held on Saturday 8 June, 1901, at a playing
field in the leafy suburb of Mossley Hill, a mile and a half from the school
itself.[18]

The event was always something of a highlight in the social calendar,
resembling a garden party where the invited guests could stroll and take
tea. On this occasion, seven pipers and three drummers of the recently
formed battalion, the Liverpool Scottish, whose Commanding Officer,
Colonel C. Forbes-Bell, was an Old Boy of the College, played musical
selections. The college magazine reported the impact of the spectacle.

We believe that this was the first occasion upon which
members of this Corps wore their uniform in public, and the
effect of the kilts, as the men swung past, was so great that for
a time the poor runners felt their noses quite put out of joint,
since all attention was fixed upon a sight and sounds which
made every sensible person in the crowd either exult in the
consciousness of being a Scotsman, or indulge in wildly
romantic attempts to prove a claim to the possession of some
Scottish blood.[19]

Thus it was that Noel first set eyes upon the Liverpool Scottish. Sixteen
years later he was to die in their service.

The second turning-point came during 1903. For most of that and the
previous year, Noel had been nursing an injury that prevented him from
playing rugby. It was suggested by the Chavasse family doctor, Charles J.

Macalister, that he could perhaps occupy games afternoons by assisting at an industrial school.[20] Noel agreed, and so his interest in the Grafton Street School began.

Schools like this were established under the Reformatory and Industrial Schools Act of 1861, their purpose being

> [to rescue] destitute and abandoned Boys and Girls from present wretchedness and vice, and from future criminality. The children reside at the schools and are supplied with plain food, elementary education, and industrial training, and are placed out in situations which they are found to fill satisfactorily. They are supported by voluntary contributions and capitation grants from the Government and local authorities.[21]

The institution with which Noel became involved was the Holy Trinity Certified Industrial School for Boys, at 73-79 Grafton Street, on the slopes running down to the Mersey. This was at the edge of the Toxteth area of the city, where one could move within half a mile from the ostentatious wealth of the streets housing merchants and their families to an area of Dickensian deprivation that could hardly have been worse anywhere in England. Here Noel could appreciate for the first time what it was like to live in these mean streets — Victorian slums of the worst kind, some of them, from whence the inmates of the institution came. Directed as often as not by the city's magistrates to enter the industrial school, the boys were unruly, perhaps criminal, certainly heading for lives of squalid subsistence, unless the school could intervene and break the cycle. This is what the Governor, Mr Tom Robinson, and his wife the Matron, were endeavouring to do.

Noel's contribution was immediately important. In 1903 he was eighteen years old, athletic, articulate and inventive. As well as leading Bible-reading sessions and singsongs (he was an enthusiastic if not particularly expert pianist), he organised sports for the boys and accompanied them on their annual camps to Hightown, between Liverpool and Southport. Even when he was at university, he gave up part of every summer vacation to the needs of the Grafton Street boys.

Meanwhile, life in the Bishop's Palace continued to provide all of the young Chavasses with the solid and stable upbringing that was the ideal of their social class. Each day was structured around religious observance and mealtimes. Family prayers were held before breakfast in the chapel; the Bishop then worked in his study all morning and made calls each afternoon, while Mrs Chavasse supervised the household before lunch and visited friends or church organizations in the afternoons. After dinner the family spent some time together, though the Bishop seemed a rather remote figure, retiring to his study whenever he could. The children sometimes felt like visitors there, being expected to knock and ask if he was free.[22]

Noel's father placed great value on the home. In his sermons its importance was often stressed:

> Every movement which tends to make the home more bright, more orderly, more cleanly and more healthy, above all, more full of love, which helps to ennoble the privilege and the dignity of bringing up little children, which exalts marriage and family life, which teaches its divine origin and restful happiness, which makes, in a word, a parent a better parent and a home a truer home, ensures national contentment and national greatness. If the home be weakened or corrupt, the life of a nation is poisoned at its very springs, for it is the greatest factor in the formation of the character of its people.[23]

Thus, like his brothers and sisters, Noel acquired the strongest possible belief in and commitment to the family, and the beginnings of an earnest and unwavering patriotism.

From his mother there emanated a charming eccentricity that also played its part in the development of Noel's character. Mrs Chavasse had a penchant for exotic animals and there was always a series of pets running about in the Palace. One of these was a marmoset called Poppet. It seems to have belonged to Noel first and was allowed complete freedom to wander and climb at will; many were the visiting clergymen, sitting in the drawing-room waiting to see the Bishop, who found themselves suddenly leapt upon by the animal. Another pet was a mongoose, Rikki-Tikki, which had a habit of getting into the plumbing system, and on one occasion escaped on to the roof of the Bishop's Palace just as a group of angry Protestants was marching through the square. Leaping about between the attic windows, hotly pursued by several of the Chavasse children, the animal attracted the attention of the marchers to such an extent that they were completely distracted from their cause and the procession dispersed. They were protesting about Bishop Chavasse's alleged popery in carrying a crook in clergy processions.

Four hens, including one called Trousers whose leg feathers were so filthy that no one could face eating one of her eggs, a cockatoo (Beauty), two canaries, four rabbits, a dog called Puff, and four cats completed the menagerie.[24]

The kindness of the whole Chavasse family soon became legendary. Servants were treated generously and with an eye to their welfare; if a scullery-maid could not read or write, Mrs Chavasse taught her. The children's relations with the younger servants were as equals, from playing hide-and-seek in the garden to teaching a page boy to ride a bicycle. The Palace was difficult to keep clean, its front door opening directly on to a street thronged with horse-drawn vehicles so that dirt was constantly being brought in on the boots of visitors. It was also cold, every room being heated by one or more coal fires, and every piece of coal and every drop of hot water had to be carried to the three upper floors, the dust from so many fires adding enormously to the work of the staff. But the Chavasses were nothing if not considerate. The Bishop himself was quite willing to get down on his knees and clean his own hearth, and May, who had a notable collection of dolls, dusted them and washed their clothes herself.[25]

Often the Palace was thrown open to the children of local clergymen for parties. Noel and Chris helped with the games, while the Bishop sat the younger children on his lap during the more boisterous activities and Mrs Chavasse played the piano for singsongs — a far cry from the stuffy image of Edwardian bishops.

In 1904 Noel with his brothers and sisters formed a concert party called the 'We Are Seven Amateur Band', which had printed programmes announcing that Noel would play such favourites as 'Mulligan's Motor Car' on his flute. Chris excelled in recitations, violin and concertina, Marjorie and May sang duets, Bernard played the cornet and Dorothea accompanied at the piano. Aidan was designated 'Drums, Etc.' Money raised from an entrance fee of one penny was donated to missionary work.[26]

Family holidays were taken in Wales or Northumberland, the number of children often being augmented by the four Barnt Green cousins. At the age of fifteen Noel was developing a fluent and readable style of letter-writing, in spite of occasional interruptions by illness. In August 1901 he wrote to Grandmother Maude from a holiday cottage at Clynnog, Caernarfon:

> Thank you so very much for your letter and postal order — it is worth being ill to be remembered, and I am thinking of all the things I should like to buy with it when I get back to Liverpool, it is a very pleasant occupation. I am writing this letter in bed but I am dressed and came downstairs to my frugal dinner, for both the doctor and Mother insist on starving me, though I am dreadfully hungry. I am sorry to say Marjorie has jaundice as well as me and I am afraid will be poorly for her birthday. All the rest are in good health except Aidan who has had a slight chill, but he is alright now and has gone with Dorothy and Father to Pen-y-Groes to get some medicine while the others went for a long walk along the shore and brought in skulls and shells which were washed up in a storm we had yesterday. We brought Rikki

and Cocky with us [pet mongoose and cockerel] and they are both enjoying themselves, but Rikki is rather frightened of the sea though I have made him paddle in the rockpools to strengthen his legs![27]

Unfortunately, neither Mrs Chavasse nor her husband enjoyed robust health. There is some evidence that Noel's mother suffered from a goitre, or enlarged thyroid gland (she always wore high-necked dresses and a wide choker). This caused her to experience fatigue and nerves. Sometimes she lacked even the energy to come downstairs and spent days in her boudoir. Nevertheless, she was President of the Liverpool Mothers' Union for the whole of the twenty-three years during which her husband was Bishop, and opened garden fetes and attended bring-and-buy sales with a will. Few Everton Football Club supporters today notice, in the shadow of Goodison Park, a foundation stone in the wall of St Luke the Evangelist's Parish Hall, laid by her on 30 May, 1908; it was only one of many.

The Bishop had a number of perennial health problems, as his daughter Marjorie recalled:

> Although he rarely spoke of it and never complained, my father suffered very much from a rupture which he had had all his life, and also from kidney trouble. A few years after he became Bishop he was acutely ill and passed a large stone... He had, of course, to be most careful what he took at mealtimes.[28]

His life was extraordinarily busy, as the Diocesan Diary as well as the local newspapers recorded. On Sundays the family worshipped at St Saviour's, Falkner Square (where Noel and Christopher were confirmed by their father on 19 March, 1902), and after this the Bishop would go elsewhere to preach at least twice on the sabbath and several more times during the week. He regarded it as his duty to visit every parish in the diocese as frequently as possible, often travelling by tram to do so. Then there were confirmation services; young men to prepare for ordination; baptisms, marriages and funerals, which he was often requested to conduct; visiting sick clergy and their families; committee meetings of the numerous organizations of which, as Bishop, he was a member — Liverpool College, the Bluecoat Hospital School, the Temperance League, the University, to name but a few.

His greatest efforts, however, were directed to one project which towered, both literally and figuratively, over everything else. He wanted to build a cathedral.

Earlier plans under Bishop Ryle had come to nothing. Ryle regarded his role as Bishop to be primarily one of 'preaching of the Gospel to souls whom no Cathedral would touch'.[29] Now Liverpool had a bishop with the vision and the energy to at least make a start. Within weeks he had established a Cathedral Committee, chaired by Lord Derby, which purchased a site just outside the city centre, St James's Mount, a hilltop visible to ships entering the Mersey Estuary.[30] Bishop Chavasse had seen the magnificent municipal buildings that had been erected in Liverpool in the second half of the nineteenth century: St George's Hall, the Walker Art Gallery, the Library and Museum. He frequently passed through the waterfront area where striking commercial buildings were going up in the early 1900s, like the Liver Building and the offices of the Mersey Docks and Harbour Board. Why should not God have such a building? And let it be huge and so placed as to be a constant reminder of His greatness.

A search began for an architect with the flair and imagination for such an enterprise. A competition was held and a Gothic design submitted by the young (and Roman Catholic) Giles Gilbert Scott was selected as the winner. A public appeal for funds was opened and work got under way.

On Tuesday 19 July, 1904, the Cathedral's foundation stone was laid by King Edward VII and Queen Alexandra, upon a dais specially erected and bearing furniture of white enamel and gold.[31] A vast concourse of 8,000 spectators and choirs from all over the diocese surrounded the dais, and all the younger Chavasses had seats on the enormous semi-circular stand. The Bishop led the service and Mrs Chavasse was seated with the Queen near the foundation stone. Noel was particularly interested to see boys from Grafton Street crowding up to the railings that surrounded the whole site; and when the royal party progressed to the Town Hall, a 470-strong guard of honour from the Liverpool Scottish lined part of the route. This was indeed a red letter day for the Bishop; a beginning had been made. As he said:

> If our generation can raise only £100,000, let it put up the choir
> or part of it, and let those who come after us complete it.[32]

From now on, he and his family were frequent visitors to watch the building in progress on St James's Mount.

In the same year, the thoughts of both Christopher and Noel were turning towards Oxford. There is no denying that they had greatly enjoyed their time in Liverpool. Noel was later to write:

> I don't look back on my schooldays with any pride whatever. I
> see now I slacked terribly, or rather worked without heart and
> so without any result. I only know that I have always enjoyed
> myself at school.[33]

But as their father was an Oxford man and many boys from Liverpool College secured places at Oxford each year, it was inevitable that they would return to the place where their childhood years had been so happily spent.

Applications were made to Trinity College, which it was felt had tutors appropriate to their needs, as well as the right ambience for young men of their upbringing. Noel wished to read Natural Sciences with a view to qualifying in medicine and becoming a missionary doctor; he had earlier toyed with the idea of becoming a full-blown Anglican missionary and was known to his family as 'The Bishop of Wangaroo',[34] but this phase had passed. Christopher's ambitions had always lain in the direction of the Church of England, so he had decided to read History and several other subjects that could be classed broadly as Humanities. Noel, especially, was not optimistic that he would be admitted to Oxford — indeed, he never did have much confidence in his own abilities. However, the good news arrived in the summer of 1904, and Trinity College opened its doors to both of them in October.

CHAPTER THREE

Return to Oxford

'My Dear Mother,' Noel wrote from Oxford on 24 October, 1904:

> Things are going quite smoothly so far, only we are very full up
> with invitations. It is rather hard work to fit in time for work and
> I cannot always mannage [sic] to get 6 hours work in, because I
> get so sleepy at night that I always have to turn in at 10.30. I
> have not missed a Chapel so far though I had a very narrow
> squeak this morning. Last Sunday we had rather a scare, we
> thought there was to be a Smoking Concert, Freshmen specially
> invited and a great many Freshers got very nervous. About four
> came to consult us, no doubt thinking that we with our episcopal
> relations were authorities on the subject. We decided to strike and
> not go, but to our relief we found that it was only a College
> Meeting about a concert...
>
> I am going to watch a footer match now with Argenti who is a
> great pal of mine, because although he is awfully rich and his
> father sends him musty bottles of choice wine, he is not in the
> least fast and hardly ever touches wine or smokes. He is a very
> good rider (on Saturday he was nearly killed with his horse
> rearing and falling back on to him) and is going in for the Trinity
> Steeplechase. If he wins I am going to lead in his horse and gain
> great fame.[1]

This was the first letter to arrive at the Bishop's Palace in Liverpool following
the enrolment of Christopher and Noel at Trinity College. It began a routine
of weekly letter-writing, usually undertaken by Noel on Sundays, that
continued until his death. In the trenches during the Great War, composing
a letter home became one of the reminders that it *was* Sunday; it was also a
most poignant reminder of those golden Edwardian days of peace before the
holocaust.[2]

They soon settled in and their new life in Oxford assumed a congenial
pattern: study, sports, church and visits to or from family and friends. Their
social circle was strictly male, as indeed was the whole academic community,

for at this time Oxford did not allow women to take degrees. It was permissible for a few women to attend lectures, as Vera Brittain did before the Great War, but they were not allowed to graduate.

At Trinity, where the twins shared rooms in Kettel Hall, they were mixing exclusively with boys from public school backgrounds and privileged families; it is therefore the greatest possible tribute to their parents and schools that they emerged into the world at the end of it commendably capable of relating to people from quite different backgrounds and with very divergent values and beliefs.

From the first, the Chavasse boys involved themselves in anything and everything. They attended sermons (and sent detailed accounts home to their father), they joined the Oxford Union and met up with a number of Magdalen College School boys who they had known four years previously, and they received many invitations. Word had got round that the Chavasses were back, and old family friends were keen to entertain them. According to Noel, there were frequent 'pious teas' taken with local clergy. Uncle Tom (who was to be knighted in 1905 for his services to medicine, much to the Bishop's delight) and Aunt Frances came from Bromsgrove to see them in their rooms, while visiting their own son Arthur who had come up to Oxford at the same time as Noel and Chris and was reading Physiology at Hertford College; cousins Gwendolen, (at nineteen the eldest of Uncle Tom's children), the eleven-year-old Gladys and Esme aged nine were also familiar visitors.

Undergraduate life provided many occasions when high spirits could be unleashed, as at the Trinity 'Freshers' Drunk':

> It was quite a mild affair, only one Fresher drunk, and he is going to get ragged by some of the second-year men, because it is bad form for a Fresher to get drunk. One awful man named Gurney did not come to the Drunk, and five of us went to look him up about 12 p.m., it so happened that all the other freshers did the same, and there was an awful squash on the stairs up to his room and an awful row too. He was not in his room so his furniture was spread about a bit, nothing broken, and his coal spilt about. Then we went up to his bedroom, and found him, where do you think? Under the bed in a mortal funk, a few boots were cast at him and then everyone went out, they were too disgusted with him to touch him.[3]

Drunkenness obviously worried the Bishop, and a year later Noel made further comments on undergraduate drinking:

About Oxford being drunken. The general opinion about here is that Oxford is more drunken than a few years ago. But everybody is willing to admit that drunkenness is not considered the crime it was, and people are rather amused than otherwise at the sight of a drunken man and make every excuse for him.[4]

For both brothers, the problem of fitting academic work into this busy life had to be addressed. As far as sporting activity was concerned, Noel was compelled to take things easy for a while, as the health problem which had prevented him from playing rugby at Liverpool College still persisted. It may have resulted from a bout of rheumatic fever, for he wrote to his mother in November that he had been advised not to run in the Freshman Sports because 'the mussel [sic] around the heart was still weak and if I ran it might go another shape'.[5] By early 1905, however, both Chris and Noel were playing lacrosse for Trinity, and were proud to do so, but Noel was occasionally aggrieved by misleading reports in the local press. 'We have lost the Lacrosse match,' he wrote to his father in March. 'I got the last goal, but in all the papers it is put down to other people, it is rather rot.'[6]

As Noel's first letter home from Oxford indicates, Sunday observance was a principle all the Chavasses carried with them as a reminder of their father's teaching. Noel found himself rather worried about his cousin Arthur:

Arthur goes punting on Sundays. I told him he ought not to, but he says he does not see any harm in it, and I find a lot of men who are considered most pious go out on the river on Sunday, and what is worse, as people go to church they see undergrads going down to the river in flannels.[7]

The following year Arthur got his come-uppance:

I am sorry to say Arthur went out in his punt today (Sunday) with some friends and a lunch-basket. It poured, which was judgement. I was glad.[8]

Indeed, Noel greatly admired a President of the Oxford Union who refused to attend Trinity College debates because they were held on Sundays.[9]

But religion was not always so serious. Noel asked Dorothea,

Please tell Father I hope he will be sure to come and see us today fortnight because it is the night of our Bible reading. He can address us. I expect you here drop a tear of tenderness at a beautiful picture of young undergraduates with eager faces drinking in the words of life, while outside are scenes of drunken debauchery...[10]

Noel was quite happy, too, to play the expected role of the adventurous undergraduate:

I have made my fame here by discovering a new way out of Trinity after dark through some cellar windows under Kettle [sic] Hall. Some men are investigating it today. I have been out already but that was quite early. I only wanted to see if I could get out.[11]

And, like all undergraduates, he was perennially short of money.

I am very pleased with my battles [sic] this term. I managed to get them down to £36.4s.6d. That is at least £3 cheaper than last term. Altogether I calculate last term and vac came to almost exactly £50 which I think is pretty good considering the extra expense I had with Crosse [a cramming tutor]. Uncle Tom was awfully good and tipped us a sov. so that I am £2.10s. in pocket. I have just under £25 in the bank, could you put some more in, as the Bursar will be drawing out a cheque for my battles £86.5.0d. odd.[12]

It was the twins' twenty-first birthday on 9 November, 1905. They were delighted that their mother was able to come down to visit them, and special studio photographs were taken to mark the occasion. Their birthday present was a sum of money with which they purchased silver watches. Noel was becoming more and more concerned about his studies, but was finding that there simply was not enough time to do all that he wanted to do. In June he had written to his mother:

It has been a very humdrum term, simply work and labs all day, but still I look back on it with huge satisfaction because I did not know I could work before and also because although I have only taken three days' exercise in the last 3 weeks I have kept in very sound health. I shall not work so hard again, though, because I think you lose some of the College life not going out of your room hardly at all and I don't think we are only meant to work up here.[13]

He continued to run, but found himself being overtaken by Christopher:

Chris has got his half-blue. I haven't. He could have beaten me in the quarter-mile but did not, and the judges saw he was fresher than I was.... I am rather glad for some things [that] I am not in the running team, as now there is a chance of my getting through my Zool. Prelim.[14]

The lack of personal animosity or rivalry between the brothers pleased the Bishop enormously. 'It is delightful to think that the "foul-eyed monster, jealousy" never comes to divide you,' he wrote, 'and that it is still "we" and not "I".'[15]

From early 1906 onwards, when Noel's studies were in their second year, every letter home expressed his energetic approach to his work. Intellectually, he was blossoming. So far he had studied anatomy and physiology in theory rather than in practice, and he had not yet begun to explore the finer points of medicine, but he was happier than he had been in any learning situation before. And at last he was embarking on the work which was to lead to his life interest in surgery. He was dissecting his first body:

Every afternoon, I have to dissect away at my body, except perhaps Saturday, but I enjoy it very much and am very keen on it, and so far people say I have done him well.... [Next week] I go to the Radcliffe Infirmary to learn dispensing.[16]

Mrs. Chavasse's hospitality showed itself in many ways, not least in her willingness to receive her sons' friends as guests at the Palace for Christmas:

A fortnight today, I trust we shall have you at home. I am glad if one of your friends can stay over Christmas if he has no English home to spend it in, and we must ask some other lonely folks.[17]

The number of Noel's friends who were coming to stay increased to three as Christmas approached, but he assured his mother that 'All wish to work 5 hours a day, so we shall be quite a studious party.'[18]
He faced the examinations at the end of the year with some trepidation, but looked forward to the vacation:

I am very glad that my grind is coming to an end, and whatever happens, I feel I have done my best and deserve a jolly good holiday. 'Like Gordon, I tried to do my duty'.

Please put this on my tombstone if I succumb to the horror of trying to remember what I never knew.[19]

And a week later:

> I sent you a telegram to say I passed in Materia Medica, that was the exam I funked most. As a matter of fact, I did very well. I answered all the questions pretty well, was congratulated on my practical work, and answered all the questions.... I had a most delightful paper. I seemed to have every question at my fingers' ends and I wrote hard the whole time.... Tell Dot to buy me a song called 'The Man With Only One Hair'. It's simply ripping and not at all vulgar.[20]

At the beginning of the summer vacation, on 17 July 1906, part of the new Liverpool Cathedral was dedicated. This was the cornerstone of the Chapter House, which was to be paid for by West Lancashire Freemasons in memory of the late Earl of Lathom. The Duke of Connaught, Grand Master of the Order, led the proceedings; the Bishop was present, but his part in the ceremony was limited to saying the Benediction. He may well have been out of sympathy with the Freemasons, even though the Duke declared that their secrets 'are lawful and honourable, and not repugnant to the laws of God or man'.[21]

Freemasonry was strong in Liverpool and their £10,000 donation was not to be refused, but it is significant that no other Chavasse was present; when the Lady Chapel was dedicated in 1910 the whole family attended.

A fortnight of the summer holiday was spent by Noel, as always, with the boys of the Grafton Street School in camp at Hightown near Southport. He invited his parents to visit the boys, as the whole Industrial School Committee was keen to meet them. A day trip was made to see Grandmother Maude at Pen Dyffryn, always a popular element of the annual camp. During term time Noel was similarly involved with the Grafton Street boys. His thoughtful touches there were becoming well known. One boy, Percy Dean, a patient in the nearby Royal Southern Hospital in Caryl Street, Liverpool, received some old magazines from the Bishop's Palace, at Noel's express request.[22]

He also considered helping deprived boys elsewhere. In May 1907 he attended a meeting of the Oxford Bermondsey Mission, a group from the university who worked to raise money and resources for children in one of the most poverty-stricken London boroughs. He was very impressed with the mission, and began to wonder if he should go to Bermondsey to do the hospital placement that was part of his medical training.

There seems a great work for a medical student there, more perhaps than studying in Liverpool and looking after the Industrial School. I must say I should be very sorry to break with Grafton Street and go to London, but we must see.[23]

Always anxious about his work, Noel was filled with apprehension at the approach of examinations at the end of his third year at Oxford, even though he had done as much preparation for them as was humanly possible. During each vacation he had used whatever influence he or his family had to get some extra anatomical or other work done in Liverpool. Just before going home at Christmas 1906 he wrote:

On Monday I am going to see if I can call on Dr Macalister, to see if there is any work I can do for him, or if he will take me round the wards with him again, because I have found the work I did with him last vac. has been of great service to me this term. I am also going to write to Professor Paterson, to try and get a part to dissect at the Liverpool University this vac.[24]

Charles Macalister, as well as being Noel's own family doctor, held the post of Consultant Physician at the Royal Southern Hospital, so round the wards Noel went, behind the group of junior doctors and medical students who followed the consultant from patient to patient. Thus began his association with this hospital, and his ambition to be appointed to its staff, if fate should decree that he return to the city after leaving Oxford, rather than going south to Bermondsey. (Macalister also held the post of Surgeon to the Liverpool Scottish, another connection that Noel would make good use of in future years.)

Liverpool University Medical School beckoned too, due to the close friendship which was developing between Noel and Dr Andrew Melville Paterson, Professor of Anatomy. Professor Paterson at 21 Abercromby Square was a near neighbour of the Chavasses; the university records show that Noel was registered for his vacation classes in anatomy during 1906 and 1907.[25]

He was prepared to employ such friendships and to pull any strings that he could, provided he felt that the end justified the means. In this case, his ambition to be a good doctor overrode everything else. As Finals loomed in June 1907, Noel sent a note to Paterson to reserve another part for dissection. 'I must book it as soon as I can,' he had told his Mother, 'because I want to do a head, and they are not so plentiful as legs and arms.'[26] Even after Finals he was keen to do extra work, asking his father to use his influence with Professor Sherrington or Professor Dale of Liverpool University because it was 'very important' that he gained some practical experience in the physiological chemistry laboratory.[27]

Their spiritual life also occupied the thoughts of the twins, but there was always their father to consult. In the autumn of 1906 Noel had been reading a devotional book which prompted this request to the Bishop:

> I want to get more devotion in than just prayers and a few verses read at night when half asleep which is all I do now. And the book talked of meditation and Bible-searching and all sorts of things which seem very right. Please excuse a very dull letter but I want advice.[28]

Some months later Noel found himself much affected by a biography of General Gordon. Already familiar with tales of Gordon's glorious deeds, he had not before appreciated the sense of duty that ran through all of Gordon's actions. He thought he might use this theme in a talk to the Industrial School boys at their summer camp, and again he asked for advice from his father:

> Could you tell me of a book or tract in which I could find a talk to boys or people on doing one's Duty? I am reading the life of General Gordon and I had no idea what a very great man he was. Stead [W. T. Stead, Editor of *Review of Reviews*] says he taught men how to be good without being goody goody.[29]

And three weeks later:

> I have just finished reading General Gordon's life, on Sunday. I am very much impressed by it. I am going through the book carefully again next Sunday and am going to collect special facts and stories about him and sentences from his letters all bearing out that he had one fixed idea in life and everything else was subservient to it, and how he stuck to his Duty all the way through.[30]

Gordon became Noel's hero thereafter, for he had not only been a great general, he had also applied a passionate zeal to his work among destitute boys in England. Noel's letters from 1907 onwards frequently reiterated the theme of duty, the keynote in his admonitions to deprived boys as well as to the men under his command in war.

Contacts with Noel's old schools, Magdalen College School and Liverpool College, were maintained throughout his time at Trinity. The *Liverpool College Magazine* constantly referred to his and Chris's achievements, and as Old Lerpoolians they attended the annual dinners at the Exchange Hotel in Liverpool. They sent donations towards the cost of a pavilion on the Mossley Hill playing field, which was opened at the 1905 sports day, the prizes being presented by Mrs Chavasse while the twins looked on. In December 1906 they both returned to the school to attend a concert, and Noel asked his younger brother Bernard to 'get a ticket for me as well as for the others, but get Mother to pay for it'.[31] Every so often a member of staff would visit the Old Lerpoolians at Oxford, like the English Literature master, Mr. Forbes, in 1906 when 'a right merry evening was spent in the Chavasses' rooms to celebrate the occasion'.[32]

In 1906, the school magazine also noted that Chris and Noel were playing lacrosse for Oxford against Cambridge, and Noel had been distinguishing himself on the running track. Both played rugby during 1906, but the greatest university accolade of all was earned in 1907, when both Chavasses received their Blues for running against Cambridge. Their successes were impressive. Chris came first in the Quarter Mile and Noel was second, while Noel dead-heated with another fine athlete, Kenneth MacLeod, for first place in the Hundred Yards. In the Oxford University Sports in the same year, Noel was first in the Hundred Yards while Chris was second, and again Chris won the Quarter Mile. No wonder they were 'Isis Idols' in November 1907, when the Oxford undergraduate journal poked gentle fun at their achievements to date. Chris was nicknamed 'Push' while Noel was 'Bro':

> Their conjoint triumphs in the Hundred and the Quarter at this year's Sports, still too green in the public memory to need more detailed record, did nothing to solve the vexed problem of athletic supremacy, and we can only hope that neither next year's Sports nor Championships nor Olympic Games will supply the final solution. Pausing awhile from the triumphs on the track and in theological controversy, our Idols have returned to Rugger and are now proving themselves prolific try-getters for Trinity.
>
> A word must be said as to their varied accomplishments in private life, ranging from 'Push's' expert driving of the episcopal motor at unepiscopal speeds to 'Bro's' minute knowledge of comic opera, the poorer for his absence. Twenty-three years' patient endurance of the inevitable and time-worn jest concerning their twinhood, and the daily insult of each being mistaken for the other, have somewhat soured their naturally optimistic view of things.[33]

Noel was thrilled with the *Isis* tribute, and commented to his mother:

I suppose you have received an Isis, and see that we are Isis Idols so that I think we have reached the summit of our ambition in joining that roll of distinguished persons, including Lord Curzon, some of the Vice-Chancellors and Chancellors of the University, besides heads of Houses and who not?[34]

Christopher wrote in 1957 that Noel and he 'were not outstanding athletes' and that it was partly through being identical twins that 'we acquired a fame which our performances did not deserve'.[35] A photograph of the brothers, taken on the day they heard they had been awarded their Blues, shows them in running strip and blazers, looking solemn and strained. But Noel was able, on the same day, to write a jaunty letter home about it:

I write to tell you that we have just received official notification that we have both been awarded full Blues, so that one of our greatest desires is gratified.... Tremendous Challenge Cups have been sent to our room today. Mine is about a foot and a ½ high, and solid silver. They are to be held a year. I feel quite nervous having them in the room.[36]

As examinations loomed once again, he told his mother:

I do not think I have a ghost of a chance for a First Class, but I mean to try. And as Dr Macalister says, it does not matter if I get a 1st Class as long as I know enough to fit me to be first-rate.[37]

He need not have worried. When the Natural Science results were announced, he had indeed gained a First in Physiology. He sent a telegram to Liverpool with the news, then went to his Uncle Tom's house at Barnt Green for a few days' holiday. His parents were delighted; indeed, his sister Dorothea had 'never seen Dad so pleased about anything', as she wrote to her fiancé, George Foster-Carter.[38] But for Christopher, whose results came out a month later, the hard and unexpected truth had to be faced: he had failed in History Schools. Noel immediately blamed Chris's tutor.

I feel dreadfully cut up about Chris. I think it is most awfully hard lines and that Patterson [the Reverend M. W. Patterson, lecturer in Modern History at Trinity] is nothing else than a lazy fool. I have always disliked him. I now hate and despise him from the bottom of my heart.[39]

Chris was so devastated by his failure that he suffered a kind of breakdown.

However, with a great effort, he pulled himself together and determined to try again.

Noel could now have left Oxford and continued his studies at Liverpool University, but he decided that he and Chris should stay together. So, in October 1907, back to Oxford they came, Chris to cram and hope to raise his standard, Noel to pursue his goal of qualifying in medicine. They moved out of college; perhaps the size of their battels, or college bills, was a deciding factor. A house was found at 9 Museum Road, within walking distance of Trinity and nearer to the university science buildings where Noel would be studying. At first other students shared the house with them, but after one had left without paying his share of the rent or bills, the twins determined to be as independent as possible from now on.[40]

At the beginning of the new term, internal examinations known as Collections were held at Trinity, and this year the Chavasses did well.

> The results of the College Collections are just out and Chris and
> I have each obtained an £8 prize. People here are rather amused
> at the family taking £16 off the College.[41]

As Chris had failed his degree only three months previously, one imagines that some searching questions were being asked of the teaching staff. But Chris was determined to graduate this time, and between summer and Christmas he threw himself totally into his academic work, except for one relaxation, his old favourite, rugby. In fact they both played, as Noel wrote home:

> Chris and I have blossomed out into a new role. We have been
> asked this term to play on the two wings for the Rugby team. I
> have never played there before, but I tried today and got four
> tries. It is rather funny, I hang outside on the wing and when the
> other three-quarters get the ball they burst along until they have
> drawn men onto them, then they pass out to me and everybody
> yells 'now run', so I just run. That is all my job.[42]

A little later, he was sending home detailed accounts of every match:

> On Monday, Chris and I represented Trinity in the wings (against
> Jesus, Cambridge). We beat Jesus 35 points to 9. Of our 9 tries,
> Chris and I scored 7 (Chris 4 and I 3). We have 9 Blues in the
> team (one an international) and all the rest except Chris and I
> play for the Varsity 'A' Team.... As I am President of the College
> Athletics I have had some hard work with them, but I think I

am to be rewarded as they promise well to be extremely
successful, more so than for years.[43]

An appreciation of belonging to a group, rather than simply acting as an
individual, was also growing in him.

I must say you do get to know people well when you are both
battling and sweating to win a match for your College. Altogether
a much decenter thing than winning pots for oneself. Running for
a team is different again. [44]

Noel was exhibiting all the signs of a young man who had suddenly grown
up. Life so far had dealt him some superlative hands; he seemed not to be
capable of failure, he was liked by his fellows and gifted academically. But
Chris's setback had pulled them both up sharply, and from now on Noel felt
a great sense of responsibility and duty. 'When one enjoys life very much,'
he wrote to his father, 'one is rather afraid of not being so strenuous as duty
demands'.[45] In an attempt to remedy this he began to extend his interest in
social problems and the welfare of the poor — hardly surprising in an age
when debates about the optimum extent of state involvement in social
provision occupied every political platform and many newspaper editorials.
He had already heard Keir Hardie speak in 1905; now it was the turn of
another distinguished visitor to Oxford:

On Sunday after Hall I went to hear a Socialist named George
Lansbury speak.... I have never heard a man speak better. After
the meeting was over Pritchard asked me to come into his room
to meet the man and I was very glad to go. They all talked about
the unemployment problem and things like that till 12 when I had
to dash home and to bed.[46]

A college athletics training trip to Brighton in March 1908 filled him with
dismay at the ostentatious display and extravagance he found there, and while
staying at the Hotel Metropole he sent home his views, as he often did, to
reassure his parents that he was leading an upright and Christian life:

I don't think I have ever seen a more pagan Sunday than
yesterday. I felt quite ashamed of being in the hotel. I went to
church with Chris which made me feel very respectable, but it
was hard to realize the rest of the day that it was Sunday at all. I
think Brighton is the most unchristian place I have struck yet.

35

And

> There has been the usual crowd here today — well-known actresses brought by their admirers; a Russian princess who sent us her dog to see — a tremendous Newfoundland which requires one man simply to look after it... and heaps of French people, Jews, Greeks and all kinds of vulgar-looking English, who evidently have pots of money and nothing else.[47]

Again, as his Physiology examinations approached, Noel began to prepare his parents for the worst:

> I may say right out I don't think there is the ghost of a chance of a First. Of course, I am trying my hardest but that is only 2nd rate. I am not a person who can get 1st with a modicum of work. I have not sufficient ability. In all the exams I have so far suffered I have always worked far harder than most with no better results. In this final exam I have not even worked so long as most. All those who hope for 1st or 2nd have had longer than I have at their subject as they had done chemistry and physics at school which meant a year's hard work for me and a year out of reading physiology and anatomy.[48]

And a few weeks later:

> I do really think that so far things look quite bright for a 2nd but I am afraid all hopes for a First have vanished. I am very sorry if you and mother are disappointed, but this is a fact.[49]

Once again, however, his pessimism was unfounded. When the results were out he wrote to Dot:

> I must say I am very amused at getting a First and surprised too. I don't yet know how it was done, nor does anybody else... who all greet me with incredulous smiles.[50]

For this, Trinity presented him with some more prize money, and he bought an ophthalmoscope, saying 'Every doctor ought to have one'.[51] Chris had also passed this time, but could not technically qualify for the Bachelor of Arts degree until June 1909.

The greatest possible athletics honour was theirs in the summer of 1908. The fourth Olympics since the revival of the games in 1896 were to be held in London from 13 to 25 July, and Noel and Chris were both invited to attend trials for selection for the British team. But as Noel put it in his weekly letter home,

> We have not been in for the Olympian Trials.... On Tuesday I went to the track to train, began many fast dashes, and in one my muscle went again. So I could not run but Chris and I have had to write to the authorities saying we could not run through doctor's orders (Chris got in a fright when my leg went lest his should go), but that our legs could be right soon. We then sent our times to them (as they asked, if any competitors could not run through illness), and some of the times for the Quarter and 100 happen to be the best done in England in the last 2 years. So we have yet a chance.... Last Tuesday we were invited to run before the King and French President but of course could not accept. As we shall be in London in July it would be nice to run in the Olympian Games during that month.[52]

Their times were obviously acceptable, for on 2 June they received letters from P. L. Fisher, Secretary of the Amateur Athletic Association, inviting them to take part in the games.[53]

The grand parade of 2,000 athletes at the opening of the games took place at 3.30pm on 13 July, the athletes having been instructed to be at the White City Stadium by two o'clock. Oxford and Cambridge Blues led the parade, in front of King Edward VII, in their dark and light blue blazers and running shorts; the only uniform provided by the authorities was a white cap bearing the Union Jack. The Bishop was in London attending the Lambeth Conference at the same time, and was able to be present to see his sons' performances. No other member of the Chavasse family was there — in fact, *The Times* bemoaned the lack of spectators generally.[54]

Both Noel and Chris were entered in the 400 metres. Despite Noel's apparent concern about his leg injury, in later years Christopher declared that they were both entirely fit in time for the games. As it happens, Noel came third in Heat VII and Chris was second in Heat VIII, neither of them achieving times sufficiently fast to allow them into the next heats. Oddly, the press made no mention of twin brothers running in the same event, though it was surely something of a record.[55]

The next academic year found Noel back at Oxford without Chris. For the first time their paths were diverging, Chris studying under the Bishop for his ordination, and Noel, on his father's advice, taking another year to make sure that his grounding in anatomy was faultless. As usual, he had spent much of his summer vacation at Liverpool University studying anatomy, but now, working at the University Museum, he was doing original research with Dr Walter Ramsden of Pembroke College (who had been one of Noel's Finals examiners). The results of their research into the characteristics of albumen were eventually published in a German research journal.[56]

He was also attending lectures in ophthalmics and checking patients at the Out-Patients Department of the Radcliffe under the supervision of Dr Robert W. Doyne, the consulting ophthalmic surgeon. Noel felt all of this to be most useful, and told his father:

> You will be glad to hear that the course you have advised for me is much approved of. I am having a year in which I can soak in anatomy so that I hope the essentials will never evaporate. And one of the anatomy lecturers, a doctor here, said it was the best thing that could be done. He said most men went to the Hospital having forgotten all their anatomy, with the result that it had to be crammed up again. But I hope I shall go to the Hospital being thoroughly grounded in anatomy, besides being as well-grounded in Physiology as is possible, and having attended the best Pathology lectures and classes.[57]

In the same letter, Noel added up the total cost of his Oxford education, all paid for by the Bishop:

> I went to the Bank and found I had £115 in. That is my £100 and £15 left from the £40 you have just put in. Altogether you have (since I went to Oxford) put into the Bank £815. Of that, I have £115 left.[58]

He became quite indignant when he received an income tax form:

> As there was an envelope prepaid for an answer I replied:
> 'Dear Sir,
> Declaration A: My income with luck will be £6 per annum.
> Declaration B: I have an allowance from my father of £120 on which he has already paid income tax, and any more little bits I can persuade him to grant me.
> Declaration C: Further contributions thankfully received by
> Yours truly, etc.
> I have not been further bothered.[59]

The first of the Chavasse children to marry was Dorothea, on Tuesday 10 October, 1908, and Noel made sure he was able to get home to Liverpool for the ceremony. Her husband was George Foster-Carter, Rector of St. Aldate's in Oxford and well known to the Bishop. This was one of Liverpool's social events of the year; the Pro-Cathedral of St Peter in Church Street was filled to overflowing with the hundreds of guests. Three bishops officiated and the bride was attended by eight bridesmaids, including her sisters May and Marjorie, cousin Gwendolen from Bromsgrove (soon to be married herself) and Miss Nancy Caton, daughter of the Lord Mayor of Liverpool. Grandmother Maude's hymn *'Thine For Ever'* was sung as the bridal procession entered, while Noel and his three brothers acted as stewards. They had a struggle to control the crowds at the back of the church, trying to catch a glimpse of the bride who was given away by her uncle, Sir Thomas Chavasse. Back at the Palace a reception was held for a thousand guests, and Noel's protegés, the Grafton Street boys, provided a band to play in the large marquee in the garden.[60]

After this typically extravagant Edwardian wedding, the Bishop must surely have felt that he and his wife had at last taken their proper places on the Liverpool scene. When in the same year May and Marjorie were presented at court, the parents' self-confidence received another boost. It had been eight years since Frank Chavasse and his family had arrived from Oxford, but in Marjorie's words, 'Perhaps because of his difficulties he loved Liverpool even more than he had loved his Oxford Hall.'[61]

Back in Oxford, a new interest had taken hold of Noel. His brother Bernard was now an undergraduate at Balliol College, also reading Natural Sciences, and together they joined the Oxford University Officer Training Corps. This unit had grown out of the 1st (Oxford University) Volunteer Battalion of the Oxfordshire Light Infantry, as a result of Haldane's Army Reforms of 1908.[62] Members of the university who sought a commission could enlist in this wing of the new Territorial Force, and in Oxford as in many other towns and cities there was an enthusiastic response to the call for recruits. The *Oxford University Roll of Service* described this 'quickening of military activity in the Universities' in glowing terms:

> Partly, no doubt, this quickening was due to the tension of the political atmosphere and the imminence of the German threat. But it was wisely encouraged by the authorities, and especially by Lord Haldane, who deserves not a little credit for his patient and persevering efforts to enlist the Universities in the cause of national defence. Commissions in the Army were brought within the reach of graduates. Military History was given a recognized position among University studies. A

delegacy was appointed to superintend the instruction of Army candidates, and the University contingent of the Officer's Training Corps grew and flourished.[63]

Before attending his first session of the Oxford Officer Training Corps in January 1909 Noel wrote to his mother:

> I am trying to nerve myself for the horrible task I begin tomorrow. I am of course going to bed an hour earlier these days. I get up to attend drills at 7.30 at the Drill Hall, as I really am a Territorial now. I have arranged to go certain days with a friend of mine, and Bernard is going to attend three days too. I don't like the thought one little bit, except that I think it will be good discipline and help to make a man of me (as the Industrial boys say).[64]

A week later:

> I have attended four recruit drills this week, at 7.30 in the morning! I met Bernard there too. The Corps is very strong just now, it is over 800 men and still growing, and a great many of my friends are in it. So that Camp in the Summer ought to be great fun. I feel very virtuous being a Territorial as I feel that at last I am really doing my duty and am not a mere 'flannelled fool' or 'muddied oaf'.[65]

The Bishop certainly approved of the Army. He wrote to Bernard:

> We are pleased to hear that you have joined the Medical Unit of the Officer Training Corps and that you are attending drills at 7.30am. The discipline is excellent, and trying as you may find it at first, I am sure it will strengthen character and improve health. A Cadet Corps is being formed at Liverpool College and Aidan has joined. I hope Chris will follow such excellent examples.[66]

Noel was obviously a natural for in May he was promoted, but displayed in one letter an aversion towards one of his fellow men that reveals an unexpectedly acerbic side to his nature:

> I hear today that I have been fairly booted up in the Territorials. I have been made a lance-sergeant and so get 3

stripes on my arm. I feel both pleased and annoyed because I don't deserve it, as I have been promoted over several corporals' heads — men who have served years. It also means an awful lot of work at Camp. As far as I can see, my only merit is that I bawl out orders louder than anybody else. I am pleased, because my pet aversion is in the Corps, Mr Burridge by name (I always call him Mr, I loathe him so). I intend to use my authority and my prerogatives for abusive language on his beastly greasy head, as he slacks and lounges about on parade in a perfectly sickening way, and I refuse to have the Corps wilfully disgraced by a little beast like him, if I can possibly help it by any fatherly advice. I believe sergeants may sometimes even kick very slovenly cadets. I have stated my intention to do so, but I have been asked not to with the boots I have just bought for Territorial purposes, as they might pulverise him altogether.

General French comes to review us on June 5th so I have to attend about 4 drills a week in the early morning. If a telegram arrives from Oxford, you will know that this awful effort has been too much for a great but overtaxed heart.[67]

He later described what happened at General John French's review:

There are now over 700 of us and we had to march from St Aldate's up to Headington Park where the review took place. I am told by many onlookers that it was a very fine sight and quite inspiring. And I believe a great many more men will join next year. Really, volunteering is now quite the push thing.[68]

Though he was twenty-four years old by this time, Noel still had an almost boyish wish to feel the security of his family's support on special occasions. Unfortunately his father could come only rarely to Oxford these days, as he was now one of the bishops who occupied a seat in the House of Lords and often spent many days at a time in London. Noel wrote querulously to his mother in May 1909,

Why did you not allow Marjorie and May to come down for Eights week? We are all very disappointed. It would have been great fun if they could have come. I wish someone from our part of the world could come. Do you think you or Father could manage a day or two if he is coming down this way?[69]

But his tone in letters to his mother was not always so fractious. On one occasion he showed an affectionate humour in remonstrating with her:

> I notice you sign yourself your own mother. I never remember ever charging Father with bigamy, or marrying twice.
> Your natural son, Noel.[70]

At the end of the academic year in July, 1909, Noel made the final break with Oxford. He spent much of the summer vacation attending practical anatomy classes at Liverpool University, as he had done before, managing also to accompany 200 Grafton Street boys on their annual month-long camp at Hightown. That summer the Industrial School's monthly *Record* reported his contribution with enthusiasm:

> We tender to Mr Chavasse our heartiest thanks for the great help he was at Camp. Ever ready to organise all sorts of games, to assist in their being carried out to a most successful issue, and in a hundred ways, finding some means to add joy and happiness to our lads.[71]

He sometimes addressed the whole camp on Sundays (shades of the 'Bishop of Wangaroo'?), he presented a silver cup to be conferred upon 'The Best Tent at Cricket', and when it rained he produced scriptural stories in pictures for the boys to colour in, for which prizes were awarded. He even composed a camp song, 'Rolling on the Old Sand Hills'. As ever, a full day's visit was made to Grandmother Maude at Overton-on-Dee, and so interested was she in the welfare of the boys that a message from her was printed in the *Record*.

When boys grew too old to remain at Grafton Street, they were usually found live-in placements where they were usefully employed and would, with luck, learn a trade. That summer of 1909, on behalf of Mr Robinson, the Governor, Noel went to visit some of these boys in Yorkshire, and his report of his findings was submitted to the Chairman and Members of the Industrial School Committee:

> I can imagine no better places into which boys can be sent on leaving school. Their new parents will be their steadfast friends throughout life, they will be earning a good and increasing income; and some day they ought to marry a good Yorkshire lassie and enjoy at last the home life, of which, as children, circumstances and wickedness robbed them.[72]

Now that he was back home in Liverpool on a permanent basis, he could once again take a weekly, sometimes daily, interest in the Industrial School. But he also had to continue his studies towards medical qualification, and this took precedence over everything else, including membership of the Territorials. He was not to resume life in uniform until three more years had passed.

CHAPTER FOUR

Dr Chavasse

For both Christopher and Noel, life resumed equably at the Bishop's Palace in Liverpool, and these years seem, in the light of what was to follow, like a lull before the storm.

In October 1909, for the first time as a full-time student, Noel went through the Victoria tower entrance of the University of Liverpool in Brownlow Hill. Very near to his home in Abercromby Square, the university was a young but thriving institution, providing through its Medical School a succession of hospital doctors and general practitioners for the city of Liverpool and beyond. Here Noel met several of the leading medical teachers of the day, including Robert Jones, who was rapidly achieving a worldwide reputation as an orthopaedic surgeon. Noel was encouraged by him to work hard to achieve his ambition, and with such an example, work hard he did.

In the autumn of 1909 he took the examination in London for fellowship of the Royal College of Surgeons, but failed it. The Bishop wrote to Bernard:

> Poor Noel has been very seedy. He went up for the FRCS
> Examination looking wretchedly ill, and though he did work,
> he did not get it. He is better now and very cheerful. Very few
> succeed at their first attempt.[1]

In the following May he took it again, and this time passed with ease, to the whole family's satisfaction. As Marjorie wrote in reply to his telegram,

> Your wire has sent us all into transports of delight. Father is
> telephoning, Mother is laughing foolishly, and I am jumping.
> The servants are heaving sighs of relief 'for Mr. Nole [sic] he
> has worked so hard'. In case you are feeling too uplifted let me
> remind you that you had a tremendous pull over everyone else
> who went in, possessing as you do such a particularly righteous
> Father, Mother and SISTER, indeed my firm conviction is that
> it is entirely owing to these that you have passed.

I must close now, as I have to hasten away to weave garlands and wreaths, and practise 'See the Conquering Hero' which is to be played as you enter the house.[2]

Meanwhile Christopher embarked upon training for the ministry under his father's tutelage, and with several other young men attended frequent and prolonged classes and discussion groups at the Palace. The ordinands were also instructed in the problems of running a parish and witnessed the day-by-day administration of a large and cumbersome diocese. Finally the great day of ordination arrived. In the presence of the whole family Christopher was ordained by his father at St. Bride's Church, Catharine Street, Liverpool, on Sunday 20 February, 1910. His first curacy was at the parish church of St Mary in the town of St Helens, a coal-mining, glass-making community some twelve miles from Liverpool. Here Chris continued his sporting activities, playing rugby for the town and earning himself a considerable reputation as a character in the process.

Later the same year, the first major stage of the Bishop's plans for a cathedral for the Liverpool Diocese came to fruition, with the consecration of the Lady Chapel on Wednesday, 29 June. Appropriately enough, this was St Peter's Day and it marked the end of the useful life of St Peter's Pro-Cathedral in Church Street. Now the Diocese of Liverpool had a heart and its Bishop had a spiritual home. The whole family assembled on St James's Mount that day to witness the high point of Bishop Chavasse's ministry in Liverpool. The charming 'little' chapel (so-called in contrast to the grandiose plans for the rest of the cathedral, though in reality larger than many a parish church) was consecrated by the Bishop himself, in the presence of the Archbishop of York, who had agreed to preach. No member of the royal family was able to attend; the death of Edward VII only weeks earlier meant that the Court was still in mourning. A luncheon in the Town Hall followed, attended by the male members of the family including Noel and Chris, but not apparently graced by the presence of any of the ladies.[3]

However, Mrs Chavasse and her two unmarried daughters, May and Marjorie, led hectic lives themselves. The Bishop's wife, in spite of her shyness, was fully occupied in committee work. Marjorie drove the Bishop about in his car, a present from the diocese; she had never had a driving lesson and drove very fast but seems never to have had an accident. Both she and her twin sister May had a large circle of friends and acquaintances. They became interested in playing hockey due to companionships with young hockey enthusiasts amongst the ordinands living in the Bishop's Hostel next door, and both played for the Lancashire Ladies and for the North of England[4] from time to time. They were invited to numberless tennis matches and theatre parties, entering into every social or 'duty' activity with a will.

So Noel soon found himself involved in the student and social life of the city. At the end of the academic year he visited his old haunts in Oxford, and was tempted to stay. He wrote home:

> Dr. Ramsden very much wants me to come down again and take on a house surgeonship at the Radcliffe Infirmary and work with him again for my MD thesis. But I think it is hardly practicable.[5]

During the same trip south, he called in at The Linthurst Hill to visit Uncle Tom and Aunt Frances and in particular to see his cousins Gladys and Esme. Their elder brother Arthur was by now also working towards his medical qualifications and was based in London, and their elder sister Gwendolen had married the previous year. Between Gladys and Noel there was developing a relationship which was giving much concern to her father. He liked Noel, unquestionably, but the young man *was* Gladys's first cousin, and Sir Thomas, perhaps due to his medical and hunting stud background, was much disturbed by the thought of a possible marriage between them. In conversation with his wife he expressly forbade it, but there was probably no foundation for his fears at this time; in 1910 Gladys was only seventeen, and no such thoughts had entered her head as yet. The cousins simply enjoyed each other's company, as indeed did Christopher and Gladys's sister Esme. May and Marjorie frequently visited too, with Bernard and Aidan, and a noisy houseparty of *all* the cousins was the norm.

Back in Liverpool for the start of the new academic year, Noel registered at the University for courses in pathology and bacteriology, working towards his second MB, but seems to have finished these two subjects by the end of 1910. He then studied a large number of optional topics: infectious diseases, vaccination, therapeutics, operative surgery, ophthalmology and practical obstetrics — all except the latter proving to be of enormous value in the carnage to come. He passed each test with flying colours.

Like every medical student, he had to undertake a hospital 'placement': in his case, a position was found at the Rotunda Hospital in Dublin, and here he spent three months in the summer of 1911. This was his first time away from mainland Britain, and he was soon apprised of the differences between England and Ireland:

> The King is coming here at the end of this week and I expect we shall see a little Irish contempt. Dublin is not giving him an address of welcome ...[6]

This did not particularly upset Noel. However, he was greatly distressed by what he observed of the attitudes and activities of some priests. Never having encountered a Roman Catholic community before he could not refrain from remarking to his mother:

> I like the Dublin people very much, they are very warm-hearted, and I get quite attached to the patients. I think the Dublin children are the jolliest in the world, if you only wink an eye at them they will come and make friends.
>
> I don't like priests here. They don't seem to do much for their people, but they take a lot of money off them. A very poor woman will send a penny to the priest for a prayer for a quick delivery and they buy pictures of the Virgin from the priests, and they have to give money to build most beautiful churches. And when the Archbishop of Westminster and Father Vaughan came to a chapel here to celebrate some anniversary, everybody who entered the church had to pay at least 1/- admittance, so that the parishioners who are very poor did not get in. And yet when a priest visits a poor woman who has just had a baby, and who is absolutely starving, he offers no relief at all, but leaves it all to the Protestant doctors to do.
>
> The people themselves are not a bit bigoted, if you tell them that you are a Protestant, they say, 'Oh! one is as good as another.' They burn candle ends before little images of Christ and Mary, and think that they are as good as prayers as God looks down and reads their hearts and gives them their desires. Their talk is a funny mixture of devotional phrases and oaths. I don't believe they mean either.[7]

Noel's last year at university was soon upon him. He did work hard, but also found time to help Christopher in a project very reminiscent of the Oxford Mission to Bermondsey that he had so admired four years previously. In his parish in St Helens, Chris was becoming increasingly aware of the need, drunkenness and poverty in that crowded urban community, and was pleased to be asked to take charge of the York Street Mission in the town. He helped to establish a running club and a brass band, as well as holding Bible classes, and with Noel's assistance a sports club for poor boys was set up. Noel's years of experience with the Grafton Street boys were put to good use here.[8]

By 1912, Noel's ultimate ambition had taken a firm hold upon him. He passed his final Medical Examination in January, as his father told Bernard:

47

Noel has done very well in his Examination in London. A Liverpool doctor, who was examining, brought back word that he passed a splendid Examination. He went home [to Barnt Green] with Arthur for a week and the change and rest has done him great good.[9]

Now he wanted to follow in the footsteps of the great Liverpool medical man, Robert Jones, and specialize in orthopaedic surgery. On 15 March the committee of the Medical Faculty of the University, led by Doctors Macalister and Douglas-Crawford, awarded him their premier prize, the Derby Exhibition.[10] Dr Macalister was, of course, well known to Noel as the family doctor and also lectured in Clinical Medicine at the University; Mr. Douglas-Crawford was a colleague of Robert Jones on the staff of the Royal Southern Hospital. There would seem to be the possibility of favouritism here, but Noel's future career does testify to his ability, and there was no reason why he should have been disqualified from winning the prize just because he knew two members of the Committee. In any case the prize, worth £15, was awarded through a competitive examination moderated by others, containing both written and clinical elements.

At the same time as his studies drew to an end, Noel was learning all he could from the Great Man. Robert Jones had come to Liverpool from London in 1873, at the age of sixteen, to learn the art of 'bone-setting' at the feet of his uncle, Hugh Owen Thomas, who lived and practised at No. 11 Nelson Street. Jones qualified in medicine in 1878 and became a consultant at the Royal Southern Hospital in 1889. In the 1890s he pioneered aseptic methods and the use of X-rays or 'Roentgen rays' in this country. In 1905 he left general surgery behind and concentrated on orthopaedics, and it was at his surgeries on Saturday afternoons and Sunday mornings that Noel learnt much of the orthopaedic surgeon's skill.[11]

So at last, in the summer of 1912, Noel Chavasse had qualified as a doctor, registering with the General Medical Council on 22 July, 1912.[12]

Now there was time for watching cricket matches at the Liverpool Cricket Club and for a holiday lasting several weeks, most of them at Barnt Green, in the congenial company of Uncle Tom and Aunt Frances — and of course Gladys. Obviously their happiness was marred somewhat by the rigid disapproval of Uncle Tom and if there was anything between them it was unspoken. Nevertheless, Noel was unable to hide, in letters to his mother, the contentment he felt that summer:

We are hay-making, and having a right royal time and great peace of heart, such as I have been a stranger from for years. I feel I have dropped a burden and no mistake ... The days are so beautiful and I am so happy making hay and playing tennis all day long that I accepted a kind invitation to stay on.[13]

When he returned to Liverpool and was known to be looking for his first six-month hospital placement, both Macalister and Jones were prepared to support an application to the Royal Southern, where he had already done some locum work.[14] The hospital was situated in the Toxteth area of the city, just a short walk from the Grafton Street Industrial School, and provided medical care for the poor. Founded in 1838, the hospital had 207 beds in 1912 and was financed through the medium of a charitable fund. Subscribers or 'Trustees' were entitled to recommend patients; indeed the Hospital rules stated that:

> No patient shall be received without a recommendation in writing from a Trustee, except in cases of accident and emergency; these to be admitted at any hour, day or night.[15]

The list of Trustees at the time Noel joined the hospital included most of the celebrated Liverpool names of the day, such as shipping magnates Ralph Brocklebank and John Bibby; politicians like Robert Gladstone; philanthropists like John Rankin (who was to be so generous to the Liverpool Scottish during the Great War); and Robert Jones himself. In a separate category of subscribers was the Bishop, who began to donate the annual sum of five pounds in 1901.

Noel was interviewed for the post of house surgeon on 4 October, 1912. Robert Jones already had a house surgeon, but the Minutes of the General Committee recorded that

> N. G. Chavasse, M.A., M.B., B.Ch., M.R.C.S., L.R.C.P. was appointed as House Surgeon to Mr Douglas-Crawford, for the six months ending 31st March 1913.[16]

Together with another new appointee, Dr Hugh Pierce, Noel put his signature to the 'Rules for House Physicians and House Surgeons', thereby promising to live at the hospital, not to absent himself without permission and then only if he found his own substitute, to visit the wards twice daily when on duty, and never to act on his own responsibility except in the direst emergency. When on duty in Out-Patients, Noel and the other junior doctors had to report their time of arrival, and a further responsibility was to prepare the list of each day's operations for the consultant. Dogs were not to be kept on hospital premises.

So Noel moved out of the Palace and took up residence at the Royal

Southern, except for his official periods of leave. His appointment to the firm of Mr Douglas-Crawford was renewed in March 1913 for six months, and there is nothing to suggest that he was in any way unhappy or dissatisfied with this state of affairs; indeed, a strong friendship grew up between them. But Noel still wished to specialize in orthopaedics and was delighted when, in October 1913, he was appointed house surgeon to Robert Jones himself, now a very senior and much-respected member of Liverpool's medical fraternity. Now began the time Noel most enjoyed during his peacetime medical career, days in which he worked harder but learnt more than at any other period in his life. He also read widely and was an avid borrower of books from the fine library of the Liverpool Medical Institution in Mount Pleasant.

As a resident Noel was himself able to recommend a few patients for treatment. In 1913 he was travelling through the poorest district, adjacent to the docks, when he saw a crippled child crawling in the road. He stopped his cab, alighted and handed the boy his card, telling him to ask his mother to bring him to the Royal Southern Hospital. The boy, Robert Eager, underwent nine operations at the hands of Dr Chavasse, supervised by Robert Jones, and was finally able to walk upright and lead a full life in the Merchant Navy.[17] Even in a charitable institution like the Southern, if poor citizens had no means of attracting the attention of one of the Trustees there was little likelihood of obtaining treatment.

Christopher too was undergoing a change in the direction of his career. In the autumn of 1913 he left his curacy at St. Helens and became chaplain to his father. The Bishop was not in the best of health, and it was hoped that Christopher could lighten his burden somewhat. Brother Bernard, also pursuing a medical career, had gained a First in Natural Science at Balliol College, Oxford, in 1912 and was now studying at Liverpool University. Aidan, a strapping twenty-one-year-old and the last of the four Chavasse boys, entered Corpus Christi College, Oxford (his father's old college), and achieved a Second in Mathematics. Noel thought he should have done better: 'I feel he is a First Class man,' he wrote to his mother.[18] Aidan also obtained a Third in History in 1914 but any further studies were interrupted when war broke out. Had he lived, he too would probably have sought ordination in the Church of England.

Unfortunately, during 1913 the Chavasse family suffered two great losses. The first was the death of Sir Thomas. At fifty-eight he was a fit and fearless huntsman, running a string of hunting ponies at his own stables at The Linthurst Hill. Unaccountably, he was thrown from his horse while out with the North Warwickshire Hunt just before Christmas 1912 and suffered a fractured thigh. It was thought that he was making a good recovery, but suddenly on 2 February, 1913, in his bedroom at home, he suffered a heart attack and died that evening, his wife and children around him.[19] For a long time the Bishop could not be consoled, although some slight comfort was afforded him in January the following year, when he dedicated a memorial window in Bromsgrove Parish Church in the presence of the whole Chavasse family.[20] The major obstacle to a romantic attachment between Noel and Gladys was now removed, but it was more than three years before they took advantage of it.

The second blow of the year was the final illness of Mrs Chavasse's mother, Grandmother Maude, but this passing was more or less expected due to the old lady's advanced aged of ninety-four. Nevertheless, Noel, in his first year at the Southern, was very concerned about her, and did his best to help:

> I have seen Doctor Macalister and had a talk with him. He thinks that this Bismuth medicine would certainly be good. He also thinks that this weak bottle of Strychnine might help. I have only sent a small dose, because as he says a larger dose might only brighten the flame for a little, for it to burn out all the quicker ... He fears though that everything points to a general decay of the tissue.[21]

But Grannie Maude died on 30 July, and the family had another funeral to attend, this time at Chirk in Denbighshire.

Noel's work at the Southern was very demanding, but he revelled in it. This was exactly what he wanted to do, helping poor people and developing one of the most rewarding skills in surgery, that of the orthopaedic specialist. However, he found time to renew an association with an institution he had often thought of since his Oxford days — the Territorial Force. And when he talked to Dr Macalister about the idea, the suggestion was immediately made that he should try to get attached, via membership of the Royal Army Medical Corps, to the 10th Battalion of the King's (Liverpool Regiment), the Liverpool Scottish. Macalister held the position of Surgeon-Captain to the Battalion, but was about to transfer to the Reserve, and nothing would give him greater pleasure than to pave the way for this gifted young protégé.[22] So Noel applied, and was accepted as junior medical officer with the rank of surgeon-lieutenant. A slightly more experienced man, Dr Kidston, was still in post and thus senior to Noel, but he was pleased to help and advise the new recruit. So began the association with the battalion that was to be the most powerful element in Noel's life from now on.

A few weeks previously, the Territorials had been somewhat ridiculed by Lord Rochdale. 'To put the present Territorial Force against trained Continental troops was,' he said, 'like putting a village eleven against a county eleven.'[23] The Liverpool Scottish could never have agreed with this view. The battalion was raised in December 1900 and had over the years become a familiar sight on parade in Liverpool. When King Edward VII visited the city in 1904 for the laying of the Cathedral foundation stone, the battalion 'lined the streets, taking up their position on either side of Castle Street, from the Town Hall to St George's Street'.[24]

In September of the following year, the King inspected them and told them how he particularly remembered their fine physique.[25] With the Haldane Army Reforms, the battalion ceased to exist as a volunteer battalion and became instead a unit of the newly-organized Territorial Force. It was now designated 'the 10th (Scottish) Battalion The King's (Liverpool Regiment)', and was a unit of the South Lancashire Brigade TF, in the West Lancashire Division. At a royal review at Knowsley Hall by the King on 5 July, 1909, new colours were presented, and they were consecrated by Noel's father.[26]

By the time Noel joined in 1913, the battalion had its own headquarters at 5 − 7 Fraser Street, off London Road, a very busy part of the city. The buildings contained a miniature shooting range, lecture room, armoury, magazine, gymnasium and the usual messes for officers and sergeants, as well as a sizeable canteen for the men, all three complete with their own billiard tables. Non-military activities were numerous and of a type to suit the new doctor perfectly:

> In the Liverpool Scottish it has always been realised that manly games and sport are of value in assisting to develop soldier-like qualities amongst all ranks in the battalion; accordingly every encouragement is given to all members to indulge in games and all forms of sport.[27]

The battalion fielded rugby and football teams, while the officers competed in an annual golf competition; another annual event was the athletics competition between them and the London Scottish. Summer camps involving two weeks under canvas helped to foster an *esprit de corps*, as did pride and respect for their only Victoria Cross holder, a veteran of the Boer War, Donald D. Farmer. Still only thirty-six years old, Farmer was an uncle figure to the younger men of the battalion, and soon became well-known to Noel as he learnt his way around Fraser Street.

Morale was also boosted by the notion, deliberately cultivated in this battalion as in many others, that its members were special, different and privileged. Recruits had to have a Scottish parent or grandparent; they had to stand at least five feet six inches tall and measure at least thirty-five inches round the chest; and they had to pay an annual subscription of 10s. per annum to battalion funds. Training would involve a commitment of at least forty hours in the first year and ten thereafter, and a fortnight's camp was *de rigueur*.[28] In fact, the vast majority of members of the Scottish came from white-collar occupations and had an education that was superior to most people's; many had attended school until fifteen or sixteen and had served periods of training with banks, shipping firms, insurance companies and the like. With the men's similar backgrounds, it would not be too far-fetched to liken them to Lord Derby's 'Pals' battalions, whose recruitment was to play such an important role in the early months of the Great War.

The Commanding Officer, Lieutenant-Colonel W. Nicholl, welcomed the new young doctor on 2 June, 1913, and within weeks Noel had his first experience of a parade when King George V and Queen Mary visited the city. The battalion colours were carried by two young officers who were close friends of Noel's, Fred Turner and Robert 'Dum' Cunningham. In August he attended his first camp, along with the officers and 609 other ranks, at Denbigh, an experience he approached with some trepidation:

> I am off to camp on Sunday next for a fortnight. I am a little nervous about it. I rather feel I am being chucked into the deep end of soldiering at once. I shall have to struggle a bit before I float. I have ordered a horse, a nice confident one, who will step out with the band and obey words of command. I have had three riding lessons. The Sergeant Instructor is an old patient of mine and takes great pains. Tomorrow I am going to be put over the jumps. I have not had a fall yet but they are working up to me. They put me on a more disagreeable beast every time.[29]

And from the camp itself:

> I felt very raw at first, but I am getting knocked into shape now. The mess is very quiet. Most of the fellows seem to be teetotal and a lot of them are young married men, who seem to be a very respectable class.

Having reassured his parents he went on:

> As luck would have it [his first patient] was the Brigadier, who thought that he had lumbago, but who really had ruptured some fibres in his back. ... The fellows in the ranks seem a very good lot taking them all round. They are certainly very respectful. I don't think I have heard any bad language. On the whole I should say that they were pretty free from it.
>
> Tomorrow are the Sports, but I am not allowed to run in them,

because I am only attached [sic] to the Scottish, I am really R.A.M.C. I am in it but not of it.[30]

The Bishop knew the rigours of army camp very well, for he was himself Chaplain to the 5th Liverpools and had been with them at Denbigh Camp only three weeks earlier.

Once again the summer meant Barnt Green to Noel. 'I should like to go very much as it may be the last chance I get of going there,' he wrote to his father.[31] Perhaps he simply meant the last chance that summer, for a junior doctor's leave was limited; it may also have been that there was talk of Aunt Frances selling up and leaving the Linthurst Hill, the large house with its stables not being so necessary now that Sir Thomas had passed away. If there were any such discussions, they came to nothing.

In September he passed his first Territorial examinations, in preparation for which he attended classes of instruction at the Fraser Street headquarters on Monday evenings. His spiritual welfare also was augmented by his association with the Scottish. Church parade took place at regular intervals, preceded by a Commanding Officer's Review in Sefton Park and a march back towards the Church of St Andrew in Rodney Street. The Chaplain, the Reverend J. Hamilton, was in the habit of delivering a sermon full of patriotic rhetoric, such as the one heard by Noel Chavasse on St Andrew's Day (30 November) 1913:

> No other nation, in any period of the whole world's history, has done so much to weld more closely the links of human brotherhood, while infusing the whole, consciously, and very often unconsciously, with much of that sweet and refining influence which Christianity can impart. ... Shame on the man who belittles his country — such a country as this! And shame on that citizen who can, yet who will not, do what in him lies to maintain and defend Her benificent rule and dominion! All honour to those who freely offer of their substance to her! All honour to those who give themselves to her service without fee or reward, who recognize that the cause of Britain is a sacred cause, and who are willing to lay down their lives, if need be, on the altar of devout patriotism, for Her Dear Sake![32]

In less than a year, such exhortations became only too necessary. But Noel was so involved with meeting the many and various demands upon his time and energies that he paid little attention to the gathering stormclouds in Europe. For him, 28 June, 1914, was just another day at the hospital; he did read *The Times* every day but saw no more significance in the

1. "The three-storeyed house at the end of a terrace in New Inn Hall Street" (p.1).

2. Christopher and Noel in 1894 (*J. C. Chavasse*).

3.   "The family of seven children was now complete" (p.4). *Left to right* Noel,
Bernard, Dorothea, May, Aidan, Marjorie, Christopher, *circa* 1897 (*J. C. Chavasse*).

4.   Noel diving into the Cherwell at Magdalen College School Swimming Sports,
circa 1898 (*J. C. Chavasse*).

5. Mary Fawler Maude,
Noel's maternal grandmother,
wrote the hymn 'Thine for ever,
God of Love' (p.7)
(*J. C. Chavasse*).

6. Bishop F. J. Chavasse at his desk in the Palace (*J. C. Chavasse*).

7. 19 Abercromby Square, "the very place for the residence of a bishop" (p.11). The slightly elevated roof distinguishes the Palace from the neighbouring houses (*Liverpool City Libraries*).

8. "Liverpool College was a school for Liverpool's 'young gentlemen'" (p.14). It is now a girls' comprehensive school (*S. Lawler*).

assassinations in far-off Sarajevo than did millions of other Britons. Slight changes being made to the uniforms of the Liverpool Scottish did quite unwittingly prepare them for war:

> A supply of khaki aprons has been sanctioned, and these will be issued before camp, and will be worn instead of sporrans for field work.[33]

But the officers were preparing simply for camp, not conflict. The nominal roll of the unit listed 913 men and officers in July, almost at full strength.

So Noel signed the Leave Book at the Royal Southern for the last time, booking himself out from 2 to 16 August, 1914, and set off for Hornby Camp, north Lancashire, with his fellow junior officers. Dr Power, the locum who was to undertake his duties during those two weeks, waited in vain to be relieved. Noel Chavasse never returned to the hospital.

CHAPTER FIVE

For King and Country

> At eleven o'clock last night England declared war on Germany.
> We now know exactly what our position and responsibilities are
> in the horrible period which now has to be gone through. We
> must accept the position and shoulder the responsibilities with
> British fortitude and determination. The honour, dignity,
> integrity and future fortunes of the British Empire are at stake
> to a degree never before conceived possible.[1]

Thus the *Liverpool Daily Post and Mercury* announced the outbreak of the
Great European War on 4 August, 1914. The overall feeling was one of relief,
now that the days of tension and suspense were over.

Noel and his battalion had arrived at Hornby Camp on 2 August, in spite
of the alarm felt by the authorities at the news that France, Russia and
Germany were already mobilizing. The battalion hardly had time to unpack.
At 2 o'clock on the morning of 3 August, a telegram arrived for the
Commanding Officer, ordering an immediate return to Liverpool, where
they arrived in the early evening. Camp had been struck so quickly that the
men did not have time to draw the pocket money they had deposited with
the camp bank, run by the Young Men's Christian Association, and
arrangements had to be made to reimburse them or their families back in
Liverpool.[2] After parading at Fraser Street the men were dispersed to their
homes, with the proviso that they might be called back at any time.[3] Noel
made his way up the hill to Abercromby Square to await developments.

His father was still on holiday in Northumberland, but his three brothers
were already at home. Bernard, for the whole of July, had been cruising in
the Irish Sea on his sloop *Wender* with two friends, and Chris had joined
them; on 1 August, however, they had decided to cut their holiday short.
Aidan was about to return to Oxford to embark upon a theology course, but
decided simply to put his affairs in order and then apply for a commission
in the King's (Liverpool Regiment) if war should break out. Having been a
very active member of Liverpool College's Officer Training Corps and the
Oxford University OTC, he felt this should pose no problems.

The four brothers discussed war and rumours of war, speculating about what parts they could play. They were not left wondering for long. Later that day the regular and territorial troops were mobilized, and on 4 August Britain declared war on Germany.

For the Scottish, mobilization meant frenzied activity, equipping the men, medically examining more recruits to bring the battalion up to strength, and collecting horses for transport duties. Noel assisted Dr Kidston but was still uncertain as to whether he would see service as a regimental Medical Officer. Chris was keen to join the Army Chaplain's department and was hopeful of serving with the same division as Noel. By 5 August they could stand the inactivity no longer and decided to take the bull by the horns. They caught a train to London to go to the War Office in person. The great anxiety for young men hoping to take part in the action was that it would all be over within a few months. As the local newspaper reported,

> A couple of maiden ladies from Birkenhead have resolved to remain in Switzerland 'until the end of the war', but anticipate being home before Christmas.[4]

May, on holiday in Northumberland with her parents, was in touch with her twin sister by telephone, and both offered their services as nursing assistants to a Mrs Melly of Liverpool, who had set up a committee for the purpose; but she replied that there was no demand for untrained women. May sent Marjorie, who was staying at Pen Dyffryn, the family news on 6 August:

> We are in rather a state of anxiety at present, as Noel has offered for active service as Doctor, and Christopher as Chaplain — Noel has been accepted and they both went up to the War Office last night — Chris went too, as he wants to be gazetted to Noel's regiment. What Bernard and Aidan will do, we don't quite know yet, but I believe Aidan has ideas of offering...but he has said nothing yet. I shouldn't wonder if we go home next week, as Chris and Noel may have to sail any day, for we have to defend the Belgian frontier, and the Germans are already crossing it. At Liege they have been crushingly beaten back I believe, and the Newcastle paper says that a German officer who was wounded and taken prisoner expressed great surprise at their splendid resistance, as in Berlin it was understood that they could not offer any resistance at all....I will wire you any news that is serious.[5]

Unfortunately, Chris found that he could not be appointed to the same division as the Liverpool Scottish, but he was immediately accepted into the Army Chaplain's department as Temporary Chaplain 4th Class, and came home to prepare for service with IV Army Corps. Soon the whole family was back at the Palace.

On 7 August the Liverpool Scottish were recalled to Fraser Street, and thereafter went into billets, some of them in the Shakespeare Theatre where Sam Moulton, who was later to be appointed groom to Noel, slept proudly in a box.[6] Others were sent to the Liverpool Stadium and made themselves as comfortable as they could around the boxing ring in the centre.[7]

On 8 August Noel suffered what he thought was a desperate piece of bad luck: the Royal Army Medical Corps ordered him away from the Liverpool Scottish and sent him to Chester Castle, where he was to examine recruits. He told his mother, who with the Bishop had cut short her holiday,

> We are passing a great number of recruits — we have to keep at it 9 hours a day, and are very sleepy afterwards. The Territorials seem about to be used, so I am in hopes.[8]

The speed with which events had occurred found Noel, like many another young officer, away from home and without what he regarded as the basic essentials of life. He went on:

> I am allowed to wear mufti in the evenings here. So I wonder if Miss Stokes [the housekeeper] could root about my room and send me my best grey suit, 4 stiff turn-down collars (in round collar box), 2 limp white shirts, a black knitted silk tie and a large gold safety pin in upper draw [sic] right of chest of drawers by bed.

Two days later,

> Thank you very much, the parcel arrived this morning. Unfortunately, it seems in the travel to have come into contact with a case of herrings, and arrived very greasy and part of the herrings had soaked through at one corner, and I smell a bit of herrings, which people don't seem to like during this hot weather. The P.O. people sent up a damage form which I signed so I can get compensation if I want it.[9]

Back in Liverpool, the Scottish, like all Territorial Force battalions, had been asked whether or not they wished to serve overseas. Colonel Nicholl immediately offered the services of the battalion. Noel was in Chester when he heard the news.

I should really be very happy here, if we did not feel so restless, because I feel I am being useful. I am examining recruits, and tomorrow I am going to start Vaccinating them. ...I hear that the Liverpool Scottish and the Field Ambulances of Liverpool have all volunteered for the Front, I don't know if they will go or not, but as the senior Medical Officer [Dr Kidston] will, I suppose, go with the Scottish, and as I am a regimental doctor and not attatched [sic] with any of the Field Ambulances, I am terribly affraid [sic] lest I may be left in England on one of these rotten recruiting jobs.[10]

The worry of 'missing out' is revealed in his spelling, which always became more idiosyncratic than usual at times of stress. As yet Noel did not know whether Kidston was also going to volunteer for the front; he fervently hoped not. Meanwhile, he tried to take a more positive attitude and began to put his affairs in order in case he was sent abroad at short notice. He informed his father:

Today I had paid into your account at Liverpool £40, which was due to me when I became a Territorial. I am writing this in order to tell you how to spend the £40. Do not spend it recklessly or extravagantly. It will grieve and vex me to hear that you and Mother have gone on the bust with it.

£20 are owing to you already, you kindly lent me that to buy my initial outfit, when I joined the Terriers in a hurry. With the other £20 please pay off at once the two bills owing to Flight [his military tailor] — one for a civilian dress suit and the other for a mess dress suit. ...

£5 is still coming in to me, for mobilization. I earn here about £5 a week. Of that I spend £2 board and lodging (first rate food), and 1/- a day on a swim before breakfast and a row up the Dee after work is over. The rest I shall send you weekly to pay off the little minor debts. I want to leave England with a clean slate behind me.[11]

He had already asked the Colonel to keep his name in mind if the Scottish should be designated for foreign service, and was still hopeful. In fact, the Scottish were first offered the chance of going to Egypt but the Commanding Officer turned it down, hoping instead that they would be sent to France, perhaps to guard lines of communication.[12] The idea that territorials would be in the forefront of active service had not yet sunk in. Nevertheless, the British press was greatly impressed by the willingness of the Territorial Force

59

in this, its first real test, and held its fighting spirit up as an example to others. This appeared in *The Times*, 26 August:

> That there is good and willing material is proved by the admirable conduct of the Territorials, which has never received the public recognition it deserves. ...Yesterday, Lord Kitchener told the House of Lords that 69 Battalions have already volunteered for service abroad. That is the right answer to German libels on the national spirit. But, proud as we may be of it, the rest of the nation has no right to shelter itself behind their sacrifices and live at home at ease while they bear the burden.

Meanwhile, Noel was preparing for all eventualities:

> I am really trying to train myself in every way I can to be useful, and am reading hard, all about the hygiene of a fighting army, and all about typhoid fever. ...I have a great longing to take care of a regiment. When I go out with the Scottish boys I feel quite paternal, and love keeping them fit and dressing their minor injuries. I think it is the pastoral spirit, for the care and cure of bodies instead of souls, although I do care for their souls too — only it is not my business specially to cater for them.
>
> If ever I get sent to the Front with a regiment I shall almost shed tears of joy. ...
>
> We pass from 50 to 100 recruits daily and vaccinate them afterwards. Two of us vaccinated 175 of them last Sunday. ...I do envy Chris going off so soon, but I think this dog is going to have his day soon too.[13]

The Bishop wrote to Marjorie:

> Chris has just been summoned to report himself at Woolwich on Thursday. He is to go to a Base Hospital in Belgium or France. Aidan is going to Oxford today to see the O.T.C. people about a Commission. Bernard has heard that no more doctors are needed at present and has gone to Oxford on the same errand. Noel is still at Chester. God grant that the war may soon cease. The great wrath must at this very moment be raging.[14]

On 20 August, Christopher became the first member of the family to clatter in uniform down the circular staircase and out of the front door of the Palace. A family dinner the previous evening was the last time that all nine Chavasses were together. Noel managed to get over from Chester but had to return late the same night, and wrote rather wistfully to his mother:

> I suppose Chris went off in great spirits. When the war is over I expect the family gathering will be more cheerful, if we can afford enough food for so many.[15]

Mrs Chavasse was much troubled by a painful knee at this time, and Noel wrote to Robert Jones at the Royal Southern Hospital:

> The knee is still very swoolen [sic] but does not grate so much on moving it. There is a good deal of oedema of the leg which goes away after she lies down. ...I have told her that in the course of the next few weeks I should like her to consult you again and see what you think about it. So I think you will be hearing from her soon. I shall not feel happy going away unless I know that she is in your hands while her knee is still in this critical state.[16]

By this time the Liverpool Scottish had been sent to Edinburgh where the battalion formed part of the Forth Defences. The men were living in a bell-tented camp in the King's Park, near Holyrood Palace. Noel now learned that Dr Kidston, the senior Medical Officer, had not volunteered for foreign service, and that he, Noel, was to be attached to the battalion. He joined them in Edinburgh in early September, but he remained cautious as to his long-term future with them, especially as it seemed that Kidston was now wavering.

> I am still going to leave my name on the books at the War Office, because Dr Kidston is now quite keen on going on foreign service, only he cannot do so now because I am appointed to take his place. So if you find an opportunity of mentioning my name to Lord Derby I hope that you will take the chance. The officers are talking quite seriously. Most of them are very rich but they all think that the war will do England a lot of good, and that it wanted pulling up.[17]

Once again Noel was prepared to pull strings if he felt his purpose justified it, and the friendly relationship that existed between Bishop Chavasse and Lord Derby was worth exploiting. Frederick, the sixteenth earl, and his wife Constance had known the Bishop and Mrs Chavasse well, and when their son Edward became the seventeenth earl in 1908 an even closer affinity developed. Lord Derby sat as Chairman on the Liverpool Cathedral Building Committee; he was a Trustee, alongside the Bishop, of the Liverpool Bluecoat Hospital School; he had close connections with both Liverpool College and Liverpool University; and he had encountered Noel on several occasions already. As Chairman of the West Lancashire Territorial Association, he determined, as soon as war was declared in 1914, to recruit as many men as possible to answer Kitchener's call.[18] After October 1915, when Prime Minister Asquith appointed him to the post of Director-General of Recruiting, Lord Derby's influence benefited the Chavasse family on more than one occasion, but this time it was not necessary for the Bishop to approach him; Noel did go overseas with the Liverpool Scottish, just as he wanted to.

Meanwhile, news came of Chris, whose first post was as Chaplain at Number 10 General Hospital at St Nazaire.[19] As the wounded men came in from the retreat from Mons, his days seemed to consist entirely of ministering to the dying and conducting funerals. He reported the stories told to him by some of the men, as tales of the 'Angels of Mons' spread through the British Expeditionary Force.

Noel was eager to follow him across the Channel, but on a more homely note he was still tidying up his finances.

> If you send me an account of all I owe you, besides the £7 I sent at Chester and the £5 you lent me, I would send you a cheque as I can now easily settle up everything. If I die you will be a rich man for my pay is princely.[20]

(As a lieutenant, Noel's rate of pay was £25 per month, which compared most favourably with his salary at the Royal Southern Hospital of £50 per annum.) He was concerned too about the whereabouts of an item pertaining to his personal toilet:

> I have left my strop on the door of the bathroom. I should like to have it soon because it is a good one, and I don't want Bernard to get it. Everyone here is trying to grow a moustache so I am having a go too.[21]

The last photograph taken of the Liverpool Scottish officers before they embarked for France shows that the young men had indeed almost all grown moustaches. However, this adornment did not last long in Noel's case; within weeks he had removed it. Like so many of the things he did, this was an experiment, simply to see if he could do it; once he found that he could, he lost interest and looked round for another challenge.

In the camp at Edinburgh, he was soon faced with a much more serious problem, that of the health of the men:

> Sick Parade is at 6.45 a.m. I found this parade a perfect mob, but by first warning and then reporting slack corporals we now have quite a sharp parade. I don't think it is good to be too strict with sick men but they must keep some sort of rules.
>
> I am vaccinating the men against typhoid, the whole Battalion, over 1000 men. The men react badly and need bed-rest for 2 days and have high temperatures (103). 2 had to go to hospital.
>
> We have had a great many sick, more than any battalion around, and I have been interviewed by colonels and generals about it. They all say our lines are model lines for cleanliness and sanitary accommodation, and we think that the sickness, colds and influenza, is due to their being clerks, unused to roughing it and unused to kilts. We are the best for inoculation and vaccination. I am making these compulsory for every man who goes abroad. This week we leave canvas and go into the Marine Gardens at Porto Bello. We are billeted in a large ballroom. I would rather stay here but it is very cold and Edinburgh winds are very cutting.[22]

So crowded were his sick parades that he worried about not identifying serious complaints:

> About 100 attend, and have to be sorted out in about an hour. I am so afraid that I overlook a bad case in the hurry. As one instance, two men have both been operated upon for appendicitis, for what appeared when they reported as simple colic, and might easily have been treated as such if not examined carefully and conscientiously.[23]

The Commanding Officer, Colonel Nicholl, as well as the Medical Officer, was making determined efforts to make the men fit. Lieutenant A. M. McGilchrist, who served in the war with the Liverpool Scottish, became the battalion's official historian, and provided a description of the intense activity in the camp:

> Training was now begun in earnest. A severe programme of work was laid down calculated to weed out the weaklings. ...The day started at 6.45 a.m. with an hour's physical drill which frequently took the form of company races to the top of Arthur's Seat. After

breakfast, company and battalion training continued till 4.30 p.m., and lectures after tea were not unknown. ...The Battalion throve on the hard work, every man was keen and a genuine trier, the inter-company rivalry was prodigious, and the rapidity with which partially trained civilians were turned into a very fair imitation of whole-time soldiers was really astonishing.[24]

Noel was also concerned to polish up his riding skills, as became an officer, and to train a band of stretcher-bearers.

> I have joined a riding school here taken by a sergeant. It is all bareback riding and we have to manoeuvre like cavalry. Two days ago a big black brute in front of me fell out to the side and lashed out with his heels and caught me on the knee. There is hardly any mischief done except bruising. I fancy there is a little dent in the [knee] cap where the edge of the shoe caught me. I thought when I got the smash the cap must be smashed as it made such a row. I like the chance of drilling with the men. I think it a good opportunity of seeing their point of view and getting to know them without lowering one's rank. ...
>
> I also have a squad of 18 men, stretcher-bearers, to make proficient in first aid. I am getting very fond of them and they are enthusiasts. I have 5 men who look after the water-carts and 9 men as sanitary policemen who see that the camp is kept sweet and clean.[25]

There is an indication here that Noel felt more comfortable in the company of the men rather than with his fellow officers. It may well be that the drinking of alcoholic beverages had something to do with it. In the Officers' Mess drinking would be the normal and expected behaviour among the subalterns. Noel had been brought up in a rigorously teetotal household, and although he did gradually relax his views as the war went on, in these early days the free use of alcohol by his colleagues came as a shock. Of course, the other ranks drank too, very often in large quantities, but as an officer among them Noel would not be expected to join in. In addition, his experience with the Grafton Street Industrial School, and with the men he had met in the Oxford Volunteers, gave him an easy familiarity with other ranks and it is not surprising that he became so popular with them.

On 9 October, orders arrived for a move to Tunbridge Wells in Kent, prior to overseas duty. But several cases of serious illness struck, and the journey south on the 10th was almost postponed:

Last week in Edinburgh was a rather anxious one. There was an epidemic of rather nasty sore throats, so to make quite safe I swabbed their throats and had them examined for diphtheria...but on the eve of our departure a throat developed in the lines and one other on the morning we went. We were nearly stopped by R.A.M.C. Generals and I was getting into a row with the lesser lights, when the General (Surgeon) sent for me and told me I had done all right.[26]

With many of the men in camp at The Dell, Ferndale Road, and the remainder and the officers billeted in large houses and small hotels, the remaining three weeks at Tunbridge Wells before sailing to France were taken up with kitting out and practical exercises. At first, Noel was under the impression that they would be at Tunbridge Wells for months:

We are part of the 2nd Army Corps, and I hope we shall be sent out sometime in the Spring. I don't think we shall be really ready before then. ...I am going to do my best to prevent any man who refuses inoculation from serving abroad, as I don't think it right that after all the rest have submitted, they should have any risk from ignorant and superstitious shirkers, and of course all the inoculated men back me up in this and give the weight of public opinion....[Letter breaks off here.]

[Later the same day] We have received very unexpected but very excellent news. We have been ordered to France and we go on Friday. I am all but ready for anything and my medical stores are all in excellent order. We shall, I suppose, be sent first of all to the lines of communication and I expect will remain there for some time. But it is a great honour to be sent out so soon, and we were getting rather disheartened over it.[27]

In spite of his earlier optimism, he was very hard up:

My pay was due yesterday but I have received nothing yet. I am so short of cash. ...I should like very much a £5 note, as at the moment I am penniless and I have a few things to get yet. Before I left Edinburgh I bought a complete new outfit of thick woollen underwear so I am quite well off really.[28]

Now that orders had been received, final issues of kit were made. All leather accoutrements were replaced with webbing equipment, and each man handed in his sporran to be replaced with a khaki apron. Rifles were also given in, and new 'short' rifles were issued.[29] Men who had not completed a musketry course were not allowed to go overseas, and this meant that the last 300 recruits had to stay behind, as did Colonel Nicholl, whose health was failing. The new Commanding Officer was Major G. A. Blair.[30]

On the last night spent in England, Noel, no doubt like most men in the battalion, wrote for the last time letters that were free from the thought of censorship. The notion of imminent involvement in war was indeed a sobering prospect, and he began his last message home with a reproach for the War Office:

> The War Office have kept the Territorials on obsolete equipment and ancient guns until ordered away, and then in two days everyone had to be fitted out fresh in everything.

He went on to a farewell to 'Old England', his earlier enthusiasm somewhat muted now:

> Tunbridge Wells is full of Liverpool, the 1000 foreign men all have their people hanging around the town. They have all rushed down at the news of our sudden call-out. Wherever I go I can see little parties of the Scottish, generally a huge kilted man, on one side of him a small mother evidently on the point of tears, on the other side a stoutish, middle-aged father, puffing furiously at pipe or cigar, and also evidently very much upset.
>
> The house gate where A Company live (the Public School Co.), is surrounded by well-dressed ladies and gentlemen waiting for their sons to get off duty. They hang around for hours sometimes. When the sons appear they carry them off in taxis and feed them at the hotels. Every one of the parents is bearing up wonderfully, and all seem quite satisfied that their sons should go, but I think the sight of people bearing up well to be one of the most depressing I have yet struck.
>
> I was very sorry indeed not to be allowed to come up to see you all before I left, but I could not really have spared the time. I had to see that all my RAMC men were outfitted for the war. I have wired to Dot to see if her working party can provide them with wooly [sic] comforts. I feel in loco parentis towards my little lot and don't intend that they shall die of cold. You feel very warm towards people who are going to rough it with you (even the rotters) and when they are only lads and they are after the same job that you are you feel more soft towards them still....
>
> I feel glad that I am going with the Scottish. You will find that

66

heaps of people in Liverpool and district will be looking out to see where we go and how we get on, besides yourself. Dr. Gemmell has 2 sons as officers, Mr. Harrison (Cathedral benefactor) has a son a Captain, and there are many more. I am sending you a group of officers taken yesterday. Some of the Captains are feeling going away very much. They are nearly all young married men, with a few little children each. The wives and kids are here. I cannot help feeling what a lot these men are giving up. Before the war they were rich, easy-going, rather careless, but very sound men. Now all their ease and carelessness is gone and they are all roughing it and giving all up most cheerfully and very bravely.

A great many of the Scottish, who did not volunteer for foreign service because of home ties are now rushing up to be examined, and to offer themselves now the real call has come. As one poor chap said to me, 'I tried to keep off it, sir, because of my wife and kids, but now I cannot bear it any longer.' He was only about 25 years old. I think the fighting stuff is still in England.

Goodbye, my dear Father. I am going to do my best to be a faithful soldier of Jesus Christ and King George.

Your loving son, Noel.[31]

CHAPTER SIX

Marching Away To War

On the morning of Sunday, 1 November, 1914, the Liverpool Scottish lined up at Tunbridge Wells railway station to await their train for Southampton. Those relatives and friends from Liverpool who were still in the town, visiting members of the battalion, crowded round the ticket barrier to wave their last goodbyes, and as the 829 men and twenty-six officers got into their carriages the pipers played for the last time on British soil.

Noel had no one to see him off, but his mind was fully occupied with the difficulties to come. He had written to Dorothea the previous evening:

> Thank you for the parcel of clothes for my RAMC boys. They are not Liverpool Scottish lads, but are detached from a St Helens Field Ambulance (5 of them) to look after water carts etc. They are poor boys and are not well off like most of our Liverpool Scottish, so they need better clothing and are very grateful. This is our last night in Old England. I don't quite know what lies ahead, and I rather dread the thought of roughing it through the winter, but I have got devoted to the battalion. I have inoculated and vaccinated them, had all their teeth put right, and settled up their feet, and I think now that as far as fitness goes, they want a lot of beating.[1]

At Southampton, their transport ship was waiting at the quay. She was the 8,000-ton SS *Maidan*, a welcome reminder of Liverpool, being owned by the Brocklebank Line; a few members of the Liverpool Scottish had worked as clerks for the company. The battalion boarded so quickly and efficiently that they came in for particular compliments from the Military Landing Officer in charge of the embarkation. Also on board were the Queen's Westminsters, and the easy but temporary acquaintanceships of war were soon made. The ship was very crowded and sleeping places for the men were at a premium, but the Chavasse good fortune prevailed. That night Noel wrote a postcard to the Bishop:

> I have received great and unexpected kindness. The Captain

[William Peterkin] gave me his cabin, so I had a rare sleep of 10 hours, and feel like a giant refreshed. He is a Birkenhead man. I must ask Dot to call on his wife. The chief steward's brother was a patient of mine in the Southern Hospital. He sent me up tea this morning.[2]

The *Maidan* cast off at 7.30pm, sailing at full speed without lights in order to avoid submarines in the Channel. She was accompanied by other transports and escorting destroyers and reached Le Havre at 7am the next day, 2 November. Unfortunately, her captain missed the tide, and put to sea again, cruising around the bay until 10 o'clock that night. Even at that late hour the people of the town flocked down to the quay to watch, but the ship merely tied up for the night and the men did not disembark until the next morning. It was 3 November, and hardly dawn, when Noel set foot on French soil for the first time.

The battalion formed up and were marched through the town, passing a hospital and seeing war-wounded leaning out of the windows to watch them go by, to Number 1 Rest Camp, a bell-tented camp on the higher ground outside Le Havre. Here, equipment was checked and the men had time to write letters home. For the first time, they had to write with the battalion censor in mind — a frustrating restriction which only rarely uncovered a genuine lapse in secrecy that could conceivably have been of succour to the enemy. Officers found it embarrassing to have to read their men's intimate messages home, but at least it prevented those exaggerated accounts of army life which might have caused unnecessary alarm amongst families. Noel, as Doctor, and the other officers simply had to sign their envelopes on the outside, and were generally trusted not to include sensitive information.

Next morning, Wednesday, 4 November, the Liverpool Scottish repacked their kit and marched down into the town again, this time to the station, where after a wait of four hours they boarded the cattle trucks that had already become familiar to thousands of Tommies of the BEF. Bearing the words '*Hommes 40, Chevaux 8*', these wagons were to be home for the next twenty-seven hours. The train did not even leave Le Havre until seven in the evening. However, as Noel told his father, 'The Officers were very comfortable, 4 in a carriage, but some of the men were packed in cattle trucks.'[3] The train had forty-eight trucks pulled by one engine and the journey to St Omer was therefore slow and tedious.

At Rouen, Red Cross nurses provided cups of hot chocolate; the boredom was further relieved when the train stopped for a time outside Abbeville, and the Doctor amused the whole train by stripping off and standing under a water tank at the side of the track, while a fellow officer pulled the plug and gave him a cold shower. Lieutenant Bryden McKinnell, who was fast

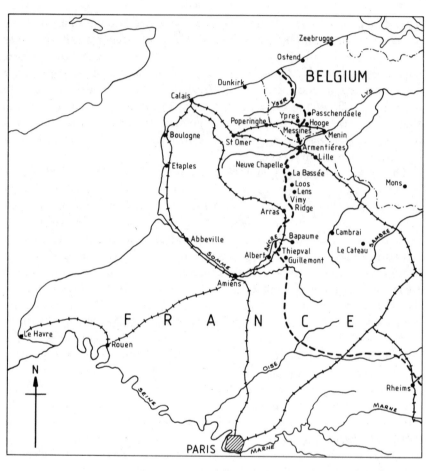

Zeebrugge

Ostend

BELGIUM

Dunkirk

Calais

YSER

LYS

Poperinghe

Ypres

Passchendaele

Hooge

Messines

Menin

Boulogne

St Omer

Armentiéres

Lille

Etaples

Neuve Chapelle

La Bassée

Loos

Lens

Vimy
Ridge

Arras

Mons

Abbeville

SOMME

Bapaume

Cambrai

ANCRE

Albert

Thiepval

Guillemont

Le Cateau

SAMBRE

Amiens

F   R   A   N   C   E

Le Havre

Rouen

OISE

Rheims

SEINE

MARNE

N

PARIS

MARNE

0 10 20 30 40 50 miles

– – – – – – Approximate line at the end of 1914

THE WESTERN FRONT 1914

70

becoming a close friend of Noel's, recorded in his diary that he would have loved to join in, the weather was so hot and sunny, but as he could not find his towel he had to forgo the pleasure. (The officers each had a valise or canvas bag, normally carried on the mess-cart and containing kit weighing thirty-five pounds, but they soon developed the knack of carrying essentials in the uniform pockets. Thus they would be independent if the valises went astray. Encounters with officers returning from the front confirmed the wisdom of this. The Liverpool Scottish subalterns were also advised by these veterans to dress exactly like the men, and to wear no swords, as officers were often singled out for special attention by the enemy.) This shower-bath at Abbeville was just the first wartime example of Noel's preoccupation with keeping himself and his men clean, an obsession that was to intensify as the war ground on. He certainly described this occasion as 'one of the bathes of my life' and it even found its way into the Regimental History.[4]

The French people who approached the train during its frequent stops generously supplied coffee and rolls, and pestered the men and officers for 'souvenirs et biscuits'; articles of uniform and equipment had to be carefully watched over. That day's *Daily Mail* could be purchased and was enthusiastically passed from man to man, keen to read the war news.

At 9.45pm on 5 November the train reached St Omer and there followed a three-mile march through pouring rain to billets in a chateau at Blendecques. Lieutenant McKinnell reported that the men were 'full of good spirits':

> Even marching from the station yesterday through the crowded streets, they marched past as if they were marching from Sefton Park, but finer and steadier than ever Liverpool people saw them march.[5]

He believed and hoped fervently that the Liverpool Scottish would 'get into it shortly', and that if they did a great boost would be given to recruitment back in England.

Unfortunately this chateau was for one night only. The next night found officers and men sleeping in a barn — comfortable enough, except for the first incursions by the body louse. Two battalion mascots were acquired, tiny black and grey kittens, which Noel fed on bread and milk.[6] This pleased his animal-loving mother greatly when she heard about it.

The two weeks spent at Blendecques were used for training in various techniques of attack, though under freezing conditions. Lieutenant McKinnell commented:

> Seems very queer doing the ordinary camp training within sound

of the enemy's guns. Still, it goes to show how matter-of-fact everything right up to actual fighting is, the romance and excitement generally attached to troopships, troop trains etc. being *non est* except in the writing of novels.[7]

Noel's diverting letters were eagerly awaited back home at the Bishop's Palace:

> We hear from time to time the far-away boom of the guns. They must be deafening close to. The aviation depot is here. Aeroplanes circle round our heads nearly all day, coming and going to the Front, reconnoitring and also patrolling the air, because a German aeroplane dropped a bomb near HQ not so long ago. These aeroplanes remind me for all the world of pigeons circling round the cote before going in.[8]

An added hazard was the habit of the German 'aviators', in Taube machines, dropping darts about four inches long and made of steel. One of the Scottish officers acquired one as a much-prized souvenir.[9]

From these earliest days, it was obvious that the class distinctions that were so much a part of Edwardian England were to continue, and even be reinforced by the war. Men travelled, ate, slept and washed separately from the officers. At Blendecques the men had beer to drink, the officers had wine. The town itself was off limits to the men, while officers could stroll around there at will. In his diary Lieutenant McKinnell made clear, with a disarming lack of self-consciousness, his views on women and the working class:

> [Captain] Fred Harrison and self walked into town. First we went to a barber's and were shaved by a woman. The town is quaint. A point we all noticed is the preponderance of the working class and so few real nice people about. It was wonderful to see the blend of uniforms, French, Belgian, Eastern khaki and a lot of kilts. We had a long search for a bath. The public ones we found shut, but after a lot of trouble and with the use of what little French Fred Harrison knows, we at last found one in a hotel. Then we went to another hotel, and ordered a big dinner. No cigs, or chocolates could be bought, the whole town being cleaned out by the troops who are constantly passing through. How the motors raced about the narrow streets...[10]

The battalion's guns were tested in a quarry some three or four miles outside

Blendecques. Beetroot heads were put up to fire at, being the nearest likeness to a German, in the view of the junior officers, and great amusement was caused when they jumped up or burst when hit. Soon, however, local farmers began to complain of the noise and stray bullets, and the practising stopped.[11]

Noel was already tremendously impressed by the friendliness and hospitality of the French people. Now quartered in an empty house, he was 'sleeping in a large French bed' and a bowl of fresh pears was put on his table every day. His orderlies were given soup every midday by local well-wishers and he was able to get plenty of fuel for fires to keep the men dry. His day began early:

> At 6am I have sick parade. There are a good many sick, our chaps, though fine fellows, don't yet know how to stick it, and give in for the least thing. We also have the old soldier who wants a day of rest. He gets castor oil and duty if I can catch him... Not one man wants to get nearer the Front, but all are willing. We did have a few fainthearts who malingered and said they were not fit, but I got rid of all I could of these. The rest of them will have to be driven (I could count them on one hand, they are so few).[12]

Noel was getting a reputation among the men for not tolerating malingerers; but a greater worry was the onset of winter, and with it the first experience of trench warfare.

> They mean to make us as warm as possible, and the men are all to have fur-lined waistcoats and wooly [sic] things.... We expect to be moved to the Front at any moment.... The men (apparently) will be in the trenches alternate 24 hours, changing with a fresh lot of men during the night. I am behind at HQ, probably a dug-out where I sit and wait for the wounded to be brought to me. I believe that doctors are not allowed in the trenches, so really I shall run very little risk during the war, and I do not intend to run any risk at all unnecessarily, my blood is not heroic, and my form neither proud nor, alas, childlike. In fact, I am getting fatter than ever on active service diet. I am told the feeding at the Front is absolutely splendid and in the trenches there is a *Daily Mail* for every 10 men.[13]

In the light of later events, these remarks bear a sad irony. But Noel was nothing if not an optimist. He fully intended to save every single one of the Liverpool Scottish in his care from the effects of illness or injury, if it was within the power of medical science to do so.

One of his major worries, even before the front line was reached, was the danger of tetanus. The disease was well known and doctors were fully aware that it was particularly likely to occur following the contamination of wounds with manured soil or with infected dust or animal or human faeces. Given the conditions in which men lived in France and Flanders, it is surprising that there were not many more cases. There was no vaccine until the 1930s; however, the Government had regarded the disease as serious enough to merit the setting-up of a Tetanus Committee early in the war, with the express function of securing adequate supplies of anti-tetanus toxin. This serum would be injected as a prophylactic measure, after men had been wounded, and Noel Chavasse was one of the first doctors to use it routinely when any of his men received injuries. In total, eleven million doses of the serum were given during the war, and only a very few of the injured developed the condition. Considerable numbers of horses and mules did, however.

On 17 November a proud duty was performed by the battalion. Field-Marshal Lord Roberts who, on the outbreak of war, had been appointed Colonel-in-Chief of the forces of the United Kingdom from overseas, the Dominions and India, died on 14 November. Having visited Indian troops in the field, on his way back to Sir John French's headquarters at St Omer he had caught a chill which developed into pneumonia. A short funeral service was held at the Hotel de Ville in the town, and the Liverpool Scottish were 'told off' to form part of the guard of honour outside. Twenty six-footers were chosen to follow the coffin, making an impressive sight, under the command of a junior officer, Lieutenant Fred Turnbull, a good friend of the Doctor's. In bitter cold and driving rain, the rest of the battalion lined the Grande Place and nearby streets.

> When the cortege was 100 yards off the men presented arms, then reversed and then rested on reversed arms, whilst the officers rested on their swords... all with their heads bowed down. It is the most impressive drill in the textbook as it is carried out so slowly and stately. Then came the gun-carriage covered with the Union Jack and flowers. I could see French, Gough, Smith-Dorrien, Lindsay, Robertson, Joffre and their Royal Highnesses Prince Arthur of Connaught and The Prince of Wales. [He was] very young-looking and small but very clean and smart-looking. Following these were more Staff and Lancers and British troops, also Gurkhas and other Indian troops. Amongst the Staff were various Indian Princes.[14]

Lord Roberts' body was taken home to England for burial at St Paul's

Cathedral with full military honours, King George V attending the service in person as Chief Mourner.

Noel was not present at the funeral but he did see General Sir John French, Commander-in-Chief of the British Expeditionary Force, quite frequently. However, as he remarked drily, French was in the habit of driving up to the front by motorcar but made sure he came back to St Omer to dine in style each evening.[15]

From the moment Noel landed in France he had conducted an active correspondence with his twin brother. Christopher had been involved in the war since mid-August, as an Army Chaplain at Number 10 General Hospital, firstly at St Nazaire and then for a short time at Rouen. Like Noel, Christopher was a great communicator, sending off hundreds of letters to the parents of killed or injured soldiers who had passed through the hospital. However, he found that the demands of ministering to the wounded were beginning to tell on him. Noel sensed this and wrote to propose that they might meet at Bailleul, 'and Arthur too if he's nearby, because I expect we are going to be in this appalling country for a long time yet'.[16] Arthur, of course, was their cousin and close friend, Dr. Arthur Chavasse from Bromsgrove, the brother of Gladys, Esme and Gwendolen. They did meet eventually at Bailleul in the spring of 1915.

Meanwhile the battalion left Blendecques on 20 November but had to leave behind, in safe-keeping at the infantry barracks at St Omer, the pipes and drums of the pipe band and the officers' swords that they had taken out with them. (A year later these items were retrieved, the swords to be sent home and the pipes to active service with the battalion.) Another loss was that of the Commanding Officer, Major Blair, whose health was not up to the arduous campaign ahead and who was ordered to return to England. The young officers were sorry for Blair; he was now going to miss out on the adventure. His place was taken by Major J. R. Davidson, an expert in drainage engineering and a useful man to have call upon in the months ahead.[17]

Bailleul was reached on 21 November after a two-day march in wintry conditions. In spite of a special issue of short woollen drawers, the Scottish uniform was proving to be one of the Doctor's major problems. Many of the men were still wearing their spats; boots and puttees had been promised but insufficient pairs had arrived. Spats allowed the ice and snow to penetrate the men's civilian shoes, which they were obliged to wear as no other footwear was compatible with spats. When 400 pairs of boots and accompanying puttees did at last arrive, the men had to set off on the long march without time to break the new boots in. The snow-covered roads, with solid ice beneath the snow, caused the smooth-shod horses to fall continually, and many of the men, unable to keep their balance, suffered cuts and bruises. In addition, the kilts when wet froze solid, the pleats being transformed into icy spikes which lacerated the men's legs. When the material thawed in the warmth of the billets, the lice became extra active and prevented the men from sleeping. As yet there was little that Noel could do, but he had plans in mind for the next time they stopped for any length of time.

He wrote on 22 November, with his usual idiosyncratic spelling: 'Tomorrow we are to march towards the firing line so that the men may see shrapnall (sic) burst.'[18] On the march they met men of the London Scottish (1/14th (County of London) Battalion, the London Regiment (TF), the first territorial battalion to see action in the war), against whom the Liverpools in peacetime had often played sporting fixtures. These men, fresh from trench duty, had grim, white but determined faces. They told the Liverpools that their Corps had done very well, and had undoubtedly saved the line which the Germans would otherwise have broken through, but they believed the press had greatly exaggerated their exploits.[19] The British newspapers were reaching the troops in this area on the same day as they were issued in London — and they were free. The Medical Officer of the London Scottish reaffirmed to Noel that RAMC personnel were not expected to go into the trenches, and he hastened once again to reassure his family as to his safety.[20] The battalion also passed columns of French troops, whose uniforms made the Scottish laugh — 'so like "Musical Comedy",' McKinnell observed.

> They were dressed in red riding breeches and big blue cape coats
> and large silver helmets with horse-hair streamers, but only
> imitation top-boots.[21]

As they slithered along under the wintry skies, the men were heartened to observe an air battle, a 'dog-fight', in which the British pilot decided the issue by dropping a bomb over the side of his machine and by good fortune hit the propeller of the German plane. They cheered when it spiralled to earth.[22]

On the same day, Saturday 21 November, the battalion crossed the border into Belgium. As Noel remarked, 'and so we have earned another medal (hardly won)'. He met an old friend from Oxford on the road, greatly excited to be going home for his first leave, who advised him that 'A doctor must always try and save his skin, and only take risks when circumstances demand it.'[23]

The main purpose of this kind of comment was to relieve the anxiety felt at home, especially by Mrs Chavasse. All four of her sons were now in uniform. Never a robust woman, the strain was already beginning to tell, and for much of the war she was an invalid who kept to her rooms on the first floor of the Bishop's Palace. May was making her own preparations to depart for France, so the real strength of the family rested with Marjorie, soon to be the last daughter at home, and with Dorothea, who, though married and with a growing family, was near enough in Birkenhead to be a real support to her parents and indeed to her brothers and sister at the front. So it was to Marjorie and Dorothea that most of Noel's requests were sent. He wanted many items to add to the comfort of his men: balaclava helmets, gloves, socks, 'woolies' (sic). For himself, a reminder of Oxford days: 'my running blue sweater, to keep me warm at night, some shaving soap, ordinary soap, matches, fieldglasses, chocolate, and possibly some more vests'.[24]

Noel had already begun to scrounge on behalf of the men. When they suffered with sore feet, 'a Major of the Ambulance gave me a gallon of castor oil and now their boots are very soft'.[25] Years after the war, General R. E. Barnsley of the RAMC remembered that 'Chavasse somehow managed to keep a cow, commandeered somewhere between the lines, in order to give his patients fresh milk.'[26] Certainly his reputation of being able to get hold of the impossible began to grow from very early in the war.

In some ways the war was becoming, at least for the officers, an extension of their civilian social life. On Tuesday 24 November, Lieutenant McKinnell described a luncheon at a hotel in Bailleul:

> At the table were Chavasse, myself, several French officers, a French Tommy (territorial), also a colonel, major, a parson, a doctor and several other English officers, two aviators and some peasants. First one and then another of the English found out that they were old friends, and had been stationed together ten or twelve years ago in China and India stations. This meeting of friends absolutely forgotten must be continually happening out here. Their conversation across the table was very interesting.[27]

Near Bailleul on the morning of 25 November, the battalion was drawn up for inspection by General Sir H. Smith-Dorrien, the General commanding II Corps, who was accompanied by the Prince of Wales (referred to by Noel, with an eye to the censor, as 'an illustrious young man lately attached to Gen. French's staff').[28] Although it was raining the Scottish wore no greatcoats, and the inspecting party took off theirs as a sign of courtesy. The General, after complimenting the Liverpool Scottish on their appearance, expressed his opinion that all the British and French had to do was to pin down the Germans in the West during the forthcoming winter; then the Russians would smash through to Berlin in the spring of 1915 and the war would be over by the summer. This came as a great surprise to the assembled troops — they had had no idea the war would last so long![29]

From now until New Year's Day 1916, the battalion was part of the Regular 9th Brigade, consisting of four battalions — the Lincolns, Northumberland Fusiliers, Royal Scots and Royal Fusiliers — under Brigadier-General W. Douglas Smith, which in turn was part of the 3rd Division under Major-General A. Haldane.

Billeted near the village of Westoutre for a few nights, the prospect of imminent direct experience of trench warfare was one that excited Noel.

> Here, I am billeted in a Belgian Church. 300 men sleep here too... really, the men were very good and reverent, and I have not heard any swearing in the Church. This morning while washing behind a little screen of chairs in a bucket, the village folk trooped in and 2 priests held High Mass with the men sleeping in straw all around.

Quite an experience for the son of a Low Church Anglican Bishop! He went on:

> I am very happy. I feel I am where I ought to be, and I am really trying hard not to be selfish and to live for the men, but as you know with personal discomfort this is an effort, especially as it is my duty to keep as fit and as hard as I can. Anyway, I am getting bigger in the chest and less in the paunch, so all is well.

And, with surprising jocularity, he added a postscript:

> Today I had a Post Mortem on a Sentry of Army Service Corps who fell asleep on duty (probably). His gun went off and burst his head to bits. My first real tragedy and before breakfast too.[30]

Like many young officers, Noel coped with the initial hardships and horror of war with a flippant exterior; his later reactions were to reflect more obviously the searing impact that the conflict made upon him.

The night of 26 November was spent at Westoutre. Lieutenant McKinnell reported the task of

> making charcoal to be used in the trenches like the Japs did [in the Russo-Japanese War of 1904-5], that is, a little wood

smouldering in a bucket with a blanket over, so no smoke is visible.[31]

Here the men were ordered to remove their cap badges, shoulder-plates and all other means of identification. Instruction was given with regard to behaviour in the face of the enemy and certain trench warfare rules were emphasized, such as 'No Smoking' and 'Day and night every other man will be on sentry duty' — rules which, in the event, were impossible to enforce. The Liverpool Scottish, relieving the Highland Light Infantry, had to provide 150 rifles for the front line, 100 as supports, and two platoons as local reserves, only 400 yards from the firing line, behind a slight rise. Because of constant aerial observation, the men could only leave shelter at night. Shelling went on all day and at intervals during the night. The text-book maxim 'Never go near buildings when artillery is about' was immediately rendered meaningless. Snipers were an added hazard; they were reported to have penetrated the Scottish trenches, dressed in British khaki uniforms.[32] In those circumstances the inside of a trench was the safest place to be, and the support trenches were, unusually, more dangerous than the front line.

Now the Medical Officer and his orderlies had to operate, for the first time, the standard RAMC procedures for dealing with the wounded. The Regimental Aid Post would be the most forward position for emergency medical care, and it was the stretcher-bearers' job to collect the wounded and escort or carry them there, where the doctor, in theory, would be waiting. After preliminary dressings the wounded went further back to the Advanced Dressing Station, then back again to the Main Dressing Station. Those in need of specialized treatment or an operation proceeded out of enemy artillery range to the Casualty Clearing Station, which was often the size of a large hospital. Right at the rear, in places like Etaples and Boulogne, were the enormous Base Hospitals, and from there a man might hope to be evacuated to England. Now that the Scottish could expect their first casualties, Noel waited anxiously for their arrival.

On Friday 27 November the battalion marched up to the trenches, through the ruined and deserted village of Kemmel. Noel described the experience:

> ...and from a partly shattered house came the strains of a waltz played on a pianola. This by some officers in a perilous billet there... In a field we met the Regiment we had come to relieve [Glasgow Highlanders]. They had been 48 hours in the trenches without casualty. It came later, because an officer who went a little apart to drink, was hit by a stray bullet in the lung. He was hurried off in a motor looking as if he bled inside, very faint and

white but terribly alive... I suddenly heard a horrid hum and whiz close to my ear. I am sorry to say I ducked, and felt considerably startled. As I went on there were more hums, from bullets possibly overhead. I ducked every time.

[An Advanced Dressing Station was established in a farmhouse.] My stretcher-bearers were more shaken than I was, even, and did not sleep a bit, but sat round a room in silence hating the whole thing. We are all new to it, and I felt very sorry for them. Some pigs and hens were in the yard, and they chased a hen into the house and there I killed it very humanely. (One is not allowed to forage, but such queer things happen with shrapnall [sic]).[33]

As senior Company Commander, at thirty-seven years old, Captain Arthur Twentyman had the honour of taking his 'Y' Company into the firing line before anyone else in the battalion. Tragically, he also had the distinction of being the first Liverpool Scottish officer to die. His experience under fire lasted precisely twenty-four hours. Noel was greatly affected by the loss of a good friend:

We heard the sad news by telephone from the trenches. He had been overrash — he was screened by a hedge, but not sufficiently, and was shot through the heart. I feel very sad about it because I liked him the best of the whole lot, and he has always been invariably kind to me... and I miss him very much. That evening the Colonel told me he wished me to take my stretcher-bearers up, and bring him down.

At first the zip, zip of bullets hitting the sandbags close to one's head was rather disconcerting, then it became just part of the general environment. At one point we had to get past a gate where a sniper lay in wait. I went by doing the 100 well within 10 sec.... We had to rest 5 times while crossing a ploughed field as the Captain was very heavy on the improvised stretcher (2 poles and a greatcoat). On the way I saw a group of 10 dead Frenchmen. Next evening, the men came out of the trenches. The young chaps were haggard, white, and stooped like old men, but they had done gallantly.... 2 men have lost their nerve....Two days ago the King inspected us from a motor car, and now we are to go back to the trenches, tomorrow night. We all hate the war worse than we thought we could. Today, we are the supports. We are on a hill and look over a plain towards the spires of Ypres, for all the world like Oxford from the Hinksey Hill.[34]

Captain Twentyman was buried the same night in a wood just beyond the grounds of Kemmel Chateau (and now lies in Rue Petillon Cemetery at Fleurbaix). Like Noel, he was an Old Boy of Liverpool College.

As that first Christmas approached, the real horror of war had, for the first time, become only too painfully apparent. There was, however, much worse to come.

CHAPTER SEVEN

From Kemmel to Ypres

The Kemmel action put paid to Noel's expectations that as a medical officer he would stay behind and not be in any danger. This was not the last time that his athletic prowess helped to save his life, and it was to be only the first of many such nights spent in danger and fear. A week later, in another of his regular letters home, he gave this graphic account:

> Our men have had a terrible experience of 72 hours in trenches, drenched through and in some places knee-deep in mud and water. To see them come out, and line up, and march off is almost terrible. They don't look like strong young men. They are muddied to the eyes. Their coats are plastered with mud and weigh an awful weight with the water which has soaked in. Their backs are bent, and they stagger and totter along with the weight of their packs. Their faces are white and haggard and their eyes glare out from mud which with short, bristly beards give them an almost beastlike look. They look like wounded or sick wild things. I have seen nothing like it. The collapse after rowing or running is nothing to it. Many, too many, who are quite beat, have to be told they must walk it. Then comes a nightmare of a march for about 2 to 4 miles, when the men walk in a trance... and in about 3 days, they are as fit as ever again.[1]

No wonder that the Bishop had some of Noel's letters printed and privately circulated amongst friends and colleagues back in England. Noel himself was of the opinion that his brother Christopher's letters were so moving that they should be sent to the papers, but there is no evidence that this happened.

The arrival of the mail from home was always an exciting event, but in the Kemmel trenches there were no facilities for dividing it up; it had to be sent back down the line intact to await the battalion's return to camp. McKinnell described Noel's aid post, only 1,500 yards from the enemy:

> [Chavasse] is in a doctor's house, most marvellously fitted up.

The owner must have gone in for research work; and as everything has been left behind (in terrible disorder, having been looted several times), our doctor is in paradise.[2]

By now, many of the men wore odd headgear, having lost their Glengarries, and puttees instead of spats — an interesting sight, worn with the kilt. This irregularity of uniform helped to fuel the rumours about spies that were circulating everywhere. Early in December, a man dressed as an interpreter came along and engaged men of the battalion in conversation. His questions to them were put in perfect English, and as he tallied with a description of a wanted spy he was put under arrest. McKinnell had to let him go because all his documentation appeared to be in order, but he thought it was a great mistake to do so. A few weeks later McKinnell noted, 'A spy was caught in this village [Kemmel], while we were there, telephoning to the enemy. He was dealt with.'[3]

It was in the harsh and cold reality of the Kemmel trenches that Noel observed something new:

> Just now we have several cripples with an interesting complaint of the feet, brought on by the men having their feet in water and mud for days at a time. The feet are very tender, and the men cannot walk, then when they take their boots off their feet swell like balloons. It is some circulatory trouble, and I think it is the beginning (or threatening stage) of a gangrene of the feet which was noticed in the Balkan wars, and which was probably some of the so-called frostbite in the Crimean War.[4]

Trench foot had arrived. It was to be the curse of the infantry soldier and would exercise all the best endeavours of the Medical Corps for the rest of the war. As far as the Liverpool Scottish were concerned, their ranks were reduced from 829 men and twenty-six officers on 27 November to a total strength of 370 in the first week in January. Only thirty-two had been killed or injured in battle; most of the rest had succumbed to trench foot. McKinnell described the experience of trench warfare that led to the large numbers of disabled men:

> Soon, we got the order to advance, one platoon to the support trenches. We doubled along and eventually got into the trench, myself and 40 others. The trench was over the knee in mud, and I had great difficulty in moving the men along it. Several stuck fast and we had to dig them out.... I had to run across the fire-trench in front as the communication trench was full of

water. What a sight! I never realised what war really meant till I got up there. Our men were absolutely unfit to make an attack, having been sitting in water for two or three days. A stream of water ran the whole length of the trench, so I had to have every second man baling out water. It rained all the time, and every ten minutes seemed an hour. We had a keg of rum, which I passed along the trench in two water-bottles at mid-day and again at night. It was very much needed, as we were all soaked to the skin and shivering. We were relieved at 6.30 p.m. in a terrible fog. The men had just to clamber out of the back of the trench and run. My greatcoat was so heavy that it toppled me over and I fell five times on my way back.[5]

The proper name for the affliction was still being discussed in *The Lancet* a year later:

'Frostbite' is inaccurate, as all experience goes to show that it is wet-cold which is the principal agent in its production. [In the Balkan campaigns] frost was present in only ten per cent of cases. 'Water-bite' has been suggested and is correct, but has an unfamiliar sound.... 'Trench-foot' conveys no suggestion of cold, and is at best a descriptive makeshift. At present we see no alternative to its use.[6]

Nevertheless, *The Lancet* preferred 'local frigorism'. Chavasse, an avid reader of the *British Medical Journal*, was content to use the phrase 'sore feet' until the BMJ began to talk of 'Trench Feet' in April 1915.

Whatever disagreement there may have been about a name for the condition, all were agreed as to the seriousness of the symptoms. There was also widespread agreement that they had been detected in military campaigns of the past, even as far back as Napoleon's Russian campaign of 1812. What made it so critical on the Western Front in the winter of 1914-15 was the appalling conditions in which men had to fight and live. As the *Official History of the War* pointed out:

The troops arrived... at the entrance of the communication trench more or less fatigued, and bespattered with mud and wet; and in the days before trench boards were in general use the effort of marching through a long communication trench, sometimes half a mile or more in length, was a feat of endurance which was attended with an immense expenditure of energy. When the men eventually arrived at their destination, having waded through mud and water sometimes reaching the waist, they were already wet through, and had then to remain at their stations with little power of movement, owing to the depth of the cold semi-liquid mud which often was at a temperature near freezing point.[7]

The part of the line that the Liverpool Scottish had had to occupy in the Kemmel sector provided precisely this experience. When at last the boots were taken off, the feet were white and dead. The swelling might extend up the leg as far as the knee. Men often had no idea that there was anything wrong with their feet as they could feel no pain, but occasionally, when gangrene had set in, a toe or as much as half a foot died. Again, when blisters had burst and become infected, the socks stuck to them and lumps of skin came away when the socks could be removed, sometimes only after prolonged soaking in warm water.

Noel's priorities had to be dry socks, warmth and cleanliness; in his letters home he was asking for pairs of socks by the hundred long before the BMJ recommended in December 1915 that each man should have at least two pairs of socks, one dry pair always being available to replace wet ones. Tetanus was often also present, so it was perfectly possible for a man to die of the results of trench foot. Early treatment consisted of rubbing the feet with a spirit of some kind — Noel proposed to use the men's allocation of rum for this purpose, but a threatened rebellion in the ranks prevented him. More sophisticated management of the condition was to come later in the war, and Noel was always in the vanguard of new treatments; as early as December 1914 he was asking for 'soda salycilate' tablets, or aspirin, fully two years before its efficacy in the management of trench foot was described in the BMJ.[8] However, the incidence of trench foot was never again as common as in that first winter.

Meanwhile, the 'Doc' had plenty of other demands upon his skills, even if Lieutenant McKinnell believed that the numerous members of the battalion reporting sick were doing so because the Scottish were so much better educated than the ordinary Tommy and therefore had a more varied imagination to draw upon! Now that they were seeing front-line service, there were bullet wounds, shell-splinter damage and shrapnel injuries to deal with. Noel wrote home:

We found one of our men shot through the thigh. By the time I had got the muddy clothing out of the way my hands were filthy and I had no water to wash them. All I could do was to pour iodine into the wound and put on clean dressings with forceps and give the poor fellow some morphia.... Meanwhile, one of our officers was sniped through the forearm. It was a beautiful wound, just bad enough to send him home for Christmas. He went away very pleased with life, chuckling.[9]

Not all casualties were so happy, but Noel regarded each case as one to be investigated and learned from. On Christmas Eve he was particularly busy:

Our little dressing station, in an inn, was a picture that night, not a very pretty one either. The light was only a few candles (3 in all) and the window was all closed and shuttered.... In one corner were 3 flock mattresses, and the rest of that side of the room (the pub room) had straw put down. On the bar table we laid out our bandages and iodine and other dressings. Four men staggered in with a stretcher and dumped it down in the middle of the room. On it lay a man groaning, he was in his greatcoat and in a mass of mud. A bugler holding a candle gave the light and we had to cut the filthy coat off the poor fellow, then we cut away the kilt, and so came upon the wound, a great slash in the back muscles, how made I do not know. All I could do was to paint the wound over with iodine, swab it with pure carbolic and bandage. His legs and feet were a mass of mud. We cut his boots and puttees off and a bugler rubbed away at his feet, but we could not get them warm. We gave him hot Oxo and cocoa and then some morphia and he seemed fairly comfortable except for cold. I am using the hot water bottle (rubber) that was sent to me for warming the men's feet, and another rubber bottle would really be a comfort. After this, man after man arrived. One could really do little for them. The wounds one had to dress were not the clean punctures I had imagined gunshot wounds to be, but because of the near range they at first made one think they had been made by explosive bullets. Because, to take an instance of a wound in the fleshy part of the thigh, the entrance wound was neat and punctured, but the exit was a gaping burst, a big hole that I could put my fist into, with broken muscles hanging out. As a matter of fact, I believe that at such near range, the bullet turns over and over, and practically bursts its way out.... My S.Bs have been mentioned in orders for their good work and I feel very proud of them, as the whole Bn. thinks they have worked splendidly.[10]

The bugler holding the candle was Sam Moulton, a twenty-year-old who had volunteered for the Scottish and been medically examined by Noel on 7 August, 1914. As Bugler he had to carry his officer's ammunition and rifles, and so stayed near to the Company Commander. Moulton, however, was

9. "In 1903 the three Chavasses swept the board" (p.16). Noel is at left, Christopher in the centre (*J. C. Chavasse*).

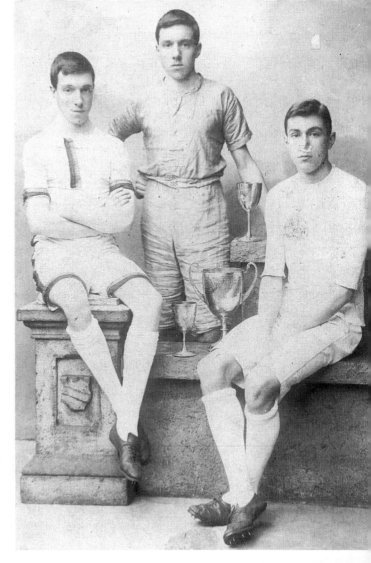

10. "Noel dead-heated with another fine athlete, Kenneth MacLeod, for the first place in the Hundred Yards" (p.32). *Left to right* Chris, W. Brass, Noel, MacLeod (*J. C. Chavasse*).

11. "The greatest accolade of all was earned in 1907 when both Chavasses received their Blues" (p.32).

12. "They were delighted that their mother was able to visit them" (p.27). The twins' 21st birthday, 9 November, 1905 (*J. C. Chavasse*).

13. Bishop Chavasse "wanted to build a cathedral" (p.21). King Edward VII laid the foundation stone in 1904 and the building was completed in 1978 (*S. Lawler*).

14. Family group at the Bishop's Palace, 1913. *Standing left to right* Bernard, May, Christopher, Noel, Marjorie, Aidan.
Seated left to right Dorothea, the Bishop, Mrs Chavasse, the Rev. G. Foster-Carter (Dorothea's husband) (*J. C. Chavasse*).

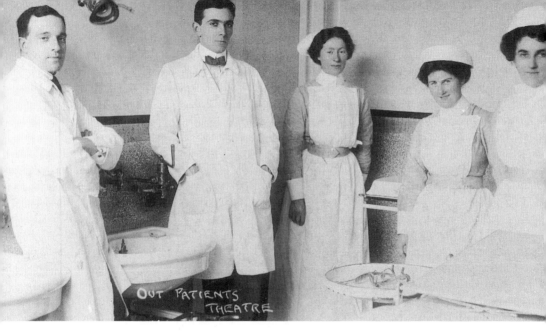

15. "Noel *[left]* took up residence at the Liverpool Royal Southern Hospital" (pp.49-50) (*J. C. A. Quinney*).

16. "I have had three riding lessons . . . They put me on a more disagreeable beast every time" (p.53). Denbigh, August, 1913 (*J. C. A. Quinney*).

under the illusion that something of a 'cushy number' was to be had by keeping close to the Doctor and he volunteered his services in that direction. By 21 December he was a stretcher-bearer, had a comfortable billet in an *estaminet* and helped the Doctor generally to look after the wounded. His diary records:

> I helped to carry the wounded into ambulances after they had been inspected... I saw some terrible wounds, just like a burst sausage and treated with iodine. Iodine was the be-all and end-all, closely followed by Number 9s (laxatives).[11]

However, the role of the stretcher-bearer could be as hazardous as that of any other soldier. Stretcher-bearers did not, for obvious reasons, form part of the leading wave in any attack, and while their colleagues were awaiting orders to 'go over the top', they had freedom to move up and down the trench or to remain in dug-outs or advanced aid posts. But in the aftermath of battle their actions were often heroic, and many received awards for bravery during the war. The Liverpool Scottish stretcher-bearers were no exception.

Albert Collins, a private in the Liverpool Scottish, was inspired to write a song about the stretcher-bearers, to be sung to the tune of 'John Peel'. It contains a reference to Noel Chavasse:

> Have you seen the stretcher-bearers of the famous Liverpool
> Scots?
> When there's any trouble going they are quickly on the spot,
> With their haversack and stretcher, you can bet they're blooming
> hot,
> And they're all good lads at rising at the morning.
>
> Then a word about the cocoa, which the bearers make in pots.
> Every night you'll see it ready, and it's always steaming hot,
> Then a multitude of sick men come and drink the blooming lot
> And the bearers have to starve until the morning.
>
> Then the sick men who come hungry, and there's nothing for to
> eat,
> Are all welcomed by the Doctor, who soon gives them all a treat,
> He will give them his own bread and butter and some potted meat
> And he'll have them fit as fiddles in the morning.[12]

By the end of December Sam Moulton was in charge of the Doctor's 'medical cart', a hand-drawn contraption that was used to move medical supplies when a new dressing station was being established. (This medical cart had been, in 'civilian' life, used in Liverpool for carrying the *Liverpool Echo* round to the shops and street newsvendors each evening.) Moulton also rapidly forgot his bugling function and, when not actually stretcher-bearing, became groom to the Doctor's horse, a strong-willed beast called Tit. She had been a milk-float horse in Everton, Liverpool, and caused him endless trouble. Noel was very keen always to present a smart turnout, but Tit did her utmost to frustrate this by rolling in the mud at every opportunity. Sam Moulton that winter was often 'fed up, frozen up, and far from home', as he put it in his diary, but nevertheless his life at the front was a far cry from that of most members of the Scottish who spent days at a time in the firing-line.[13]

In spite of physical discomforts that were in marked contrast to their previous lives as civilians, the junior officers, fit young men with a taste for adventure, made a joke of everything. Lieutenants Dickinson, Cunningham and Turner, good friends of Noel's, were becoming known as characters. Shortly before Christmas 1914 their arrival in the front line trenches was observed by McKinnell:

> They all swanked up, taking very little heed or cover, joking all the time. Cunningham had gone out of the trench to look at some drainage and one of those beastly dazzling flares was shot up by the Germans. Our instructions were always to throw ourselves flat, but experience shows it's not necessary. However, Cunningham threw himself down. Turner, who was lighting his pipe in the trench, roared with laughter, 'Old Dum's turned his toes up at last', he said (the shots had whistled over him). But Cunningham only got up and banged his foot on the ground, saying, 'Quite spoiled my two days up here.' He had got his coat wet! This is the spirit which prevails among many and does an enormous lot of good to keep the men cheery. By taking due precautions and taking things in a light spirit — however forced — the men are made to think less of the actual danger.[14]

Morale-boosting among the men was undoubtedly a fundamental function of the officer at war. But of these young men only Cunningham survived the conflict.

The state of the trenches in the Kemmel area was itself an additional hazard of the war in that sector. There were no dugouts, no duckboards, no pumps, and few repairs had been undertaken to remedy the damage caused by weeks of shelling. Even sandbags were not available for most of the time, so that the process of building up the parapet in front, or strengthening the parados behind, was made far more difficult. After heavy rain or during a thaw the waterlogged state of these trenches was unbelievable. A non-commissioned officer with the battalion, Sergeant W. G. Bromley, commented:

> These so-called trenches lay behind a hedge about 100 yards in the rear of the firing-line, and were simply ditches covered in a haphazard manner with boards, straw, earth etc. About every twenty feet or so there was an opening roughly four feet wide — and as the 'dugouts' were only about three feet high, and oozing in mud, they could hardly be described as 'cushy'.[15]

Food was short too (so much for Noel's confidence that provisions would be 'absolutely splendid'). Basic food in the line was bully beef and biscuits, and the miserable conditions were certainly exacerbated by the lack of hot food. All rations had to be carried up to the line at night, for obvious reasons, but the rough and shell-torn terrain caused problems of its own. When hot tea was being transported in dixies, it had to be carried for a mile and a half and what was not spilt was cold by the time it reached the men. Hot meals such as stews were impossible to provide, because in these early months no field-cookers were available. Sam Moulton recorded in December 1914 that since landing in France they had not seen bread, and lived solely on army biscuits, Tickler's plum and apple jam, tea and cheese.[16] When bread did finally appear, eight men had to share one loaf, which meant they had about one slice each for breakfast, dipped in a little bacon dripping if they were lucky. No wonder Sergeant Bromley described with relish how potatoes were, on occasion, foraged from deserted farms and roasted over a coke fire in the trench.[17]

In Kemmel village itself, when in reserve, the men and officers patronized the various *estaminets* and could purchase omelettes and coffee. And Noel Chavasse's letters home contained many requests for items to improve life for the men:

> Please send candles and good penny paper novels for the men so that they can get through the long winter evenings in their barns happily, instead of being in darkness and dullness from 6 p.m. to 7 a.m.[18]

Life was somewhat more agreeable at Christmas 1914. The battalion had the good fortune not to be in the line on 25 December. On Christmas Eve Noel was in a billet in a ruined building with McKinnell, and the two of them slept head to foot on a small mattress. When they woke, they went out for their usual cold baths, but decided not to bother in view of the freezing temperature. At midday the battalion paraded in a nearby field and received gifts of chocolate, Oxo cubes, writing paper and pencil, sent out from Liverpool by the wives and relations of the officers. The Commanding Officer, Lieutenant-Colonel Davidson, said there was only one thing he wanted to know — were they downhearted? The whole battalion roared 'NO!' The battalion pipes were borrowed from the store at St. Omer, and the pipers played almost for the first time since arriving in France, as bagpipes were not usually permitted. Only four pipes turned out, the fifth piper having been killed the previous day. Their uniforms were tattered and torn, but the men pressed them to play again and again. A carol was sung, then up galloped a pair of horses and a transport waggon full of Princess Mary's Christmas gift tins, each containing pipe and tobacco, and there was a Christmas card for every man from the King and Queen. Lord Derby, by now Director-General of Recruiting, but with a special interest in the Liverpool battalions, had sent plum puddings for all ranks, and for the officers a hamper containing green turtles, ready-to-eat turkeys and cigars. There was also a cigar for each of the non-commissioned officers. The men had special rations of rum, bread and fresh meat.[19] More than 250 sacks of mail had been received, containing tons of foodstuffs — so much, in fact, that Sam Moulton was sick after eating too much. Indeed, normal daily rations were not drawn by most of the men for the next day or two, they had received so much food from home.[20]

On New Year's Eve the battalion marched to Kemmel where it was placed in immediate reserve and had to supply fatigue parties. Some men were allotted the task of pulling wood from ruined houses; doors, shutters and floorboards were used to make fascines (bundles of wood wired together for men to stand on in the trenches) and hurdles. Others dug reserve trenches or made drains or repaired roads. Lieutenant-Colonel Davidson, together with the Adjutant Captain C. P. James, Major Thin and the Doctor, sipped what McKinnell thought was 'beastly' rum and sang 'Auld Lang Syne'. At midnight, rockets, guns and star-shells were fired by both sides. McKinnell dismissed any thought of fraternization with the enemy:

> All sorts of stories have been circulated regarding the meeting of the enemy and British troops between the trenches. Luckily the troops holding our immediate line of trenches just waited until the Germans got out of the trenches, then they let them have it, rapid fire; it stopped any of this 'scratch my back and I'll scratch yours' sort of nonsense.[21]

Noel's letter to Dorothea after Christmas reflected his main concerns as the new year opened:

> Thank you for the singlets. The men really do not have much chance of getting them washed, so that a constant change of singlets is really the best way of fighting the constant plague of vermin. On the whole, I think we are not so bad, but I have to plan and plan how to keep the poor things clean. Often there are only about two pumps for the whole Battalion. We are in a ruined village. I have collected tubs, and by making friends with the cooks have managed to give hot baths to about 100 men in the last two days. At the same time I overhauled their underclothes, and whenever I spotted one (I am getting a very practised eye) I had the garment soaked in petrol. It was dry by the time the wearer was. War is really very amusing — the same old trivial round and common task. I still pare corns and administer caster oil.[22]

Later in the year, Noel described the drawbacks of using petrol to defeat the body louse:

> A poor young doctor had lice from a dug-out. He rubbed himself over with petrol and then put on pyjamas and went to bed. There he set himself alight and rushed through the camp in flames. He has since died of his burns. He was only 23 years old.[23]

Attitudes to the enemy were hardening. Although Noel rarely castigated the Germans, others did. McKinnell thought that the British stretcher-bearers were marvellous but the Germans were 'swine'. He saw more Germans in the flesh than the Medical Officer as he spent much more time in the front-line trenches. He witnessed an incident where a wounded British officer lay fifteen yards from the enemy trenches, and two stretcher-bearer parties each consisting of four men were all shot dead trying to rescue him, and he was wounded five times. In the end he died and his body was never recovered. McKinnell declared in his diary: 'There must be a crooked strain among some of them that should not be.'[24]

Noel's spiritual life, and his concern for that of his men, figured often in his letters home. It was as if the intense experience of war gave him pause to examine his own motives and to look for new ways of helping his fellow man. He had not been able to attend Holy Communion since leaving Liverpool the previous August, and this worried him considerably. At Christmas he was at last able to attend a service conducted by the padre, and announced to the family that he was also holding church parades of his own for the Liverpool Scottish and requested some hymn sheets for the purpose. Other men's troubles always found a place in his thoughts and he tried in many different ways to minister to their needs.

> What did the men more good than anything else was a boxing-match and a concert that were held at the Rest Camp. There were several good bouts between our men and then of other regiments. The boxing was very good and clean but the men were not in very good condition — the Rev. Gillingham, the cricketer, came over and judged. A temporary stage was rigged up and there was some really good talent. I think these did more good than any amount of number 9s.[25]

In the same letter Noel mentioned that a 'very impressive' service had been held featuring Kipling's 'Hymn Before Action'. This hymn expresses a bellicosity one would not associate with a man who loved humanity as Chavasse did:

> The earth is full of anger,
> The seas are dark with wrath,
> The Nations in their harness
> Go up against our path;
> Ere yet we loose the legions
> Ere yet we draw the blade,
> Jehovah of the Thunders,
> Lord God of Battles, aid!

However, we have to remember, with a kind of culture shock, that the rightness of England's cause was never in question for this generation of officers, at least not in the first year of war. That being said, very rarely did Chavasse criticize or condemn *Germans*; what he denounced with all his power was *suffering*, however it was caused. He felt deeply for a 'great big fellow' who, at church parade, wept a little and surreptitiously kissed the flyleaf of his prayerbook, on which his mother had written an inscription.[26]

Junior officers of Noel's class and army status often, by their own admission, 'slacked' or 'fooled about'. The death of one of their number, however, was an experience that deeply affected them all. Noel's good friend Lieutenant Fred Turner was killed on 11 January. Noel went out with his stretcher-bearers to fetch him.

He lies buried in the Church ground here. The stretcher-bearers have made his grave very nice and a Pioneer friend has made him a beautiful cross.[27]

Turner was a graduate of Trinity College, Oxford, and had known Noel and Chris for several years. These young men were being scarred by the loss of friends from before the war as well as by the loss of comrades and acquaintances gained exclusively through service life.

On 24 January news came that another young officer, Second Lieutenant P. D. 'Togge' Kendall, had been killed. Shot in the shoulder, he had been lying wounded when he was hit by another bullet which ricocheted off a tree. He was buried in Kemmel churchyard next to Turner. Their fellow officers mused sadly on the strange circumstances that led to the one-time rugby captain of Scotland (Turner) and an England rugby international (Kendall) being buried side by side in a small Flemish churchyard. Noel and his orderlies laid out Kendall's grave too, as best they could, and placed a cross at its head. (In subsequent shelling, both graves were lost, but these officers are commemorated on special memorials at Kemmel.)

Such were the close relationships that often grew up between officers and men that a similar sadness was felt when an other rank was killed. One of these was Private Basil Teague, shot in the head on 22 February, 1915, and taken to the Casualty Clearing Station at Westoutre. A group of officers asked Noel to take them in to visit Teague, and McKinnell found the sight of him most affecting:

> Poor fellow! There never was any hope for him; even if he had lived, he would have been an absolute living corpse, not able to speak. The Doctor spoke to him, calling him by name, and though now he is only vegetable matter, such is the marvellousness of the brain (though so little remaining), that he opened his eyes and looked at us. I never felt or was moved by anything so much before (and I have seen some terrible sights here!). I seemed to realise all of a sudden the terrible price some of us have to pay for war; and all the sorrow, mourning and tears that are necessary to build a lasting peace. I felt myself reel, and rushed out into the open air. We hadn't walked for ten minutes before we were laughing and joking and thanking God that we were able to do so. For is it not one of the greatest boons which we acquire out here that any sorrow, however great (and which would upset us for a long time at home), is quickly lifted from us?[28]

Noel himself commented:

> Head injuries are very distressing, as the men live for so long
> with frightful mutilations, although happily they are
> unconscious. One man [Teague] lost the whole side of his head
> and a large part of his brain, yet he lived and was semiconscious
> for 2 days. His brother arrived, with the other Liverpool
> Battalion at the Front, the day he died, and about the first duty
> of the poor fellow on arriving was to attend his brother's
> funeral.[29]

Prolonged strain of this kind was bound to take its toll. When leave was
announced there was great relief and excitement, although the prospect could
weigh heavily upon a man who was in the slightest bit superstitious: what a
temptation for Providence to intervene and prevent the longed-for trip back
to Blighty! But early in February, several of the Scottish officers set off for
England, their first leave of the war. Noel travelled with McKinnell (who
found difficulty in carrying his valise, which contained a 4.5 howitzer shell
as well as other souvenirs) and three others, sailing from Boulogne to
Folkestone and then proceeding by train. In less than twenty-four hours
they were home amongst their families, so far from the Western Front that
they might as well have been on another planet.

Noel's brother Christopher had a few days at home, too; it was one of the
rare occasions when their leave coincided. Apart from visiting old haunts and
renewing friendships, they called in to see their old school, Liverpool
College. The school magazine had already recorded, in December 1914, the
war service of hundreds of Old Boys who were now in uniform — indeed
without them, the King's (Liverpool Regiment) would have been
hard-pressed for officers.

> They are men who have patriotically answered their country's
> call to defend our national existence and national honour. The
> College is proud of them. The heavy casualty lists have,
> unfortunately, contained the names of some who have lost their
> lives on the battlefield. Their relations and friends have to mourn
> the loss of gallant gentlemen; the British Army of gallant officers.
> But they have died the finest of deaths.[30]

More optimistically, the next issue of the magazine recorded:

> We have been delighted to welcome the brief visit of C. M. and
> N. G. Chavasse, the former a Chaplain to the Forces, the latter

a Surgeon-Lieutenant attached to the Liverpool Scottish, both fresh from the Front. They pictured to us very vividly the appalling rigours of trench-life, and the cheerfulness of the British soldier under these awful conditions.[31]

Noel also took the opportunity of visiting the Royal Southern Hospital, where young Robert Eager, recovering from the ninth operation on his feet, was greatly impressed to see his erstwhile surgeon in uniform. Noel dashed down the ward and swung Robert round in the air, declaring to everyone in sight that he had 'made another soldier for England'.[32]

It was hard to describe the Western Front to people who had not experienced it. McKinnell noted sombrely:

> Everybody too optimistic and confident of success. No doubt of success in the end, but many reverses before that, and hundreds of thousands of more men required. Pleased to see that everybody looked so well, though they all worry far too much over the individual. We British never seem to be able to get into the way of thinking entirely from the point of view of 'the Country' and that if a man gets killed for 'his Country', it's an honour, and not an event to be mourned over. No mourning should be worn and all sympathy should be spent on the wounded. Those are the ones that suffer and are always too soon forgotten, especially if maimed.[33]

Before long, that singular honour, 'Pro patria mori', was to be won by the great majority of the young men in the Officers' Mess of the Liverpool Scottish.

Back at the front, a more settled routine was being developed, both in and out of the trenches. As supplies became more reliable, Noel could assume that certain treatments and facilities would be available and he could train his medical orderlies accordingly. This was an important part of his work and he took it very seriously, delivering short lectures to the orderlies as and when the opportunity presented itself. He might concentrate on 'Wounds' one week, on 'Care of the Feet' the next, and 'Chest Infections' after that. He himself received frequent encouraging letters from Robert Jones, who would send out his latest ideas on the treatment of battle injuries.

It was a commonplace in the British Army to translate 'RAMC' as 'Rob All My Comrades', but this kind of epithet was worlds away from the Liverpool Scottish experience of their own Medical Officer. In his dressing station Noel had the walking wounded helping his staff by collecting firewood, cleaning the building or dug-out, lime-washing the walls for added cleanliness, and ensuring that whenever a tired trench party arrived back they would be met with at least a hot drink and the chance to get warm. He was gratified to hear that Medical officers in other battalions were adopting the idea too. At the beginning of March he wrote:

My own dressing station has been a great success. I have been working at it, collecting furniture and windows for it and cleaning it up, till it has become a veritable little home away from home and the sick men love it. I have a large kitchen which I turn into a little convalescent hospital — here I have about 6 - 8 men suffering from flue or mild complaints, which render them unfit for the trenches. They do very well and enable me to return to duty a lot who might otherwise be lost....

On the brick walls hang 2 sacred pictures and an oil painting. We have chairs, table, a cupboard filled with china. Every night we keep cocoa brewing, and people drop in all night long and get a hot drink. We have tried to dig out the floor — a layer every day.... In our room this evening there was a wild scene. A Captain and 2 subs. from the regiment billeted in the brickfields came in and we had a musical evening. The officers then tuned in with 12 miners and they all drank cocoa and very dilute brandy in the inner room.... Outside the door, there lay muffled up in their oil sheets, rigid and still, two poor men who had laid down their lives that morning — we are, I think, mercifully numbed, or who would ever smile here? They say that after three months an officer loses his nerve, from sheer nervous drain, but so far I have, please God, a good hold on myself, and am doing my best to cheer up the poor officers as they come back wearied from the strain of trench work.... I have won several good and affectionate friends up here, and am perfectly happy and in good health. I made my bed very deliberately and am quite content to lie in it and so far have felt no ill effects whatever, thank God. My great fault is irritation when a bit over-pressed with work (which some scrimshanks have found to their cost). I ask God daily to give me courage and patience for naturally I am not overburdened with either.... I feel much happier now that something is happening.[34]

The 'something happening' was that the Liverpool Scottish had moved to the Ypres Salient on 10 March. They had left the 3rd Division, whose Commanding Officer, Major-General A. Haldane, had addressed them by letter on 2 March:

To part with such a fine battalion is a grievous loss for any General.... but I shall look forward to having the Liverpool Scottish with me again. They have invariably done their duty in a thoroughly soldierlike fashion and to my entire satisfaction, and I feel confident that wherever they go they will maintain the good reputation which they have so quickly earned in the field.[35]

In Ypres there were reminders of civilization and of a life left behind in England, in another world; but here too was action and greater danger than the battalion had faced so far. Noel Chavasse was not alone in relishing a situation which promised more movement and more involvement; however, he could hardly have imagined how searing was to be the impact upon him and his men of the almost featureless few square miles around the ancient walled city of Ypres which, it had been decided, would never be taken by the enemy, no matter what the cost.

CHAPTER EIGHT

In the Salient

Ypres... 'Wipers' to the British Tommy. The name of the town is sufficient by itself to evoke all the horrors of the Western Front. To have been to Ypres had a certain cachet among the troops even by early 1915.

In medieval times Ypres was an important town because of its contribution to the Flemish cloth trade. Indeed, one of its principal buildings, the famous Cloth Hall, was a landmark that could be seen for many miles across the flat Flanders plain. Also visible from afar was the spire of St Martin's Cathedral, which since the Middle Ages had indicated the town's importance as a religious centre. However, the war was to bring to Ypres a new kind of fame. The town barred the way to Calais and the sea and stood at the centre of a major communications network. Road, rail and canal links converging on Ypres ensured that it would be worthy both of prolonged attacks by the advancing German Army and of determined defence by the British; in 1914 its population numbered only some 18,000, but it became a point of principle to the British that Ypres should not fall. Indeed, both sides displayed a reckless disregard for the seemingly unending loss of life.

After the famous retreat from Mons in August 1914 and the subsequent battle of the Aisne, the Allied and German forces desperately tried to outflank each other in their race to the sea. In mid-October Sir Douglas Haig's I Corps advanced beyond Ypres, while Sir Henry Rawlinson's IV Corps made for Menin. There followed the first battle of Ypres, which was fierce and deadly while it lasted, but had ground to a halt due to the onset of the winter weather by mid-November. So important was Ypres in the eyes of the Allied commanders that a salient or bulge in the Western Front was formed round the city in order to protect it.

In the spring of 1915 Britain decided to persevere with her efforts in Flanders in order to encourage her two allies, France and Russia. At the same time, the naval bombardment at Gallipoli began in mid-February, and the Mediterranean Expeditionary Force was ordered to the Peninsula from Egypt, the first landings being made by British and ANZAC forces in April. Unfortunately, heavy losses were sustained by the Allied in both areas — at Neuve-Chapelle (Belgium) in March 1915, and at Gallipoli following the landings.

THE YPRES SALIENT

The battle known as 'Second Ypres', in which the Liverpool Scottish were involved, resulted in the enemy occupying the whole of the Passchendaele Ridge and territory including the villagers of St Julien and Hooge as well as Hill 60 to the south. Ypres was under a more pressing threat than at any time during the war so far.

When the Liverpool Scottish marched into Ypres on 10 March, 1915, they found a town which had been shelled and had suffered quite considerable damage, but which still functioned as a commercial centre. According to the regimental historian,

> The damage was largely confined to the vicinity of the Grande Place and to the houses near the two easterly exits from the town, the Menin and Lille Gates. The Cathedral and the Cloth Hall had suffered, and the latter had been completely gutted by fire, but there was still stained glass in some of the windows of the Cathedral, and it was a fairly simple matter to climb up ruined stairs into the tower of the Cloth Hall. Most of the civilian population had gone, but enough were left to give the place quite a busy air. These were mostly of the shop-keeper class who were prepared to take a certain amount of risk in order to separate the fabulously well-paid British soldier from some of his wealth. There were several restaurants, teashops and *estaminets* open, where good food and drink could be had — how and where the owners got their supplies was something of a mystery. A good trade was done in the shops, where picture-postcards, lace and knick-knacks of all sorts could be bought, while the tobacconists must have made small fortunes. There was even a first-class photographer's shop which was well patronised.[1]

Some of the officers dined in one of the restaurants, paying 'famine' prices according to Bryden McKinnell. Within days they had developed a routine: drinks at 'Marie's' (named after the barmaid), lunch or dinner at 'Julia's', and tea at the 'Patisserie'. There was even a bus service running to take the troops back to their camps along the Poperinghe road.[2]

Two companies of the Scottish were destined for the trenches in the front line at Hill 60, while the remainder were in reserve, billeted in the infantry barracks in Ypres. As early as 21 February, Noel had managed to ride over to Ypres to see it for himself and picked up some chips of marble and bits of stained glass as souvenirs for his father.[3] He even acquired one of the hands from a church clock-face.[4] Now he was able to set up his dressing station in the infantry barracks, with the hope of staying in one place for long enough to do something really worthwhile for the men's comfort. He discovered that action to reduce the plague of lice was already being organized by the Army authorities:

> In the barracks I found a washhouse and a copper. I also found 4 big tubs....I can wash a company (about 120 men) a day; they appreciate this very much — all they have to do is bring a pail of cold water from the town moat....Every time we are resting, the men march to some baths rigged up in some schools. There, each man is given soap and a clean towel and they have a hot scrub in a tub. They give in all their dirty underclothing and are given clean. If necessary they get a complete refit. Also their kilts are ironed. Meanwhile, their blankets are given in, and exchanged for blankets which have been stoved for an hour. In this way the man is cleaned and gets clean clothes and blankets.... This seems to me to be the only real attempt to rid the men of vermin; the wonder of it all is, the small place in which it is all done. Belgians wash and iron, the rest is done by cookers and two field sterilisers, and blankets are dried in oasthouses where in peace times they dry hops.[5]

Of all the obnoxious aspects of war on the Western Front that soldiers had to endure, the prevalence of the body louse was probably the most distasteful. Disregarding distinctions of social class or military status, lice afflicted everyone. Medical literature frequently commented upon the problem:

> (Men) get covered with lice, chiefly *pediculi vestimentorum*. These cause great irritation, and rob them or sleep when off duty. The lice inhabit chiefly the shirt, pants and trousers, in which millions of eggs are laid in a very short space of time.[6]

Apart from the irritation, it became apparent that the lice caused skin problems such as boils and impetigo, whenever the surface of the skin was broken by scratching. (Not until 1918 was it discovered that trench fever, a disease with influenza-like symptoms which could incapacitate men in epidemic numbers, was traceable to the excreta of the body-louse.)[7] In the meantime, various proprietary products were widely advertised as being capable of dealing with the problem:

Every Soldier Needs Kennedy's Kill-Lice Belts
From All Chemists

1/6 Each   3 Belts 4/-[8]

Noel experimented with the fumigation of blankets with formalin, but along with many other MOs he realized that the only certain method was careful bathing and laundering. His washing and bathing systems became more and more sophisticated as the war progressed.

His friend Bryden McKinnell, during his first spell in the trenches at Hill 60, warned of another problem: flies. 'To my mind,' he wrote that March, 'flies are going to kill more than bullets unless we advance before the hot weather.'[9]

In Ypres the men managed to make the best of the situation, as soldiers will. Sam Moulton recorded in his diary:

> The first time in Ypres was like a picnic as regards food — there were plenty of shops — lovely cream cakes, cream slices, cream horns, all sorts. So if we had no money we exchanged what we could for all sorts of things — we went out after tea and spent our money in the cake shops. We swapped tins of bully beef for bread with the civvies — they went mad for bully beef and we were very glad for the bread — army biscuits were as hard as the hobs of hell. Bully beef works wonders — the civvies offered to clean the stables for a tin of Fray Bentos. It is getting scarce now that everyone seems to have taken a great liking for it.[10]

Noel made several real advances in his quest for 'comforts for the troops'. Late in March he sent ten pounds to his father, requesting that he use it to purchase a gramophone:

> I am going to put a man over it and he shall take it round to any billet that applies for it. I want you and my relations, if they will be so kind, to give me some records for it. The officers and men will do the same. We found an old gramophone at our headquarters here, and if you had seen the C.O. and Majors listening with delight to the squeaky wheezy old thing you would understand how the men would love to have one to go the rounds of their billets.[11]

Within a week the gramophone had arrived, together with a few records. Noel particularly enjoyed 'Comfort Ye My People' from *Messiah* — it was so 'lifelike'. In the constant stream of requests home, a regular item was candles and 'refills for the electric lamp'. He also asked for books and magazines, especially *Nash's* and *Strand* magazines so that he could continue with some serials he was following. As for more serious reading, he asked for pocket editions of a Shakespeare play and a Dickens novel; he received

Richard II and *David Copperfield* and professed himself satisfied: 'I feel I could never be dull anywhere.'[12] While on leave he had left his prayer book at home, and asked for Marjorie to send it on: 'It has buried so many men.'[13]

For the men in his charge, he wanted liquorice and menthol lozenges for their coughs, and of course there was a permanent request for socks. In one letter he asked for 1,000 pairs; they arrived within a few days, thanks largely to Marjorie's efforts.[14]

The war was never far away, however. An exciting but tragic time was experienced by one company commanded by McKinnell, holding a point overlooking the railway line at Hill 60:

> I had some good revolver practice in the railway cutting. We were busy trying to hit their trenches with rifle grenades and I had been chatting with Barker, when what I had been waiting for happened. There was without warning a terrible roar, and everything shook, and there, 200 yards from me, on the left of our trench, a mine exploded.
>
> I ran at top speed along the trench to the left. The men were splendid and as cool as possible, attending to the wounded and oiling and loading their rifles. None of them were afraid, but all were in a terrible temper; in fact, one of my gunners, Smith by name, tried to get over the parapet and at the Germans with his bayonet. I got to the left in a few minutes, and found the whole of the salient, including a house, fire trench, support trench and a platoon of men had disappeared, and in their place was an enormous crater. The enemy's own trench was blown in too. ... Our casualties in three days were nearly forty. Poor Rawlins was killed, and Davidson, the C.O.'s brother, shot through the hand while he was getting him into the trench.[15]

As well as dealing with the aftermath of events like these, Noel always had plenty of occupants in his sick billets. One of them was Private E. J. Finlay, who remembered:

> For all Doctor Chavasse's care and love of his men, one must play the game with him. While carrying rations along an interminable long trench I collapsed with a fever and was escorted to the Medical Dug-Out to await the Doctor. In his gentle, and almost feminine way, he just says, 'Good gracious, we must get some Mother Seegal's Syrup for you', and down I went to a sick billet, the best in the village, with a wire bunk over a flooded floor, and another sick companion who devoured 98% of a food

parcel (while I looked on, and on my 21st birthday). The Doctor visited us and asked me how I felt, and I agreed that I was feeling much better, and he was just said, 'two or three more days' rest will help you'. The other 'case' complained that he was 'not too good', and the Doctor quietly said, 'I think you are fit enough now so you had better go up the line this afternoon'. But in the daily uncertainty of life in France and Belgium, with so much horror, I vow that Noel Chavasse made life easier by everything he did.[16]

Noel often described his work when writing home. For example:

In a large hut I have about 10 men lying up with minor complaints. I have made palliasses from bread sacs [sic] and straw which I found here, and they get a good slop diet — bread and milk, cocoa and Bovril. In this way I can check the drain away to the hospital and give men who need it a bit of a rest. The weather during the last week has been glorious and has revived the men wonderfully, besides drying up the ground. It is worth being alive now, and as I have never lived in the country so long before, every day delights me....

We have now about 4 men whose brothers have been killed. I feel very sorry for them, they almost have a widowed look. I generally try to get them off trenches for a bit afterwards.[17]

This compassion for the suffering of his fellow men was never far from the surface. One of the duties which he took very seriously was the writing of letters of sympathy, or simply of explanation, to relatives. One such letter survives:

Dear Mrs. Jones,

I am very sorry to have to tell you that your son Private Jones of our battalion, and one of my Stretcher Bearers, was WOUNDED today.

I am afraid the wound is a serious one, and it will keep him lying up for a long while, but I hope it is not a dangerous one. You will no doubt hear from the hospital telling you more about it, but I shall make enquiries myself and will try and keep you posted.

I will try and explain how it happened. We are billeted in a ruined town and the battalion was being bathed. Your son had gone to dress any small cuts and sores the men might have. He had just gone outside for a few minutes when some heavy shrapnell [sic] burst overhead and he was struck on the bottom of the neck, at the back and on the right side. I saw him almost directly afterwards and was glad to find that he was not in great pain, and that he was comfortable and very cheerful. He was taken away by ambulance car almost immediately and will have received skilled attention very soon after he was injured. The wounds, there were three of them, were rather deep, and will I fear give your son a weary time before they heal. You will I hope soon have him back in England, and help him through.

He, I know, will always bear it bravely. Your son had not been on my section very long, but in that time he has done splendidly. He was very brave, and anxious and ready to do his duty. He was always cheerful, a great virtue out here, and even in the trenches kept himself smart and clean. I never saw him downhearted, he was learning his work splendidly, and his strength was of great use in carrying away his wounded comrades.

His loss will be felt very keenly by us all, for we were all very fond of him, and I myself trusted him and relied on him, and shall miss him very much. His comrades are very upset.

In conclusion, I beg to offer you my sincere and respectful sympathy, and I pray God that your son may soon be restored to you, and may make a good recovery.

Believe me
Yrs. faithfully,
Noel Chavasse
Capt. RAMC and
M.O. the Liverpool Scottish

You will, I know, respect this letter, as *private*.[18]

Such detailed information can only have given comfort to the man's family; but the letter also encapsulates all those qualities in a man that Noel held as his ideals, with duty predominating.

He also made full use of his athletic prowess. An unnamed soldier in the Liverpool Scottish witnessed the following incident:

While on duty as a signaller at Battalion H.Q., I received a telephone message from the front line, 'Man severely wounded in head, could doctor come up at once?' In daylight, only the communication trench was used, and it took at least 20 minutes to reach the front line.

To my surprise, a few minutes after giving the doctor the

message, the front line sent word, 'O.K., the Doctor is here'. Instead of using the communciation trench he had sprinted up the road — in full view of the enemy — in order to reach the wounded man in the shortest possible time. [19]

Near to Hill 60, the Commanding Officer of the Scottish, Lieutenant-Colonel Davidson, put his engineering background to good use. He designed a dug-out — a 'glorious' one, according to McKinnell:

> It contained one big room with two bunks and one room for telephones and one for men to sleep in; a long passage to a kitchen and open-air sitting-room, and on to big dug-outs for Headquarters people; the whole construction being the finest I have ever seen. The Brigadier was very struck with it and means to take a General to see it. It has specially been called the 'Davidson Dug-Out'. The C.O. was able to come and go to the fire-trenches in broad daylight and in perfect safety. It must have been very interesting to him as he has never seen any of our trenches by day before as it would have meant staying up all day. We had the Brigadier and all sorts of 'Brass hats' visiting us. The C.O. was very keen on making patent sniping loopholes and shooting grenades. His engineering training is standing him in good stead.[20]

On his visits to the front line to treat the wounded, Noel found this dug-out invaluable. But invariably his route took him back to Ypres, usually at night when movement could be undertaken more safely. A dramatic description of the Grande Place at night was recorded for posterity by his friend McKinnell:

> What a strange sight, a clear sky, new moon, and half a battalion in kilts lying on the Square in front of the fam̃ous Cloth Hall, the ruins making a most impressive sight, every three or four men clustering round a candle and drinking hot tea supplied by our field cookers. Silently glides past a battalion of Frenchmen in their quaint uniforms and heavy paraphernalia, which they are invariably encumbered with. Then our pals the Lincolns pass and we get up and follow, our men singing at the tops of their voices all the way back.[21]

On 2 April, 1915, the Liverpool Scottish left Ypres. The battalion often returned there during the next three years, either into billets or passing through and out by the Menin road, and the gradual disappearance of recognizable features in the city was indicative of the heavy bombardment it underwent. But for now their duties took them to other parts of that terrible salient.

In the new area, the St Eloi sector, the Scottish rejoined the 3rd Division, 9th Brigade. For seven weeks, half of the battalion were in the trenches while the other half were billeted in huts behind Dickebusch. In order that the reserve troops could be got up to the front line quickly in an emergency, it was decided to construct dug-outs in a wood near Voormezeele — nameless until, according to Private Frederick Jackson, the Doctor christened it 'Scottish Wood': 'He got the Pioneer Section to affix a wooden name-plate to a tree by the road.'[22]

Noel's aid post here proved to be a godsend more than once. Bryden McKinnell had occasion to use it when he was too tired to walk back to his own billet, and was scolded by Noel for lying down on a (looted) bed still dressed in his mud-covered uniform.[23]

The area around St Eloi was 'lively', because the Germans were sending over vast quantities of high explosive aimed at Ypres. As Noel told his family,

Every now and then there passes overhead a thunderous shriek, like an express train tearing through a small station. This is followed by a dull roar, these are the real Jack Johnsons on their way to level an ancient city to the ground. I don't know what thunderbolts of wrath were hurled on the cities of the plains, but they could not have been more terrible than those forged by the Hun. We hear them pass all day and we hear them crash and looking over tangled and shell-pocked fields we can see great pillars of smoke and dust rising from the tortured city.

It is wonderful to see how quickly but how graciously Nature tries to hide the hideous scars made by man in the countryside. I have now lived for a month in a shattered village 400 yards behind our trenches. When we came at the beginning of April, all around was a stark, staring, hideous abomination of desolation. The place was a ruin and wreckage of homes, with an awful collection of refuse left by French troops and a stink of decaying organic matter.

Now the shells of the houses are being veiled by blossom, in the rubbish flowers are forcing their ways up to the sunlight, and a kindly green veil is being drawn over all the unsightliness and shame of the outraged homestead. Meanwhile, between the bursts of cannonade, the birds sing ever so sweetly and are building everywhere. I found a nest only yesterday in an old dug-out. Every morning I walk across green fields, drinking in the sunlight...[24]

Here, as in many places on the Western Front, the supply of clean and plentiful water was a major problem, as in the case of a nineteen-year-old stretcher-bearer who was wounded and whose pulse had stopped:

> There began a very grim but exciting fight for his life. I had no apparatus, but with the aid of a morphia syringe, during the day I got 3 pints of salt solution into him. I think it says a lot for my orderlies (untrained clerks), that although the water we draw is muddy and smells a bit, yet they filtered it with such care and boiled it and took such pains that not once did he develop an abscess though that often happens in hospital.[25]

Sadly, the young man died later in the Casualty Clearing Station. A further hazard to water supplies was noted by Noel on 16 May, when he described in his weekly letter home how the Germans across no-man's-land had poisoned a stream — an action he judged to be 'rather pitiful'.[26] Later he evolved a complicated filtration method for recycling water:

> We have had to dig a well. This has been a great success, and we have enough water to go on with. We now have a supply of souhage [sic] pits and pass the soapy water through charcoal filters, and so run the waste back into the pond to be used again. It is not a very nice idea, but as creosote is put into all the water and the sunlight acts upon it, all the germs ought to be killed, and really it is very clean after filtering, only still milky with creosote.[27]

Nevertheless, infected water was no respecter of persons, and the Commanding Officer, Lieutenant-Colonel Davidson, contracted paratyphoid and had to be sent home to England via the huge hospital at Versailles. He was absent for two months and thus missed the battle of Hooge which decimated his battalion in June 1915. Meanwhile, command was taken over by Major E. G. Thin.

From time to time Noel met up with members of his family. In November Christopher had been transferred from No.10 General Hospital to No.6 Casualty Clearing Station, and by Easter 1915 was at Merville, some eight miles south-west of Bailleul.[28] He was greatly saddened by some of the duties that he had to perform as padre. On 9 April, for example, he had to counsel and perform the last offices for a private of the Scots Guards who was shot for desertion early that day.[29]

On a lighter note, like Noel he ordered recreational activities for the men, like the boxing contest that spring which the poet Julian Grenfell was prevailed upon to judge. Soon after this, Chris was transferred to Ypres and often took the opportunity of ministering to the Liverpool men in the pastoral sense. Noel reported to the Bishop:

> I was very surprised a few days ago to get a wire to say Chris was quite close. He is only about a mile away and I went and had lunch with him today. It was as good as a tonic to see him again. He came to where the men were in dug-outs afterwards and held a short service for them. He gave them a rattling good address. It was only voluntary but the whole lot turned out as far as I could see, and I hope he will often come. Of course, Chris is not in our Brigade but I think he will be given carte blanche to do what he likes, if he will do it.[30]

A few days later Noel saw Chris again, on Whit Sunday, and attended his service of Holy Communion. Their brother Bernard, who had enlisted with the RAMC, served first in Egypt and then in Gallipoli, before arriving on the Western Front in 1916. The youngest brother, Aidan, was a lieutenant with the 11th (Pioneer) Battalion of the King's; Noel saw his battalion passing by one day but Aidan was not with them. However, the Bishop and Mrs. Chavasse were acting as a clearing-house for family news and kept everyone in touch with what the others were doing. The Bishop himself had for some years been Chaplain to the 5th King's and so had yet another point of contact with the Army in France and Flanders.

Noel's unmarried sisters, Marjorie and May, were engaged in their own wartime activities, doing things and seeing places that girls of their class could not have dreamed of in peacetime. Their Aunt Frances was in the process of opening a hospital for convalescent soldiers, the Beaconwood Auxiliary Hospital at Rednal, Worcestershire, of which she was to be the Commandant. Marjorie decided to go there as an assistant, working as a ward-maid alongside her cousin Esme. Gladys Chavasse, Esme's sister, was there too, but as a VAD (member of the Voluntary Aid Detachment) she wore the Red Cross on her uniform. At the hospital there were some twenty-five nurses in all, and Aunt Frances was held in such high regard for her work that she was awarded the MBE in the War Honours List of 1920. Marjorie was only there intermittently, however, as she was often needed back home at the Bishop's Palace in Liverpool, particularly as her mother's health was slowly deteriorating.

May, meanwhile, had determined to take a much more ambitious course. In November 1914 the suggestion had been made to a gathering of Liverpool citizens that they should contribute to the care of the wounded at the front. Within weeks, a number of Liverpool merchants had contacted the War Office and offered to supply a fully equipped hospital. The offer was accepted, making Liverpool the only city or town in the Empire to provide such a hospital, which was designed, built, equipped, staffed, managed and financed entirely by its own citizens. The hospital was 'mobile', being made of creosoted wooden sections that could be taken down and moved as necessary, and capable of holding beds for 156 officers and 196 other ranks. The War Office granted a site at Etaples and the hospital was constructed. The first staff, including May Chavasse, travelled out to it in March 1915.[31] Her role, as she was not qualified in any way, was that of 'Lady Helper to the V.A.D' — a ward maid. She served there until 1918, and supplied yet another stream of letters about the experience of war to add to the piles of correspondence from Chris, Noel, Bernard and Aidan which the Bishop's secretary was carefully filing away.

Aunt Frances and her daughters periodically wrote to Noel and sent him parcels too. In May he wrote to thank her for 'a most splendiferous cake' and for a parcel of books:

> I have a hut away back by our transport and there I send the seedy men. So I have left some of the books back with them and formed a little library for my Convalescent Home. The rest I have up here, and if men come out sick from the trenches I give them one to go back with. They fairly snap them up.
>
> Today we had to go into a dug out, because some small shells (not crumps but crumpets) were hitting the house. So I took the magazines and also a box of Abdullah cigarettes, which Gladys so kindly sent me and really had quite an enjoyable hour — especially as the shells soon left us and went to worry someone else. Please thank Gladys very much for her kind present. It has been very much appreciated.
>
> Just now we are having another low German attack — of German measles. It may really prove rather serious, but I think we are checking it. I am really enjoying myself very much just now. I love the country round us, the grass is beautiful and the flowers are springing up and birds building everywhere....[32]

There is no doubt that by the spring of 1915 Noel's thoughts were turning more and more to his cousin Gladys. At twenty-two she was nine years younger than he, but they had grown up together and had always been good friends. Perhaps it was the dangers of war, or the sadness of suddenly losing comrades, together with the complete separation from the life he had known, that made Noel, along with thousands of others like him, want more than anything else to have something permanent to look forward to. In short, Noel wanted someone with whom he could spend his life when peace returned. He knew that Gladys was the one — but as yet he dared not declare himself.

CHAPTER NINE

Hooge

During May 1915, the Liverpool Scottish remained in the St Eloi sector, billeted in Dickebusch and Voormezeele and serving in the front-line trenches. This was the first spring of the war and, as McKinnell commented,

> One can almost see everything growing, especially the weeds. They are going to evolve another problem, as they are beginning to completely hide the trenches and in between on the "No Man's Land" they are growing so thick and high that we will have to keep a sharp lookout for the ubiquitous sniper who will probably crawl right up. A yellow mustard flower is the worst offender....[1]

The enemy's first gas attack, using the killer chlorine gas, at St Julien on 22 April had caused much alarm, even though it was far enough away from the Scottish to do no more than cause a few eyes to water. Noel had a somewhat ambivalent opinion of this new means of warfare.

> I think the Germans are having their last kick. But I fancy we shall hold them all right in spite of their rotten gas. I must say that although I think that they have no excuse for breaking conventions which they have signed, yet I do admire their skill in making and using the gas. It is certainly a fine way of taking trenches.[2]

It was feared for a time that the salient might have to be given up, so fierce was the fighting following the gas attack, and to this end a new line was dug and the fire-trenches were cleared of all stores and ammunition, prior to a speedy evacuation. The withdrawal never took place. As the regimental historian commented: 'How many lives might have been saved later on if the Ypres Salient had ceased to exist in 1915!'[3]

Sam Moulton, Noel's groom, recorded this account of the Doctor's activities in May:

> Every day I have to go to Stink Village as it is known (really it

is Voormezeele) with the Doctor's horse — he meets me there and proceeds to the Black Hut in Dickebusch and has a sick parade. Half the Bn. are in the trenches at St. Eloi. Later on in the day I make my way back to Stink Village, wait for the Doctor to ride up from Dickebusch, then I ride back to the Transport Lines in Dickebusch. I used to go as far as the cross roads on the other side of the village — it is a straight road from Dickeb., about 2 miles. Right at the end of the road, there was a German Observation Balloon — they couldn't help but see me on a light grey horse ride up every morning and they must have seen the Doctor ride back.... I believe one or two shells came over later on.[4]

Spending such a comparatively long time in one sector allowed relationships to be struck up with other units. Noel described how the Artillery challenged the Scottish to a game of stump cricket:

It was a curious game, because there was an aeroplane watcher — if he saw a Hun aeroplane he blew his whistle and fielders and batsmen fled to a little copse, in which the onlookers sat.[5]

He also attempted to provide some more permanent amenities for the men. For example, on 19 April he asked his family to send seeds, 'sweet peas, nasturtiums and some others that grow quick for little gardens by the huts'.[6] Unfortunately, the men were not there long enough to appreciate the results.

His feelings about the war, now in its tenth month, were optimistically expressed in his letters.

I am now in the proud position of being the only regimental doctor who has not broken down — and as for me, I am like 'Johnnie Walker' (if you know who he is) and still going strong. I am very glad I am so fit because I have a tremendous attatchment [sic] to the regiment and could not bear to leave it. As for the war itself, it is beginning to bore me a bit — and I shall not be sorry when it is over.

It seems unlikely that the Bishop, as a lifelong teetotaller, would appreciate the reference to a whisky advertisement! The letter continues in a darker tone:

The striking of munitions workers for a half penny extra a day, while poor jaded and terrified boys of 18 years of age are shot for shirking the cruel hardships of winter trenches — fills us with dismay and rage. Why should trench-exhausted men be driven to collapse while boozy and cushy slackers at home are cajoled only? At the same time, we have a feeling that Germany is very hard pushed and that with proper ammunition we shall soon win.[7]

Like Wilfred Owen, Siegfried Sassoon and many others, as the war went on Noel was becoming more and more aware of the enormous gulf that existed between the Home Front and the fighting forces. Men sentenced to death by court martial for cowardice did not often cross his path, but he felt deeply for them, especially the other ranks; there is some evidence that Noel had less sympathy with officers in this situation, believing as he did that they should, above everything else, show an example to their men. He wrote home in September, 1915:

> Today a poor fellow was brought to me with a bad wound of the leg (most of his calf shot away). He had dropped out on the way to the trenches (he comes from a first class Highland Bn.) and crawled into a dug-out where I am afraid he shot himself (he said he was cleaning his rifle — they all say that). When he gets well the poor chap will be court martialled and either shot or given penal servitude, I fear. It seems like tending a dead man but it can't be helped. He seemed a poor specimen of humanity.[8]

He and his twin talked about the heart-rending scene that Chris had witnessed at an execution the previous April. This was kept secret from most civilians at home, as it was not in the public interest to broadcast what was happening.[9] On the Western Front, however, it was official policy to make sure that 'for the sake of example' such executions should be publicized widely amongst members of the British Expeditionary Force.[10]

On leave, soldiers could not begin to show their families what it was really like. Many doctors refused to recognize that there existed such a thing as shell-shock and branded all such cases as cowardice. Civilians at home were inclined to do the same with anyone who condemned what was happening in France and Flanders. Consequently, many soldiers turned in on themselves and for decades afterwards refused to talk about the horror. Noel and men like him were perhaps fortunate in their ability to voice their feelings in letters to a receptive and sympathetic audience.

Early in June, the Liverpool Scottish had to provide working-parties to dig support trenches behind the line at night. These trenches were dug so well that daytime visits from 'Brass Hats' became a nuisance, because officers had to take time to show them round and justify every little thing that had been done. The staff officers seemed entirely unable to appreciate that very often companies of the battalion had worked all night and needed to be able to rest during the day. Daily routine in the trenches was described in detail by McKinnell:

Before breakfast, I had to go round the trench with Major Anderson from end to end, which takes an hour. The trench in many parts is very narrow, and the men start making their breakfasts. They are supplied with rations for two days, and these consist of 1 lb. bread, 4 lbs. cheese between two, tea and sugar, also a little bacon and some biscuits. Coke is also supplied. The men are adepts now at cooking, and make most savoury messes, such as toasted cheese, and they completely alter the identity of a 'Machonochie' meat ration. In a small meat ration tin they light carefully prepared chips of wood or a little grease or candle. Then rifles and ammunition have to be cleaned, and all the time a certain number have to keep watch. I issue orders to the Sergeant-Major, and everything depends upon how competent a man he is as to how the work is done. He arranges all details such as which men he wants and for how long. As far as the men are concerned, set meals cease to exist and they appear to eat during any time they are not on duty or working. I have breakfast at 12.00 p.m., (ham and eggs, bread and butter, tea and honey). I have only one more meal, which takes place at 9 p.m. The Germans generally start shelling at 6 p.m. At night patrols are sent out and contents of rubbish bags buried, and the work that cannot be done during the day is carried out.[11]

To reach these trenches, Ypres had to be passed through, an experience described graphically by Noel's groom, Sam Moulton:

The Doctor rode Doreen [a new horse] and I marched with the Transport limbers. Ypres was a mass of ruins and smelt something horrible — so different to what it had been on our last visit, when it was clean and hardly shelled. There were no shops or civvies left, just soldiers, dust and rubble.[12]

Noel was by now developing quite a correspondence with the four young children of Professor Jesse Alfred Twemlow, a lecturer in 'Palaeography and Diplomatics' whose acquaintance he had made while studying at Liverpool University. The family lived at Number 64 Upper Parliament Street, a short distance from the Bishop's Palace, and frequently entertained Noel when he came home on leave. In a letter to Madeleine Twemlow, he also described Ypres (though not naming it for fear of the censor), after thanking her for a parcel of gifts including shortbread and mint rock:

> At the time of writing I am in a trench on short rations which we don't like half as much as shortbread. We had to go through a city of which you have heard a lot and it is now all knocked to pieces, it is practically only a rubbish heap. You pass between rows of empty houses all gutted by fire and only bits of the outer walls standing, some are absolutely levelled to the ground, and one passes between heaps of smouldering rubbish. When we went through there were two big fires blazing and the whole city is given over to the flames. The smell is appalling. I was afraid a great many people are buried in the cellars under the debris.

There followed a vivid account of his life under fire in this new area:

> As we carried our stuff to the trenches we had to pass through a little copse. It was about 11 p.m. and in the copse a nightingale sang most sweetly. This was most remarkable because bullets were spattering through the trees all the time and frequently shells burst quite near so that its song was drowned. But it did not mind and continued singing all the time. It sings every night and I love to hear it.
>
> When we got to our dug-outs we found we had a hot spot because they are played upon by a machine gun. We found this out to our cost two days ago because as one of my poor stretcher-bearers was chopping up some wood to boil some tea the Maxim gun suddenly let off and a little shower of bullets kicked up the earth all round him. One bullet pierced his head and he dropped unconscious. He lived still when we put him onto the ambulance, but we hear he died on the way to hospital. I have now had 4 stretcher-bearers killed and one wounded, and one has had to go home with a strained heart and another because his nerves gave way after a very bad shelling. That is 7 out of 16 already.
>
> Last night I had a bad but necessary job. I had to crawl out behind part of the trench and bury three poor Englishmen who had been killed by a shell. I am going out after another tonight. This is the seamy side of war, but all is repaired in the feeling of comradeship and friendship made out here. It is a fine life

and a man's job, but I think we shall all be glad to get home again.[13]

This was one of the many letters from Noel that a child would find full of interest. Whatever the destination he was able to make them suit the recipient, and it is not surprising that letters like this were carefully preserved.

It was in June that Noel heard about the first member of the Chavasse family to become a war casualty. His cousin Captain Francis Chavasse Squires, serving with the 1/3rd Sikh Pioneers, was killed in Aden on 7 June, 1915, aged thirty. He was the son of the Bishop's sister Ada and her husband the Reverend Henry Charles Squires. All the Chavasses were devastated by the news, including Noel:

> I was very grieved indeed to hear about Frank. I had read about a scrap at Aden and knew he was there. I thought he had a safe billet there. I saw also that 2 officers had been killed but did not know that it had been poor Frank's hard fate to be one of them. I do feel sorry for Aunt Ada and the girls.[14]

On 10 June the battalion was informed that leave was about to be granted. Names were asked for, so five junior officers were put on the list (all five had risen from the rank of private), then four company commanders and twenty noncommissioned officers. Naturally, a very merry evening followed, but in the middle of a training session next day official word was received: 'Leave postponed.' Obviously they were going into action. Thereafter, the battalion was moved to a bivouac camp at Busseboom for special training. When the training turned out to be bomb-throwing practice and learning how to deal with barbed wire, no one was in any doubt that an attack was imminent. In fact, the 9th Brigade was to make an attack on Hooge and the Liverpool Scottish were to assist. At least the suspense was over. McKinnell even felt privileged 'to be among the chosen few to do a special job'.

The battle of Hooge (more correctly called the first action at Bellewaerde) took place on Tuesday 16 June, 1915. The objective was to capture the enemy trenches which lay between the Menin road and the Ypres-Roulers railway where a salient had been formed, bulging into the British line. The attack was to be in three stages. The regimental historian described the battle plan thus:

> First, the Royal Fusiliers, Royal Scots Fusiliers and Northumberland Fusiliers were to assault the enemy's front line of trenches.... Then the Lincolns and the Liverpool Scottish

were to go through and capture the second line... After this, the three battalions which had taken the first objective were to go through again and capture the third objective — [a line] from the south-west corner of Bellewaerde Lake... a double leapfrog.[15]

Each battalion involved had to carry 400 bombs, 125 wire-cutters, six signalling screens and ten small flags so that the bomb-throwers could indicate their positions. To assist in the work of consolidation after the objectives had been achieved, spades were also carried — fifty-one in the case of the Liverpool Scottish. Each man, apart from having his own haversack on his back, carried 200 rounds of small arms ammunition, two days' rations and two sandbags tucked into his belt.

The Officers' Mess was filled with laughter and jokes as they tried to lighten the anxiety felt by all. McKinnell completed a last poignant entry in his diary before going to sleep:

> We have a trench to take, in fact the enemy's second line, together with the help of the Lincolns. Am afraid it's going to be a very difficult job. Men all cheery and we all rag each other as to how we will look with wooden legs, or tied up in an oil sheet. All the plans have been explained today, all stores have been issued. Hope we win. Unfortunately the Huns must know almost everything, as it has been widely discussed. I am beginning to suspect it is done with an object. Sacrifice a Brigade here and push hard somewhere else. However, we are going to justify our existence as Terriers and men — we middle-class businessmen!
> GOD SAVE THE KING[16]

Noel's detailed description of what happened at Hooge, written on 20 June, so moved the Bishop and Mrs Chavasse that the Bishop had it printed and privately circulated. It was headed by the word ICHABOD, a Biblical reference (I Samuel iv,v.21) meaning 'The glory is departed'. This codeword signifying his utter despair after Hooge would have been immediately understood by his father:

> I have not been able to write for some time, but I have much to tell you now. All leave was cancelled, and we were told confidentially that in a few days the Battalion would take part in a charge on the German trenches.
> So we prepared for it. The men charged 'dummy' trenches, and practised bomb-throwing. The machine gun officer went through all his guns, and I took all extra precautions. The men were in excellent spirits, and sharpened their bayonets and cleaned their

rifles most industriously. Sick men tried to get well for it, and a sick Officer who heard of it came out of hospital; but they all realised its gravity.

On June 13th. (Sunday) a Parson came over, and 130 men paraded for Holy Communion. Eighty men went to the Presbyterian Communion, and about fifty to the Roman Catholic Mass. The Holy Communion was very simple, yet very impressive. There was just a common table with a fair white linen cloth over it, and a square of men kneeling round it. As I looked at the scene, and at the quiet and reverent yet set faces of the men, it seemed to me a perfect picture of prayer before battle, and I knew that every man was commending his soul to God. Nearly every Officer went, and I knelt next Kenneth Gemmell, who alas, is now missing.

We went up to the trenches from which we were to jump up on the night of the 14th. It was an eight-mile walk, and the pipers played us for four miles. There was a tremendous stream of men along the road, as a whole brigade was to attack. The men were in the best of spirits, and sang all the way. My stretcher-bearers who had had their number increased to 24 making as usual a joyful noise, and had finally to be silenced by the Adjutant. We halted at last, for we had to go up to the trenches by a by-path, and I said Goodbye to as many Officers as I could. I had been ordered to stay back on a main road half a mile behind the trenches, and felt very sore about it, but I went up to see what the ground was like.

As we wended our way slowly up a path congested with traffic another battalion passed us. It was the battalion which had crossed in the same transport as our fellows [the Queen's Westminster Rifles] and very friendly salutations passed. They were to be in reserve trenches. I had then to leave my stretcher-bearers in some 'dug-outs' behind a little ridge. Our battalion was here waiting to go to the trenches from which they would jump off, which lay about twenty yards in advance. I said no more Goodbyes, and left to go back to my dressing station. Three Doctors were to take serious cases up to these 'dug-outs', and two were to go back to dress walking cases that would straggle back during the attack. I felt very mad at being shoved back like that, but had to obey orders.

At 2 a.m. a terrific bombardment began, and went on till 4 a.m., but I was so tired that I dozed through it. But at 5 a.m., I was woken up by the first batch of wounded coming down. The first to be dressed was Lieut. Lloyd, our Irish International [rugby football]. He had been grazed on the head and was very excited. Just then a batch of German prisoners passed along the road, and he bolted after them, and bagged the cap off one of their heads. Then the wounded came straggling down. They came along a long communication trench in a steady stream. Meanwhile the Huns began to put crumps and shrapnel down the road. Our C.O. arrived with an artery bleeding in his head, which was troublesome to stop, and we had to lie him down at the back, as a crump landed too near the dressing-station for safety. Then news came that a Captain Cunningham was lying exhausted at the top end of the communication trench. So he had to be fetched down. I then found the trench blocked with men who had dropped exhausted trying to drag themselves along. The Huns were putting big shells into the trench, and making direct hits, so that in places the trench was blown in, yet not a single wounded man was hit all day. It was a weary job helping poor Cunningham down the trench. He was hit in the leg and arm, and was very brave. We got some more men back at the same time, but when we arrived at our place we found that another crump had burst just outside our dressing-station, and wrecked it, and had killed four men next door.

So we took all our men a quarter of a mile down the road to an industrial school, where the RAMC had an advanced dressing-station. I left three dressers with them, and they said they would tackle all slight, walking, cases of our battalion, while I slipped up to the trenches to see how our brave men were getting on there. I took with me besides more dressings, two bottles of lime juice, and a sackful of water bottles left by the wounded men.

We found the top end of the communication trench blocked by the wounded. I dressed 30 of them, and sent them on to the ambulance. I found the little path behind the 'dug-outs' a shambles. Our stretcher-bearers, who had carried very well all morning, were now lying exhausted, and the wounded men of our battalion were lying out in a road in front of a mud wall, with no protection whatever against crumps or the sun. One poor chap who was half naked, was blistered already, so I set about and dressed them, and then tried to get shelter for them with sandbags. You should have seen them lap down my lime juice. None of them happily were in great pain.

Then stories began to come in about chaps lying out. Then a

message came to say that the Adjutant [Lieutenant L. G. Wall] was hit, so I went out with a stretcher-bearer and two servants. We found him in a trench where another battalion were crouching in support, and his servant saved us all trouble by carrying him on his broad back. But we had to wait a bit, for during the next hour the trench was heavily shelled, and men were getting hit, so I had to run up and down the trench with my dressings, dressing people's wounds — most of which were only slight.

When I got out of the trench it was getting dusk, so I went off with a trusty man, and searched for the wounded. I knew where the charge had taken place. We found most of them in a little coppice. They lay behind trees, in 'dug-outs', and in the bottom of trenches. They were so weak that they could not call out. Their joy and relief on being found was pitiful, and fairly spurred me on to look for more. It was awful work getting some of them out of their trenches and 'dug-outs'. It was hard to find men enough to carry them away. I had to appeal for volunteers for the men were dead beat. Finally, at dawn, we got our last wounded away from a very advanced point, at 4 in the morning. Altogether, we had collected 18 men behind the trenches, and were pretty well certain that none were left.

On getting back to the dump, we found that the RAMC had failed us, and had not carried any of our wounded back. I had about 25 on my hands. Fatigues parties took pity on the poor chaps, and carried them all away one by one — except 11. Then I set to work to dress those we had carried in. I got them arranged along the mud wall, and then fell asleep sitting on a petrol tin. The battalion had been relieved the night before, but I had, of course, to stay by the wounded. My stretcher-bearers were terribly exhausted, and I sent them all away.

The attack itself was somewhat on this wise. Our brigade had to take a thousand yards of trenches. Another battalion was to take the first line. We were to rush over and take the second line, and then they were to come over us again, and take the third line. The artillery were to bombard each line before it was taken. As a matter of fact our men made such a splendid rush that they carried all three trenches in fifteen minutes, and even penetrated the 4th line. But the artillery continued to shell the advanced trenches, according to order — the smoke obscuring everything. A great many of our own poor fellows were wiped out by our own shells.

Then for some reason the people on our right gave way, and

the Germans also began to come round us on the left, so our men were in the air at both ends, and had to retire to the first line we had taken, and at one place to our second line. In this way a great many wounded fell into the German's hands, among them three great friends of mine — Kenneth Gemmell, and Captain Ronald Dickinson (the latter, I fear, dying), and Captain McKinnell, who went on leave with me. The remnant of our battalion was relieved the same night. 130 men reached the camp out of 550 who had marched out the previous day; 2 Officers (both Lieutenants) were left out of 22.

The trench is a great gain, as it commands a very extensive view of our part of Belgium.

All the next day I had to look after my 11 wounded, and to try to shelter them from the sun under the mud wall. I then made a tour of the trenches, to see if any wounded were lying out, and learnt that one had been heard to cry from a trench between the lines, and got a bullet through the shoulder for his pains. A brave Officer had slipped out and given him a drink. I also found a great many wounded Germans and English — in 'dug-outs' in the trenches, but none of our men. I reported them, so that they could be carried back at night. When it was dark I brought up a stretcher, and an Officer of the regiment holding the trenches crawled out to the 'Jack Johnson' hole where the poor Scottie was lying. When we crawled to the hole I found that it was an Officer, such a nice chap, with a broken thigh. You may be sure he was glad to see us. The other Officers went back to get the stretcher, and the poor wounded chap put his hands in mine, and we sat in the 'Jack Johnson' hole, holding hands like kids. Then we got him into the stretcher, and ran him back to the trench, where many willing hands helped to lift him in.

Just after, Germans were heard crawling in front, and we expected the trench to be attacked. They gave me a spade. But nothing happened, except that a Maxim of ours swept the ground where they were. We got him back, and dressed him, and saw him carried off to hospital.

And then I went to see another bit in front of another part of our trench. The Engineers were there already, putting up barbed wire, and they had searched the ground thoroughly, but we found and carried back a poor chap from another regiment.

Then I was beaten for a bit, but a drop of brandy made me feel all right, so I did one more little crawl to search some 'dug-outs' in front of another part of our line, but only found dead Germans.

Then I was assured again that the rest of no man's land had been searched, and no Scotties found there, so I set off to join the battalion. I arrived at the camp at 5 a.m., and slept for 12 hours, and after a meal felt as fit as ever I did in my life, but dreadfully saddened. I am missing jolly faces everywhere, and it was dreadful to see great big fellows strewn on the ground as cannon fodder.

I expect to come home soon for a short leave. 6 of our men went today, and the Officers will go too when a fresh supply comes.

I rode over and saw Chris today. He was looking very fit.[17]

To Margaret Twemlow he wrote simply:

In that photo you have of Scottish officers before we left for Belgium, I am the only one left now. All the rest are either killed or wounded or have gone home sick. But some of them I hope will come out again.[18]

Private F. A. Fyfe of the Liverpool Scottish, a press photographer in civilian life, had disobeyed orders and brought his camera with him. Wounded early in the battle, he took several photographs of the action which show clearly the artillery flags planted on the German parapets. He, of course, was lying in no-man's-land and was therefore much nearer to the action than were the artillery spotters further back.

The official casualty figures differ slightly from those Noel had in his possession when he wrote to his father four days after the battle. In fact, twenty-three officers and 519 other ranks went into battle at Hooge and the figures show that the Liverpool Scottish had practically ceased to exist:

Killed:	4 officers,	75	other ranks
Missing:	6 do ,	103	do do
Wounded:	11 do ,	201	do do

Most of the wounded were subsequently found to have been killed, and only two officers and 140 men had come through unscathed. So most of Noel's friends had died and the rest had been wounded. None of the bodies was ever found and their names appear on the Menin Gate at Ypres. However, 'the Scottish had definitely proved themselves as a fighting unit and set the seal to their previous record in the Brigade,' said the regimental historian, A. M. McGilchrist, himself one of the lieutenants who were wounded.[19]

A chilling letter was sent home by Private Angus Glendinning:

The day has passed and we have been victorious but wiped out. Some of our boys were taken prisoners, who the Huns stripped and dressed themselves in their clothes. The Lincolns found our prisoners shot and naked. Like damned fools we took prisoners and treated them well, but our boys got tortured. Our officers were heroes.

The cads had women in their dug-outs, which were full of dead, and would not fight, asking for mercy! Now we cannot muster 150. The shellfire was hellish! When going up to the firing line, the only thing one could see was dead, dying and wounded. 2,600 wounded passed through the hospital from our Brigade.

The Scots Fusiliers went up with 900 and came back with 150. Last night we were relieved, and when I met our boys they had no officers left, but all had German helmets. The Scottish did more than their share. An officer went up to a German who had his hands up and then brought them down, shooting the officer, but another man got him with his bayonet. With all our wounded left out, they turned the gas onto them, and killed the poor chaps![20]

Private Edmund Herd, also of the Liverpool Scottish, described what his company found when they reached the enemy lines. Two German officers were discovered dead in their trench, wearing British uniforms — perhaps an example of espionage, or perhaps just a vain attempt to escape. Herd, too, saw several apparently Belgian civilians, including women, behind the German lines. The German dug-outs were a revelation; they were full of luxury items like wine, cheese, coffee, cigars and cameras. Those Germans who were taken prisoner were 'in splendid condition and wearing good uniforms', Herd wrote. 'Many of them held out testaments and crucifixes when surrendering.'[21]

Not all enemy troops who wished to surrender were allowed to do so. Sergeant Bromley saw German soldiers holding up their hands and shouting 'Kamerad', but 'some of our fellows... had little mercy on them and used their bayonets freely'.[22]

Noel had been modest about the part played by him and his stretcher-bearers. Sam Moulton entered in his diary:

June 17th. It was heartbreaking to see the chaps straggling down the road — dead tired — their uniforms turned yellow with the fumes of the shells. I was left by myself, waiting for the Doctor, with his horse. I waited and waited. I finally went up to the Dressing Station on the Menin Road — could not find him there

— they told me he was still in the trenches and wouldn't be down till he was sure all the wounded had been brought in. I waited till 8 a.m.

June 18th. Doreen [the Doctor's horse] and I set off once more and saw Sgt. Rathbone at Brigade HQ and he told me the Doctor wouldn't be coming down till late that night... I went to the Asylum on the outskirts of Ypres and had been there about half an hour when the Doctor and stretcher bearers arrived and they all looked done in. The Doctor had been in the firing-line since the 15th and after the charge had been made on the 16th (early morning) he had been looking for and attending the wounded in front of the trenches. He covered all the ground the Battalion had advanced over and examined every Jack Johnson hole, and he would not give in till he was satisfied everyone was accounted for. I had to push him on Doreen's back and how he managed to stay in the saddle I don't know....

The Doctor ordered his horse just after dinner. He went to a Belgian Field Hospital just outside Poperinghe, left the horse there, borrowed a bicycle and went on to 9th Field Ambulance HQ. He was trying to trace one of the officers, he couldn't find him anywhere, he tried all the hospitals in the vicinity.[23]

This indicates the enormous concern that Noel felt for the welfare of the men in his charge, and his ability to spur on others to greater effort. The regimental historian commented:

One section deserves special mention for its behaviour during and after the action — the Battalion stretcher-bearers.... An inspiring example was set them by the Medical Officer, Lieutenant N. G. Chavasse, to whose untiring efforts in personally searching the ground between our line and the enemy's many of the wounded owe their lives.[24]

If anyone deserved some kind of honour it was Noel. But he was not alone; a list of recommended awards was prepared by the Commanding Officer, Major Blair, a list of considerable length. However, it never reached Division, from where the recommendations would have been sent on. It is thought to have been destroyed in a fire at Brigade Headquarters.[25] In spite of this, Major Blair was under the impression that his recommendations had gone forward, for at church parade on 27 June in a barn near Ouderdom the recommendations were announced, including that of the Military Cross to Noel Chavasse.[26] He had been forewarned that the announcement was to be made and for once absented himself from church parade. Private Finlay of the Liverpool Scottish recalled: 'He was missing, but later found in a little wood, weeping.'[27]

Thus it was that none of the Liverpool Scottish who received awards for their conduct at the battle of Hooge were recommended by their own battalion. Other battalions' awards for the action were appearing in the *London Gazette* by September, 1915, but there was nothing for the Scottish for months. A week after his death, Bryden McKinnell was awarded a posthumous Military Cross for his work at Hill 60 and in the St Eloi sector, as recommended in an earlier list.

Noel's Military Cross, which appeared, of course, in the RAMC list, was finally promulgated on 14 January, 1916. Because of the lost recommendations, and the very long list of names included in this despatch, there was no citation for Noel's award.[28]

In addition, one of Noel's stretcher-bearers, Private F. F. Bell, received the Distinguished Conduct Medal for his service at the battle of Hooge; so did three other men from the battalion, and ten men were awarded the Military Medal. Major-General Haldane issued the following official 'Special Order' on 17 June, the day after the battle:

> The Major-General Commanding cannot adequately express his admiration for the gallant manner in which the attack was carried out yesterday. The dash and determination of all ranks was beyond praise, and that some actually reached the objective in the first rush and remained there under most trying circumstances is a proof of their superiority over the German Infantry. That the captured ground could not be held is disappointing, more especially as the losses incurred were heavy. But these casualties have not been in vain. The 3rd Division carried out a fine piece of work and fought splendidly, and their Commander is deeply proud of them.[29]

Leave was now allowed to a proportion of the officers and men, and Noel was able to spend a few days at home, returning to Busseboom on 9 July, just in time to attend an inspection of the battalion by the Major-General and Lord Derby. After complimenting the sorely depleted battalion on their sterling work at Hooge, Lord Derby promised to use his influence to obtain more men from England, so that once the Liverpool Scottish were up to strength they would be able to go over the top again. McGilchrist was probably right to say that this statement was not particularly well received.[30] But at last this period of rest, following the spell he had spent away from Flanders, allowed Noel to give more time to the welfare of his men.

He also had time to write to friends, including young Cecily Twemlow, who at the age of twelve or thereabouts must have been interested and at times amused to receive the following:

Advanced Regimental Aid Post,
You know of what Regiment but
You don't know where exactly —
In Flanders.
July 23rd. 1915.
My Dear Cecily,

I will try and answer your questions. I will tell you what I can about Geoffrey Higgins [a young officer, missing at Hooge] at the end of the letter, because I am presently going to the part of the trench where his company is in and I can get news there. A dead Frenchman is lying out just in front of our parapet there, and he is not healthy, so after I have buried him I will find out about Higgins.

Alas, I have heard nothing about Capt. Ronald Dickinson or Kenneth Gemmell [both killed], but we have news from two more of our Liverpool 'Jocks' who are prisoners, both of them such nice chaps, and one of them writes to say that he is wounded and lying in the bed next to Major Anderson who is also slightly wounded. This comes as very good news, because I thought that he had been blown to pieces.

Just after I had got back from leave we were ordered back to the trenches. We were not able to take up much of a line, as we are only 200 fighting strength but we have a nice little compact piece of trench to manage. I will explain it to you. First, there is the fire-trench about 150 yards away from the Germans. This trench is fairly comfortable and although we have been in the trenches 9 days I have only sent 3 sick men to hospital. We draw lime-juice for them instead of fresh vegetables and meat and we send a petrol tin round on all hot days at noon and give each man a good cupful. We also give them a great treat. There are potatoes in a farmhouse close by and we buy them for the men. You should see how they fry them on little fires they make out of chips of wood in tins. But best of all a stream flows through the trench. It comes from the German lines and has been poisoned with arsenic and they must not drink it but I have got basins made out of biscuit tins by a clever Sergeant of mine, and have canvas baths brought up and the men wash three at a time.

Behind this trench is a wood and through the wood a little fort called a redoubt (I think that is how it is spelt). In this little fort are 50 men, who if the Germans break through the first line never leave it but fire on the enemy all round, till they drive them back or get wiped out.

Then close by the fort is the sapper trench and at one end of this trench, I have my Advanced Dressing Station and live in a little dug-out I have had built. In two other little dug-outs live two medical orderlies and four stretcher-bearers. These are round a little square, and in the middle of the square we are building a large dug-out with one side open, and large enough to hold four stretchers. This is our hospital. From this medical square, a communication trench goes back for ½ a mile to a road and there is also a path over the fields for night.

A way back by the road is a large house, in the cellar of which I keep a medical corporal and four men. Here I send seedy men for the night, and they can have a stretcher and a blanket and milk, eggs and bread, and are very comfortable, and soon get well. Here too I keep most of my dressings and bad cases are properly dressed here, after I have given first aid in the trench. The ambulances come here every night and take the wounded men away. Of course, any man who can walk can get back to the dressing station in the daytime down the communication trench. The bad cases must wait till night and be carried down the path.

So far, I am glad to say we have only had one casualty. The poor fellow was shot through the head. I have dressed a fair number of men from other regiments. One was shot just outside my hospital (a very handy place to get hit I told him). We have had some lovely weather on the whole, but 3 nights were very wet and then the trenches turn into slime and mud and we get very wet and dirty. But the sun soon dries us and we can always wash in our dear little poisoned stream....

I am writing this in my little dug-out. I am very cosy. It is very wet outside and the men go slosh, slosh, along the trench and so I have drawn the curtain (a sand bag) across the little window (a real little window with glass) and am waiting for my supper — fish (sardines), thick bread and jam. A fine feast, if no-one gets hit. After I have got the Frenchman covered over, I shall sleep soundly on my bed (a stretcher which shuts up whenever you lie down on it).

With love,

Your affect. friend,

Noel Chavasse.

...I am afraid that the news about Geoffrey Higgins is just the same old news. He is missing.[31]

A generous gift of money had been sent to him by a well-known Liverpool businessman and philanthropist, John Rankin. Rankin had been known to Noel since his days as a junior doctor at the Liverpool Southern Hospital; indeed, he was one of the hospital's leading trustees. He was also a generous contributor to Bishop Chavasse's Cathedral Building Fund. Now he wanted Noel to spend a gift of £50 for the benefit of the men of the Liverpool Scottish, and further sums of money were promised. Noel also had at his disposal other donations from various well-wishers. But how to spend the money? He wrote home on 18 July,

> I find by experience that the men are chiefly short of literature. . . . My idea is to supply each Company with a complete set of magazines a month, a few weeklys [sic] every week and 6 books every week. I will go round and find out what books are most popular but meanwhile I shall like Marjorie to pick out my the first weekly 30. Also a primus stove to get hot drinks for fatigue parties who come in from the trenches. I sometimes used to give as many as 50 hot drinks a night, and I want to go on with it again. I am afraid we shall be very short of fuel this winter so it would be fine to have a primus stove and a regular supply of paraffin coming out to us. I think that an endowed primus stove and a lending library will be the chief ways of spending the £50. Candles may have to be added in the winter, and perhaps a few cricket balls.[32]

Having given further thought to the men's needs, he wrote again on 6 August:

> I have a little band of 8 men and I have bought some music for them and hymn tunes. (It has cost 15/9 at Rushworth and Dreaper.) They will perform to the men when we leave the trenches and play the hymns for Sunday which ought to cheer us all up and will certainly make our service go with a pius [sic] swing.... I have also spent a few shillings on getting the men potatoes in the trenches. They do so like them. If Atora [suet] is not too expensive and is sold in tins, I shall get some for the men. They will cook it with the spuds and make chips. I wonder if you could put forward the following order for me — it is regular light literature for the men. They cannot stand

anything except the very lightest, except for a few who I try and cater for.

I would like 24 copies of the Liverpool Echo every day. My stretcher-bearers will become Echo Boys and take it round. Also 12 sixpenny books weekly and 2 Strand Magazines and 2 Nash's. Perhaps some newsagent would take this order over for me.[33]

Noel was also making more detailed arrangements for the treatment of wounded men. Distance and difficult terrain in the vicinity of the trenches often meant that men had to wait hours for medical treatment; this was one of the lessons he had learnt from the Hooge action.

I am very busy building a hospital in the trenches. It is a new scheme of my own and approved of by most people. There ought to be some sort of rough shelter to give comfort and protection to the wounded behind every trench. The dressing station proper is often so very far away.

He enclosed a drawing of the hospital with a note attached:

Will anyone present stained glass? Cunningham suggested that it should be called the Chavasse Memorial Hospital, but I thought it a very poor suggestion.... My stretcher-bearers have invented a new design of stretcher, for trenches which wind a lot. It is short, and the men sit up while their legs dangle down. I am going to show it to the Divisional Doctor.[34]

The stretcher was in fact designed by Lance-Corporal W. E. Pennington; it was patented on 29 September, 1915, three weeks after the Commanding Officer of the Liverpool Scottish had written to the War Office recommending its more widespread use. The design was certified by Noel as being Pennington's own in November that year.[35] In the event, the Divisional Doctor was greatly taken with the idea and Pennington received fulsome praise for it.[36]

In the war, as in their childhood, Noel and Chris were often mistaken for each other. On one occasion, Noel was amused that a man from another battalion confused him with 'Parson Chavasse':

Chris had preached to them once, prefacing his remarks by asking, 'Are there any St Helens lads here?' Three quarters of them were his old parishioners and they hung on his every word. An old sergeant expressed his disappointment at me being myself and not Chris as he had first thought, because he said he thirsted to see him.[37]

Chris's reputation as a sound and popular padre was catching up with Noel. A Presbyterian minister met the Doctor late in August and told him of an encounter with 'a young parson in Rouen who was certain to be a bishop some day. The parson was Chris....'[38] Noel's own impressions of Army chaplains in general were not good. As he told his father:

> Our Presbyterian pastor is a washout. He never goes round talking to the men, trying to cheer them up, but only preaches on Sunday (a real congregational minister, not a parish pastor). He is an old dear, who ought never to have come out.[39]

Another padre, Goddard, whom Noel had met before the war and whom the Bishop presumably also knew, was described in harsher terms: 'Socially poisonous as ever, and his voice a disease, but the men like him.'[40]

Noel's conviction of the value of religious observance in the trying conditions of trench warfare was becoming stronger with every month that went by.

> Now that everybody is up against elemental things like sudden death as an everyday occurrence of life, all talk and argument goes to the wall and we all go back to the simplest beliefs, which now impress themselves as facts, and prove their truth by their power to comfort and sustain.
>
> When they go into danger, our men, who are a very good average of other men, want a Fatherly God to keep an eye on them (and they seem to feel in their bones that there is such a person too), just as when they are hit, they all want their mothers, and long for home. The two wants seem to be instinctive, and death, God and home all equally real.[41]

Noel's personal religious needs were simple. The Bishop had advised all his sons in uniform that they should cultivate the power of 'ejaculatory prayer', if circumstances were such that they could not take Holy Communion or spend the usual amount of time in private meditation.[42] But Noel needed a structured service whenever possible and he tried to provide something of the sort for his men; as for himself, he was capable of voicing savage criticism if the opportunity for *his* kind of service was lost. A year later he was very annoyed to find himself at a High Church service, even though it was Church of England. In fact he left the service before it began.

> I felt my gorge rise.... I think it's rather bad form to thrust one's own notions down everybody's throats, for that fellow would have officers of all shades of opinion coming to his service, and he could only please the very few, if any. Because out here one does like a plain and simple religion to help us through very blunt and plain truths and tragedies. And besides, I put down my religion as C. of E. because I have been brought up to believe and to love the teaching of the C. of E. Prayerbook (The Book of Regulations), and I think I am entitled to have my religion according to those Regs, and not to be at the mercy of whims and fancies of any Tom, Dick or Harry of a parson....
>
> I feel I have been robbed, because the Holy Communion is the best steady and comfort to the nerves that I know.... So I hope we get a 'pukka' padre next Sunday and not the hermaphrodite because I shall not go to his show.... I wish we had a man like Chris.[43]

In August 1915 Noel was promoted. While pleased about the extra pay, he saw no significance in the elevation of rank.

> I, with many others, have got a rise. I am now a Captain and drawing very good pay. They have kindly ante-dated 6 months so I have pay owing to me. Every Lieutenant on Active Service for 6 months is getting this rise, so there is no glory attached to it. Existence is the only qualification. I am afraid that a great many medical officers have relinquished their temporary commissions, most simply 'fed up' or upset because so many of their officer pals have gone. Very poor reason one would think for deserting one's country. I find myself the only one of the Brigade who has been out with a Battalion since November last. So that yesterday I received a note to say that I was Senior Medical Officer of the Brigade. Again, the only qualification is existence, which if I carry on feeling as well as I am now ought to lead me on to dizzy heights of promotion.[44]

His optimism was misplaced: further promotion was not forthcoming. His later outspoken criticism of the RAMC, as well as his sympathy for soldiers whose nerve had gone, made sure of that.

It is noteworthy that from August 1915 onwards, Noel's letters began to be addressed to both parents, instead of just to his father. This change of style followed closely upon the few days of 'post-Hooge' leave that he had enjoyed, and it is known that his mother's health was giving cause for concern. Perhaps, like his men, he was thinking more and more of home as the war dragged on. He was not immune to the idea that one day he might become a casualty himself; after all, no one was better placed than he to see the effects of trench warfare upon individuals. And he was only too aware that most of the Scottish officers with whom he had served had been either killed or wounded. He was developing a more fatalistic outlook, apparently not caring whether the war 'did for him' or not. Within a few months, however, this was to change, as he realized that he wished to have a life after the war, now that he had found someone to share it with. But, for the moment, there was plenty to occupy the time and thoughts of this most conscientious Medical Officer.

CHAPTER TEN

A Family Affair

Belgian civilians caught signalling to German 'planes by means of a windmill. Court-martialled and shot. Rained in evening.[1]

This terse entry in Private Edmund Herd's diary indicates how easily the desperately serious side of war was relegated to the level of ordinary gossip. The material that filled dozens of boys' adventure stories was real now, but there were so many intense and unusual experiences that soldiers hardly bothered to comment. What mattered in the line were the everyday things like food, warmth, shelter, personal comfort, jokes (often of the crudest type); out of the line, sports, entertainment, perhaps religious observance. Above all there was comradeship, and each of the social activities in which the men took part, from 'chatting' lice to singing songs, from playing football to laughing at a concert party turn, built up the sense of togetherness and friendship which for many was the real meaning of the word duty. For most men and officers, the major compulsion to obey orders and not to run away was a deep-seated wish not to let down friends. The strongest loyalties were to the fighting unit, whether it be the battalion, the company or the platoon.

While Noel Chavasse, with his background, could theorize about duty, and indeed believe in it, the sense of owing loyalty to a co-operative venture was instilled into the ordinary soldier by just such 'comforts' and 'welfare' activities as he was promoting. Whenever the men were out of the front line, he was working hard for them, in ways which, ultimately, contributed greatly to their esprit de corps:

> I have established a recreation room with magazines, 3 stoves, tea and buns. The Y.M.C.A. have a cinema in the village. A gentleman from Liverpool, Mr. Place, is giving us Primus stoves, four have come already. They will be of the utmost blessing. I am getting the paraffin out of Mr. Rankin's Fund which also runs the Sick Fund and Sick Billet Fund and the Canteen.[2]

The various funds of which Noel was in charge went a long way towards creating a sense of 'family' among the men. In a sense, officers like him were undertaking a parental role, particularly for the younger men of the battalion. So it was the Medical Officer who filled their Christmas stockings, did their laundry and thought about obtaining extras in the way of food.

Meanwhile, Noel spent these weeks behind the lines in the Zillebeke Lake area of the salient, perfecting the dug-outs in which he treated sick and injured men.

> We had a draft out last week. 5 days ago 50 of them came to work in the dug-outs. We are trying to make them shipshape for the winter. While they were filling sandbags some high shrapnel suddenly burst over them and knocked out 8 of them. There were some big empty dug-outs there and they were dragged in. I felt very pleased with the way in which my men worked. The wounds were very many and some were large gashes, and all had to be carefully cleaned because shell wounds always go dirty. But as soon as one man was done they had him comfortable in less than no time. They are getting quite like nurses. They brushed out the dug-outs and had them clean, and they cleaned away the bits of wool and dirty dressings, and when a man was dressed and I had to rush on to the next, if I looked round I found the man lying comfy in a stretcher with a blanket round him, sipping hot tea.[3]

His canteen was also 'going great guns':

> We are selling a lot of Quaker Oats and condensed milk in our canteen and are giving away all the paraffin the men need for their Primus stoves. More are buying the stoves as I have guaranteed that they shall have paraffin for them by hook or by crook. The Canteen is getting famous. Men from other battalions come asking to buy but we have to refuse them as we barely have enough for our own fellows.[4]

In October he managed to meet Aidan, who had come out to the front on 16 August, and wrote home to reassure his mother about her youngest child's well-being:

> I have been twice to see Aidan. He looks very fit. He has very nice billets indeed in a gaol. He has a sitter and a bedder and a scout, what more does he want? He has to go out digging every night until 1, so he sits up late and I suppose gets up late. So he really might be at Oxford.[5]

As winter drew on, the fight against trench foot began in earnest again.

135

Noel kept a brazier going night and day in the dug-outs and rubbed the men's feet every day with what he called 'frostbite grease', which was in fact whale oil. In addition, the authorities were supplying all battalions in the line with rubber thigh boots, which proved extremely effective against the complaint. However, kilted battalions had problems with these; they had to be pulled on under the kilt which, of course, had no trouser buttons to hold them up.[6] Medical researchers, looking for the causes of trench foot, were by now blaming the wearing of puttees as well as the cold and wet. These relics of the Indian Mutiny of 1857 bound the legs between the ankle and the knee and could easily restrict the blood supply to the foot.[7]

Most of the autumn was spent in and out of the trenches in the Ypres Salient, generally in the St Eloi sector. As Noel had already told his family, drafts were filtering across from England to make good the losses of the Hooge action in June, and in late September the battalion was deemed sufficiently strong to be involved in an attack on Sanctuary Wood, which lay a short distance south-east of Hooge. Noel's account of the attack once again moved his father to have his letter printed and circulated privately:

I have been the witness of as gallant a charge as ever took place, which has ended, so far as we are concerned, in our line here being exactly the same as it was before; but two regiments at least are cut to pieces. I doubt if much attention will be paid to it in despatches; yet it was the biggest thing that has happened since we came into this tortured spot, and as usual everybody responded to the call of duty, and blood was poured out like water, and lives cast away as carelessly as old boots. I am sick of seeing men sent out to die in the mud which is the mould of former battalions 'gone under'; but it will always be a delightful honour to lend a hand to the wounded heroes, and so in spite of all, in a selfish sense, this year has been the happiest of my life.

Our Brigade was in reserve. There was a barn for the men and good dug-outs for the Officers. We had hardly laid down when a terrific bombardment took place. The Huns did not make much reply, but some shells dropped very close to our dug-outs I believe; I was too sleepy to notice much that happened. At 7.30 a.m. batches of prisoners arrived and I went out and inspected them. The first batch was pretty good; afterwards there were some very poor, low, types of men; but among them was one Officer who gazed about him with defiance and hauteur, and marched off with head erect and stiff back. He was only nineteen, but everybody liked him. In the afternoon the bombardment began again. At 7.30 p.m. we had orders to be at the support dug-out, just behind the line.

Well, we had to rush off for a three mile forced march through sticky mud. I confess I felt tired. I was with the Colonel, and when he dropped in to the brigade dug-out on his way up, I very peacefully dropped asleep in the rain outside. Now all the way up I was haunted by the knowledge that our trenches must be full of wounded men, undressed, who could not be carried away. Yet I suppose fatigue made me callous, and I tried to persuade myself that my duty lay with my own battalion, that I must stick to them, and incidentally, probably get a good night's sleep. Yet I could not forget the night of June 16th and the wounded lying strewn along the road, and crying to be carried away; their terror of shell, their thirst, and my despair when the R.A.M.C. never came; so as I plodded along beside the Colonel, I muttered prayers not to feel so tired and sleepy, and so careless of the great horror around me, and not to miss my chance to give a helping hand. And call it an answer to prayer, or self-hypnotism, or what you will, I began to feel more lively.

Finally, we reached the wood, and I got my men settled in about 11 p.m. The wood we were in was full of dressing-stations, and I wandered about till at last I hit on one. It had been the dressing-station of a Highland regiment, but the doctor and stretcher-bearers had been sent off exhausted, and the relieving doctor was trying to tackle the work. His relief when I offered our stretcher-bearers' services was very plain. The trenches, he said, were choked with wounded. He could not cope with it. The R.A.M.C. had gone to lend a hand, but they were insufficient. I asked our Colonel's leave, and he said he thought it was our duty to do all we could. So I called out my poor, sleepy, tired men, who came with splendid grace, saying that they knew how they had appreciated help given to them after June 16th. I was now wide awake and fresh as a goat. We had the communication trenches pointed out to us. It was a dark night, but lighted up by the flares shooting up nearly all round us.

The trench first led through a dreadful wood. The trees, stark and blasted, dripped with rain. Straggling briars were the only vegetation. The ground was pocked with shell holes, through which poured muddy water. A smell of death hung on the damp air. Bullets snapped amongst the splintered and blasted trees, and every now and again a shell fell and burst somewhere.

We hurried on, picking our way by the spasms of light, and

suddenly found the trench ended in a large shell hole, in which floated the body of a Highlander. A Highlander limping back from the trenches — the only thing near us — pointed out our direction, and we emerged from the wood, and saw before us a muddy, shell-stricken rise of clay, on the ridge of which were our trenches.

I have described this place in detail, because by many it is supposed to be the dreariest and most dreadful spot in the whole of that desolation of abomination called the firing line. It is indeed the Valley of the Shadow of Death. Bunyan alone could describe its weird horror. It fairly grips the heart. Half way up, among the shell craters, a little cross marks the spot where Lord Desborough's son [Billy Grenfell, brother of Julian Grenfell], I think, lies buried. Just here about a little party of wearied men who had charged so gallantly told us that close by in a bomb store two men had lain wounded and forgotten for nearly two days, so my men set off to bring them in. I believe that these poor fellows would not have been found for another two days if we had not heard of them, for no reinforcements were sent there.

It was now getting near morning, and all my men were gone, but I had a haversack full of dressings, and helped by a capital medical corporal, searched among the trenches for the wounded. Some of these were pitiful beyond words, but bore their sufferings with a patient courage, of which mere words are not worthy. I thought I might as well wash the mud away, and put a dressing on, even if we could not get them all removed at once, but the Officers near spared a man here and there. My men, though very tired, came back in the early morning for a second carry, and one by one the worst cases were borne away down the stricken slope, through the dismal wood, to the dug-out dressing station, where the doctors made good my clumsy trench efforts, and then despatched them to the collecting post, from which they had to be carried a mile through mud to the ambulance wagon.

At 4 a.m. some men came trooping along from advanced trenches, because they were not safe by day, as they were shelled. They reported that these trenches were full of wounded. These were the very advanced trenches, dug in front of our wire, out of which the men jump for the charge.

I could not bear to think of our wounded lying in trenches which would be shelled. They get so terrified. So I went up with my faithful orderly, to see how many there were. We found in one sector about nine. We got two of them dragged down. It was a long and tedious job. The trenches were very narrow, and this part of them full of mud nearly to the knees. These Highlanders had charged, and found the German wire intact. They had charged three times, and finally had got in. The Territorial Highlanders also found the wire uncut, and crawled underneath it, and captured the trenches. Did you ever hear of the like? I doubt if any of those who got into the trenches returned. For reasons which we shall learn better later, and which so far as we hear now, had better remain untold, they were forced to give way.

My dressings ran out at last. The last men I dressed were some who had crawled into a sap heart. Here I met a man who had met Chris, at Rouen, and we discussed Padres.

It was now, after eleven months at the Front, that I saw for the first time a wild Hun in his lair. We were at a place where the parapet was knocked in, when, looking across, I saw another trench, with the head and shoulders of a man above it. I said I did not know that we had a trench in front there, to which they replied it was a Hun looking over his parapet. They said they were very cheeky, and that they could easily shoot them off, but the orders were not to let the Huns know we occupied this trench.

One by one we got our wounded down and away, and a warm sun shone out for a bit. It was now that I met with my gentlemanly sniper, for when I had gone twenty yards down the communication trench, it came to an end in a large crater. I climbed out, thinking that we were in dead ground, and got three shots round my head from some place I could not see. I jumped back pretty quick. But we had to get out, and it seemed to be long shooting, so I climbed out again. Then came another shot. But, when the stretcher appeared, shooting stopped, and the four men with their precious burden, went slowly down the hill into the wood. This was the experience of all the stretcher parties. They all wended their slow way in perfect peace. So one Hun has a good heart anyway.

At 12 (noon) I ate some bacon. It tasted like the choicest meat, and never was tea more delicious or refreshing. I then lay upon what seemed to be the softest of couches, and fell into the soundest of slumber.... It took the whole of the next day to get me clean.[8]

A week later, he sent some more details about his part in the action:

That day I did a bit of a combatant's job for the first time and enjoyed it very much. Our men were rushing up relays of bombs. One party got pretty heavily shelled, and scattered, dropping the boxes and wisely seeking cover. On seeing the boxes lying about and our men everywhere, I am afraid I left the wounded to be roughly dressed by our First Aid men, while I collected a party of men from all I saw near or who passed by, and got 30 boxes each with 6 bombs in carried up to the place where they were to be dumped. I felt so frightened lest the bombs might run short — because if the supply stopped for even 5 minutes, it would mean our bombers being driven back with probably great loss of life. The thought gave me quite a turn.[9]

In accounts of this kind of devotion to duty lies the legend that began to surround the Doc: that he led 'a charmed life' and bullets would not touch him; that he deserved the Victoria Cross dozens of times over; that when he was there you were safe. His descriptions are corroborated on many occasions by the narratives of other witnesses; and while this may be, at least in part, due to a desire felt by old soldiers after the war to be able to say that they had served with Chavasse, he nevertheless does seem to have inspired in his men genuine feelings of the highest regard.

His concern for the men even after death no doubt contributed to this.

We bring our dead about 5 miles back behind the firing line now and they are buried by a chaplain. I have a stretcher-bearer who is a carpenter and he makes very good crosses. Today I am sending up a cross to within 300 yards of the firing line to mark the grave of one of our poor men who was killed on June 16th. I visited his grave only a few days ago and found his cross broken by a shell. As it is a lonely grave, we are very keen to mark them as well as possible.[10]

Officially, for the Sanctuary Wood action, he was 'Mentioned in Despatches' by Sir John French, then Commander-in-Chief of the British Army in France (though the action had taken place in Belgium). Noel was included in a long list of names sent by French on 30 November, 1915, but not published until 1 January, 1916, 'for gallant and distinguished service in the field'.[11] So this honour was made public two weeks before his Military Cross was belatedly announced (on 14 January), even though the Hooge action at which he won the Cross had taken place some three months before that at Sanctuary Wood.

In the letter which his father had had printed, Noel mentioned 'the Hun' several times, usually with a certain sympathy for the enemy soldier and very little animosity. He had so far only looked at a German across no-man's-land; as the Christmas of 1915 approached he had his first experience of fraternization. There seems to have been a definite attempt by both sides in this particular stretch of the line to emulate the now-famous Christmas truce of 1914. All members of the Liverpool Scottish knew what had happened the previous year, and now they found themselves in trenches at St Eloi, opposite enemy soldiers who appeared to have little wish to fight. The regimental historian records:

> The 1st North Staffordshires, whom they relieved, had strange stories to tell of the peacefulness and mateyness of the troops, Saxons, occupying the trenches opposite.... [A] sentry was surprised, on the morning after relief, to see a German head appear... and to hear a voice ask in very good English for a tin of bully-beef. This was thrown across to him but fell short and rolled down into the crater. Without a moment's hesitation the German clambered out of his trench and retrieved the bully. Of course, he should not have been allowed to do it but it seemed unsporting to put a bullet through a man who evidently had not the slightest suspicion that he was taking any risk.
>
> These Saxons said they were tired of war and did not intend to make themselves unpleasant. [They] even went so far as to warn the men to be careful of sniping from the flanks as they had Prussians on each side of them.[12]

Sergeant Bromley, whose platoon was involved in these exchanges, agreed with this account:

> This seemed to me a truly amazing incident, and bore out what we had often heard, that the Saxons were the least bitter towards us of any German troops. From the other sap, manned by X Company, the following night two of our fellows went out and met two Saxons in No Man's Land, with whom they exchanged souvenirs and cigarettes.[13]

Private Herd's diary indicates that the fraternization continued almost every day until the battalion left the trenches on 29 November, a classic case of 'live and let live'. The Doctor mentioned the affair only briefly, telling his parents that he had been in trouble for waving at the nearby Germans — the colonel had reminded him that they *were* the enemy.[14] Frederick Jackson who was an onlooker, later described the scene thus:

> Dr. Chavasse jumped on the fire-step, snatched off his Glengarry

and waved it vigorously to the Germans, and shouted, 'Guten Morgen!' Colonel Davidson turned to him and said, with stiff dignity, 'Don't you realise that these men are the enemies?' The Doc looked down brightly and replied, 'Oh, yes sir, I was thinking how nice it would be to open a canteen in that crater....'[15]

At Christmas, however, Noel noticed the abnormal calm.

> Christmas Day was very quiet, hostilities seemed to stop by mutual consent, nobody seemed to have the heart to try to kill or maim each other on that day, but as far as I know, there was no fraternizing, that had to be put down. I think it is a great tribute to the very firm though hidden hold Christianity has on every heart, that war has to cease on Christmas Day.[16]

Noel's concern for the men's welfare was never more obvious than at Christmas, when he knew their thoughts would naturally be with their loved ones at home. So he tried to bring something extra to the festivities. As he told his sister Dorothea, whose Birkenhead 'Comforts Committee' had supplied the battalion with so much:

> I am giving the men your socks, they are tickled at finding presents in the toes. On Christmas Day I will take a sack of sweets, chocolates and cigarettes round the dug-outs.[17]

His presents for his parents at Christmas 1915 were two anthracite stoves; he was just as concerned that they should be warm in the draughty Palace in Liverpool as that his men should be warm in their dug-outs. His sister Marjorie had successfully undertaken the purchase of the stoves, for which Noel paid by cheque, and in return he received a new gramophone and a 'bundle' of records for the men. He had also received from Marjorie a violin 'which has been a great success'.[18] Private Herd described a concert in a village hall at which Private Rutherford played the violin and 'Ben Holland sang "Un Peu d'Amour" and "Come Sing To Me".'[19]

Hogmanay was celebrated by the whole battalion. Led by the pipe band and well fortified with rum, they went to the officers' quarters and dragged Noel out of bed. Practically teetotal, he nevertheless took it in good part, though cries of 'Let's get the old Doctor' gave him pause for thought:

> I know I am 'the Little Doctor', but I don't like being 'the Old doctor' at my tender years... It gave me quite a turn.[20]

The dawning of the new year marked the end of the battalion's service with the 9th Brigade, 3rd Division. Orders came on 1 January, 1916, that the Liverpool Scottish were to be transferred to the 166th Brigade, 55th Division. This was the West Lancashire Division, being made up of units from that area. Formed on 3 January, the 55th Division had contained by the end of the war 64,000 officers and men, of whom 6,250 had died, 24,294 were wounded and 4,887 were missing and have no known grave. Eleven Victoria Crosses and one Bar were awarded to the division. Commanding it was Major-General Sir Hugh Jeudwine.[21]

In saying goodbye to the battalion, Brigadier-General Douglas Smith of the 9th Brigade remarked:

> I know I shall miss you very much in the future. There is a lot of hard work before us and when I look round for the Liverpool Scottish and find them gone, I shall miss them very much. I wish you all the very greatest luck, and when you come across the Germans again I hope you will give them what you did on 16 June. You were always to the fore and never behind on that day. Few people have not heard of the Liverpool Scottish... You have always been well behaved which is a great thing in a country like this, where there are so many temptations.[22]

Noel had one reservation about the move to the new division: its Senior Chaplain was the Reverend J. O. Coop, Vicar of St Catharine's, Abercromby Square, Liverpool, opposite the Bishop's Palace. There had been disagreement between the Bishop and Canon Coop for years, and the Chavasse family attended St Saviour's Church, Falkner Square instead of St Catharine's which was nearer. Noel wondered if his twin could have moved into the 55th but assumed, rightly, that Chris would not wish to serve under Coop.[23]

The year 1916 was to bring Noel into conflict with his colleagues in the RAMC and with the Army itself over exactly the issues that Douglas Smith had highlighted: behaviour of the men and the temptations that faced them. But for now there were happier developments to distract him.

When his Military Cross was gazetted on 14 January, there were great celebrations in the Bishop's Palace. This was the first award for bravery won by a member of the family. The Lord Mayor of Liverpool, Alderman A. S. Mather, whose own son Norman was to fall while serving with the Liverpool Scottish at Guillemont in August 1916,[24] visited the battalion in the trenches on 31 January, adding his congratulations to the many others Noel had received. Meanwhile, the Liverpool Scottish moved to a new area, this time in France, and they were to stay away from Flanders for the next nine months.

Heucourt was the new billeting location, and many weeks were spent here in training, particularly in musketry. Noel wrote to the Twemlow children:

> We are in France near Abbeville. HQ is in a chateau and I have a beautiful room in a tower. Our host is an old French Count. In the village all the people weave sacking. The girls do all the work. There are no young men about at all. I have a dry canteen and library and reading-room in the Calvinistic Chapel, a hot bath-house in a confectioner's shop and a hospital in an empty house. Unfortunately, just as we have settled down and are getting up football and boxing matches, we are told we have to move to another village and shall have to begin and make ourselves cushy all over again.[25]

Early in February Noel was allowed a few days' leave in England. Part of the time he spent at Barnt Green and it was now that his love for his cousin Gladys was finally allowed to blossom, with the full support of her mother and her sister Esme. Both girls had family nicknames: Esme was 'Sam' and Gladys was 'Gaggy'. It seems certain that Noel and 'Gaggy' had been left unchaperoned, at least for short periods, so that their relationship could flourish, a development whose potential had been only too obvious to onlookers, if not to the participants. When Noel returned to the front he fired off an urgent letter to his sister Marjorie, a letter not always up to his usual standards of lucidity, indicating a certain agitation:

> Now I come to the most important part of all, and while writing it, my heart do go pit-a-pat, pit-a-pat. This would be the P.S. in a girl's letter, so you can guess to what I refer. Can you please tell me where I stand and what I ought to do to make things square and happy?
>
> (1) Do the parents object much. Because the funny thing was at Brom. Aunt F. walked off with S. and left me alone with G. and left us alone whenever she could, I thought. Then, when I went, Sam sort of darted looks at G. to see if she was going to cry, so it all seems all pretty well public.
>
> (2) What are G's feelings, for I don't want to hurt them. If a good man is going to come along, perhaps that will be best and the mission field will have me too. But I don't want to see her go off with a rotter and I certainly don't want her to be unhappy, I have said nothing so far for things are so uncertain —

i. I might not get back, and if I do I may not be a whole man.

ii. If I do get back whole I shall have to settle down and get a living and perhaps I may think I ought to be a missionary or a clergyman.

So you see it is very hard. I would like to tell the girl all this, but I don't want to make her unsettled and if she only likes me in a cousinly sort of way I would let well alone. If there is more, then I think I ought to do something. So if you have got anything to tell me I would very much like to know.[26]

Marjorie was close to Gladys. Their friendship had grown during their time spent working at Aunt Frances's hospital at Rednal, although Marjorie had by early 1916 come back home to Liverpool. It seems that Marjorie gave him the advice he wanted to hear, and no doubt she wrote to Gladys too, for within days Noel had written to Gladys and had received her answer. He then told Marjorie what had happened:

I have been and gone and done it now, and I feel ever so happy, but ever so responsible. I wrote to Gladys a letter and told her the truth, that I loved her, and could not help it. But that I had not proposed because (1) I did not wish to be disloyal to Aunt Frances' hospitality, (2) I might not get home, at all, or all of me, (3) I had as yet no prospects. So I said she was as free as the wind, but someday if she wanted marriage also, 'old Barkis was willin'.' I got a letter back which nearly makes me cry. She says she can wait, and that I must be what I ought to be, if even a missionary, and that meanwhile she supposes we have what is called a private understanding. I don't wonder I love her.

Then comes a letter from Aunt Frances, full of kindness, saying she is glad there will be someone she can trust to look after Gaggy, and that I had better not mention it to my people until after the war. Could anything be kinder? So please break the news gently to the old folks at home, and don't tell anybody else. I do hope they don't mind because I am sure things are all right.

Also, I do hope Gladys really loves me, and is not merely sorry for a 'lonely soldier'. You might perhaps find this out. I expect Father will have his breath a bit taken away, but he will recover. Smooth everything over, please, my dear sister, and don't let there be any disagreeables [sic] for dear Gladys' sake. I wonder what Chris will say.[27]

The whole Edwardian edifice of courtship is revealed in these letters. The chaperone, the part played by female relatives, the reticence in revealing one's inner feelings (as shown by Noel's retreat into the persona of a third party, the fictional Barkis from *David Copperfield*), the finality of a properly made proposal. The inevitable and only destiny for a female member of the upper middle class was marriage, which explains why Aunt Frances was so glad to see her daughter settled, especially as there was no father, in Gladys's case, to look after her interests and negotiate a good match. Such negotiations were not necessary with Noel because he was 'family', and Aunt Frances was very fond of him; however, she was apparently rather worried about the Bishop's reaction, given the close family relationship between Noel and 'Gaggy'. Noel, however, though aware of possible objections, was convinced that they could be overcome, and Marjorie was to be the medium for achieving this. The family rooms at the Palace in Liverpool witnessed many earnest discussions on the subject while the parents awaited direct word from Noel. He was the first of the Bishop's sons to contemplate marriage.

Then tragedy struck. While Noel was still considering how to put his case in his next letter home, news reached Barnt Green that Aunt Frances's only son, Arthur, had been struck down with a chest infection. He was in hospital at Le Havre in France, and his mother and Esme set off immediately to be with him, arriving at Le Havre on 11 March, where they took rooms at the Hotel de Normandie.

Arthur had qualified as a doctor in 1911 and before the war had been a physician at Queen Charlotte's Hospital in London. Like Noel, he had been eager to enter the war before it was over. In October 1914 he joined the British Red Cross Society in France, and was attached to No.2 Motor Ambulance Convoy and No.5 Hospital at Wimereux.[28] In February 1915 he entered the RAMC with the rank of Temporary Lieutenant, working first at the hospital at Netley, Southampton, and then at Number 4 (Versailles) and Number 2 (Abbeville) General Hospitals in France. On 15 February, 1916, he was promoted to Temporary Captain, but a few days later he became ill and was moved to hospital at Le Havre.

Noel heard the news of Arthur's illness on 12 March, just as he was writing to his parents. He expressed his concern to them, but soon got round to the main purpose of his letter:

> I wonder if Marjorie has told you that I wrote to Gladys and told her that I would not propose to her but that I loved her, and that if
> (1) I got home sound
> (2) I got a home (having now no prospects), and
> (3) if she had not by then married a better man —
> Barkis was willin'.

I did this for 2 reasons.

(1) So that if I died Gladys might know that I did love her and was not a flirt, and

(2) in case she might marry just anybody because she thought I did not care for her.

Dear Gladys' reply was more than I could have hoped for — but still nothing is settled (except my own mind which is now contented), and she is absolutely free and can make up her mind as she likes and is not one bit compromised, and nobody except Aunt Frances and yourselves know anything about it.

So please don't publish it from the housetops, and please don't reproach me because truly I shall not mind. If only poor Arthur was not so ill I should be feeling ever so serene in the midst of the worst of worries.

So if you write to Gladys please be very nice and tell her that although she is quite free, yet if ever I do get home, and settle down, and she then makes up her mind to have me, that you will be very pleased.

And don't call me rough or impulsive, because I am 31 and know my own mind (and no-one knows how long I have kept myself in), only of course Gladys is much younger, and may not know her mind, and so is free to make it up as she likes later.[29]

Here was a man accustomed to making life and death decisions in his chosen profession, seeking his parents' approval with an almost boyish wistfulness. Gladys was twenty-two; while Noel thought she 'may not know her own mind', she was absolutely certain that she had indeed made a commitment to him, and it was final.

But on 12 March Arthur died of pneumonia, his mother and Esme at his bedside. He was twenty-eight. Lady Chavasse and her daughter attended the funeral at the Sainte Marie Cemetery in the town, making him one of the few who died in the Great War whose family had the privilege of paying their last respects in this way. The grieving women made their way homeward, sending letters containing the news to Gladys, to Noel, to the Bishop, and to May at the Liverpool Merchants' Hospital at Etaples. May could be relied upon to notify any other members of the family whose whereabouts she knew.

Noel now felt a double responsibility for Gladys, as she had no other male relative to safeguard her. He was, however, delighted to hear from his mother that she and the Bishop gave him their blessing without reservation. He wrote back at once:

I am very glad that you and Father approve my choice. I thought it all over very carefully, and of course Gladys is still free if ever she wants it. As things have turned out, I do thank God that I wrote before this terrible blow befell all of us. Poor Gladys, I think she was Uncle Tom's special daughter and Arthur's special sister, and she is dreadfully saddened.

I feel very responsible and quite realise the gravity of the step I have taken. I don't know if it is this, or if it is the bad month we had in October, when I felt dreadfully for the men. But since leave I feel a year older. I used to feel about 25 (not more) but now I feel 26 or 27. I hope God led me into the step I have taken, in the light of past sad events, it has seemed so opportune and so far everything has seemed to lead so easily from one thing to another, as if I was born for my part in the war.

I can hardly believe my good fortune because I used to think I should never get Gladys, and I don't know why she is going to have me even now because I am not much of a catch and she has been the prize of the neighbourhood.

Girls are queer and dear things. I wonder when Gladys began to be fond of me, because I cannot tell and I expected a kind and sympathetic refusal. Anyway, I am going to take care that she never regrets it, and am trying in a blundering sort of way to make myself a proper husband and I hope some day a father. The danger is in making Gladys my religion, but I seem to love my poor men, and to feel for them more than ever. But at last I have a great longing to get through with the war, before I never thought about it. I hope it will not tempt me to neglect my duty.

I expect from this letter you will see that I am in love, but then I have been for years, but might not say so.[30]

Sadly, no letters survive from Noel to Gladys or vice versa.

And what of Chris? Having served for a short time at Suzanne in the valley of the Somme he was now with the 62nd (West Riding) Division in Suffolk,[31] a posting he was not particularly happy with as he felt he was too far from the war. Noel wrote to him there, and told him of the 'private understanding' with Gladys. He went on:

I feel quite in the air with delight, because I thought Gladys was a prize far beyond me. I can hardly believe my luck. The parents have sent their blessing. Mother, I believe, is actually pleased, and I really believe Aunt Frances is pleased too. She has been wonderfully kind. So you see, old cock, I have beaten you, in the matrimonial line, in spite of your 20 minutes' start. At any rate I have got a flying start on you. So you will have to buck up if you don't want to be an also-ran and best man.

I hope you go over to Barnt Green soon; if you do, give Gladys my love and you may give her a brotherly kiss, but you must not kiss her too much.[32]

CHAPTER ELEVEN

The Road to Guillemont

Naturally, Noel was longing to get back to England and see Gladys in person. Early in April he heard that he was to have three days' leave; he had been chosen, out of the hundreds who had recently been awarded the Military Cross, to be among the few dozen who would receive their crosses from the hands of King George V himself at Buckingham Palace. His Commanding Officer, Lieutenant-Colonel J. R. Davidson, was to receive the CMG (Companion of the Most Distinguished Order of St Michael and St George) at the same time.

Noel was anxious to spend as much time of his leave as possible with Gladys, so he wrote to his parents suggesting that Marjorie could come down to London to chaperone her, or perhaps Aunt Frances could come? This would have been the only possible way for young people of their social class to meet away from home. As he said,

> Please remember what I am feeling like. I want to see my maid for as long as I possibly can, and of course I am also longing to get home.[1]

Unfortunately, Noel's presentation and the leave were postponed. He was terribly disappointed. To his parents he wrote:

> I shall be glad of a holiday. Do you know I have been in the line with a regiment for 15 months now and I seem to get tired more easily and don't seem to be so keen. It is only the faces of the men that keep me anxious to help them at all times. I do believe my work is going on better than ever.[2]

However, he added, he was getting 'lovely letters' from Gladys; 'I do believe she loves me, almost as much as I do her. I am happy all day long.'

Christopher had reacted with enthusiasm to the news of his brother's secret engagement, but Noel detected a disquieting despondency.

> I feel very sorry for Chris because I feel so happy and settled, as

17. (*left*)"Christopher . . . the first member
of the family . . . in uniform" (p.60)
(*J. C. Chavasse*).

18. (*above*)"Everyone here is trying to grow
a moustache, so I am having a go too" (p.62)
Tunbridge Wells, October, 1914
(*J. C. Chavasse*).

19. Officers of the Liverpool Scottish,
Tunbridge Wells, October, 1914. Noel is
fourth from the left in the rear rank. By June,
1915, all but he were dead, wounded or sick
(*Liverpool Scottish Archive*).

20. "Aidan was a lieutenant with the 11th (Pioneer) Battalion of the King's" (p.109) (*J. C. Chavasse*).

22. "Bernard, who had enlisted with the RAMC, served first in Egypt and then in Gallipoli, before arriving on the Western Front in 1916" (p.109) (*J. C. Chavasse*).

21. May's "role . . . was that of 'Lady Helper to the VAD'" (p.110) (*J. C. Chavasse*).

23. "Dr Arthur Chavasse . . . their cousin and close friend" (p.75). He died of pneumonia at Le Havre, 12 March, 1916 (*J. C. Chavasse*).

24. The attack at Hooge, 16 June, 1915. This photograph was taken by a wounded member of the Liverpool Scottish, Private F. A. Fyfe, a press photographer in civilian life. It shows one of the coloured canvas flags (p. 118) put up to indicate how far the attack had penetrated. The glengarries of the Liverpool Scottish can be clearly seen (*Imperial War Museum*).

25. 'The Doc' with his stretcher-bearers in rest billets in Flanders, 1917. C. A. Rudd, who died following the same incident that killed Noel, stands behind the doctor, who wears his first Victoria Cross ribbon. At least two Military Medal ribbons may be seen among the men. The glengarry has been entirely replaced by the Balmoral bonnet (*Liverpool Scottish Archive*).

26. Lady Chavasse at her 'hospital' at Rednal, 1916. In the back row are Esme, Marjorie and Gladys (*Mrs M. Knight*).

27. Noel and Christopher behind the lines in 1916, possibly at Bailleul (*J. C. A. Quinney*).

if I was where, and doing, what I ought (of course I feel fed up at times) while Chris seems gloomy and unsettled. Although I suppose there is no-one in the Army who is doing finer work, and who is more beloved, and who has more friends and admirers, or who has a more promising future in front of him. My future alas! is very much in the lap of the gods, just when I should like it to be settled too. So I should like to see Chris and talk things over very much.[3]

A short leave was granted to Noel on 10 May, although the medal presentation was still subject to delay. The Barnt Green Chavasses had a holiday cottage in the New Forest, Hampshire (Canterton Cottage, Lyndhurst), and here Noel stayed on his first night back in England. Aunt Frances and Esme were there as well as Gladys, but Noel and his 'maid' were left alone and had plenty to talk about. Gladys took several photographs of her unofficial fiancé 'getting to know the in-laws', as she put it. The two girls then went with Noel by train to Liverpool, where they met up with Chris who had also got leave. At last the brothers were able to 'talk things over'.

Back in France, Noel was, for the first time in his life, worrying about the future. He asked his father for advice about making a will — should he leave what money he had to Gladys or to Chris or to his five-year-old nephew Aylmer, Dorothea's son, for his education?[4] He was concerned at not having a definite career goal in mind for when the war ended; like many men, he was beginning to see war as less of an adventure and more of an interruption to his life. He wrote to his parents:

I sometimes feel very worried about what will happen after the war. I do so want to take the right step then.... I feel certain I ought to have been a doctor and was meant to fight in this battalion. I know that Gladys and I were meant for each other, but I cannot see forward at all clearly.[5]

At last the date for him to receive his Military Cross was fixed: Tuesday 7 June, 1916, almost a year after the Hooge action for which it was awarded. During the short leave (which he spent in London) he was with Gladys and another cousin, Hetty, most of the time, but did meet Chris in London. The encounter worried him, as his twin seemed 'sad and unsatisfied, so different to what I feel.... I think he wants to marry but has no-one in view and feels lonely.'[6] In the same letter Noel went on to describe the ceremony at Buckingham Palace:

On Tuesday I went to get my Cross. Cousin Hetty and Gladys came too but had to stay outside the gates. In we marched in file across a big hall to another room where the King was. At the door of the room one's name was called and we had to take 6 steps forward and turning to the right saw the King. Towards him came a General bearing a little medal on a very large cushion. I bowed my best, and a hoarse voice said in my ear, 'Step forward', so I took 2 steps forward and had my cross pinned on. The King shook hands and said in a gutteral voice, 'We grant you our Military Cross.' I thought it was very nice of him. I then stepped back two paces, bowed again and turned away as the next man's name was called....

I do feel sorry for leaving Gladys behind and for the first time catch myself praying for my own safety. Before, I used to think it wrong to single oneself out for special protection over and above any mother's son.

London at this time was seething with rumour and speculation about the death of Lord Kitchener, Secretary of War, who had drowned when the armoured cruiser *Hampshire* went down off the Orkneys on 5 June. The press was debating the likelihood of mine or torpedo as the cause. Because he was presiding at a memorial service for Lord Kitchener in Liverpool, the Bishop was unable to be in London for his son's investiture.

Noel was back with the Liverpool Scottish in time to mark with them the first anniversary of the charge at Hooge; there was a march-past and the Commanding Officer made a speech.[7] The Liverpool Scottish had remained in France for the whole of 1916 so far, mainly in the Rivière sector, alternately occupying the trenches and then spending days in support. They had been faced with an especially unpleasant aspect of warfare, rats.

Rats seem to have been more troublesome to the battalion during 1916 than at any time previously. These vermin thrived on discarded food, and on unburied corpses, growing to an enormous size and spreading disease. The historian of the Scottish recorded:

Never were there such enormous rats as lived in the Rivière trenches, thousands of them, enormous brutes with an utter disregard for man. The walls of the trenches and dug-outs were honey-combed with their runs and at night they swarmed over everything. The men had the greatest difficulty in keeping their food protected. It was useless to hang a loaf of bread by a string from the roof of a dug-out.... The only way to preserve perishable food was to cut it into small pieces and pack it in a mess tin.

Rat-hunting became a regular trench sport and though many men developed great quickness and efficiency with stick or bayonet there was no noticeable reduction in the number of rats.... They were erudite rats too. One of them was discovered disappearing backwards into a hole with an unopened copy of *The Weekly Times* in its mouth.[8]

Lance-Corporal H. S. Taylor remembered the rat hunts:

At the back of our dug-out were regular runways used by the rats on their unlawful occasions. You held your bayonet ready to plunge into any rat which happened to be passing. This procedure was fairly successful, but not as good as shooting with our rifles... but higher authority finally interrupted the sport and banned further mis-use of ammunition, so the rats remained, a constant source of wonderment at their ingenuity, carrying eggs upside down by the tail.[9]

Noel was later to take 'a jolly nice little fox terrier with me who will, I hope, help to settle the rat question in the trenches'.[10] The terrier, named Jelly or Jell, was given to him by Gladys; unfortunately it was no match for the rats and preferred to run away and hide.

There were some changes in kit and uniform for the Scottish during 1916. In the spring the first steel helmets arrived, but they were unpopular because of their weight. However, they did have their uses, according to Lance-Corporal Taylor: '(a) as a seat in damp or muddy conditions, and (b) for making porridge, after removing the lining.'[11]

By this time no-one in the battalion wore the Glengarry, all sporting the khaki Balmoral.[12] The Doctor, or course, being RAMC and only 'attached' to the Liverpool Scottish, should never have worn the Glengarry at all. The story persists, however, that he preferred to wear it, once finding himself in trouble for doing so:

A vigilant Military Policeman arrested Dr. Chavasse as a German spy. Although wearing R.A.M.C. uniform, the 'Doc', instead of wearing the khaki hat of the Corps, wore the Scottish Glengarry, with of course the battalion badge. On the lapels of his tunic were the badges of the Royal Army Medical Corps. ...Full marks were probably accorded to the M.P. for his alertness.[13]

A RAMC colleague recalled:

When he visited our Field Ambulance, we used to hide his Glengarry and try to induce him to wear proper R.A.M.C. uniform. This he resolutely refused to do (and quite rightly!).[14]

It is certainly true that two of the best-known painted portraits of Noel show him wearing the Glengarry, and the occasional photograph survives of him thus attired. He once wrote to Marjorie asking her to send on his 'Glengarry cap' which he had left hanging up in the hall at the Palace; the fact that he had forgotten it implies that it was a secondary piece of headgear, but it also shows that he wore the Glengarry sufficiently often for him to have his own.[15]

Throughout the late spring of 1916, the build-up towards the so-called 'big push' was the main topic of conversation amongst soldiers in the area of the Somme and Ancre valleys. This was to be the knock-out blow which would, according to General Haig,

(i) Relieve the pressure on Verdun.
(ii) Assist our Allies in other theatres of war by stopping any further transfer of German troops from the Western Front.
(iii) Wear down the strength of the forces opposed to us.[16]

The men believed that detailed plans lay behind all the preparations, and their enthusiasm for the fight was rekindled as they thought that at last this was IT!

The attack on German positions began on Saturday 1 July, an appropriate day of the week, especially as at least one young Captain (Billie Neville of the 8th East Surreys) went 'over the top' and kicked a football across no-man's land. Most British troops faced the usual problems: of carrying perhaps sixty-six pounds of equipment; of being ordered to advance 'at a steady pace'; of finding barbed wire intact and Germans emerging from dug-outs cut so deeply in the chalk substratum that they had escaped the British bombardment; of being mown down like grass as deadly machine-gun fire raked the fields. However, the Liverpool Scottish faced none of these at the start of the battle, as their division, the 55th, was not involved in the early infantry action.

On 1 July, Noel's letter to his parents was concerned with more mundane matters, like the wartime income tax increase from ninepence to five shillings in the pound:

I am very sorry to hear that you have to pay away so much in Income Tax. It will make things very short. I am glad your hulking sons are at last earning their living. I am a wealthy man now, and shall be happy to lend you a fiver at any time.[17]

Noel put pen to paper again on Friday 7 July, in his dug-out at Bellacourt, still in the Rivière sector south-west of Arras, writing this time to Cecily, another of the Twemlow children:

Aren't I a beast for not writing to you before? But you must forgive me, as we have all been very pressed lately. It is a very wet afternoon now, and I am waiting till it gets a bit better before I go round some of the trenches. I cannot get round all of the trenches now, as we are holding a very long line, so I have to do a bit every day. It is no good going round when it is raining because everything is muddy and wet, and all the men who can are in the dug-outs so that it is impossible to see what wants doing or what is wrong. The line is so long that I have two dressing-stations in the reserve trenches.

One is a huge dug-out very deep and 30 feet long by 6 feet across. It is very safe. It is lined and roofed with large logs. Yesterday my stretcher-bearers were lime-washing it to make it lighter. One of them seemed to be trying to do it by putting lime-wash on his hair and clothes and then rubbing against the logs — he was in a mess. I have another dressing station about a mile away in a culvert under the road. This has been lime-washed, and makes a very good little surgery. It is here I see my sick parades every morning. I am glad to say that we have very few sick just now, as the men are all wonderfully well.

It has been very wet too, and the communication trenches have been filled with water, so that for 10 days the men never got their feet dry, but happily it was warm and they were none the worse.

Then I have another establishment in a village about 300 yards behind our second line, and that is a bath-house and laundry. It used to be an old estaminet, now it is a flourishing institution run by enthusiasts. You go into the front door, and if you go into a large room on the right you will see two barbers busy cutting hair. You will also see some men sitting reading at one or two tables. But don't look at the tables too closely as the table tops look rather like doors, and don't ask where the wood for the benches came from.

You will see a large barrel of paraffin for the men's stoves in the trenches and petrol tins full of lime juice for them. Then at the far end is a counter, with cigs and chocolate to sell and other things too, depending on how we can get them. For this, my dear, is the Liverpool Scottish Canteen, no less.

The other door has written upon it. 'For Bathers and Staff

Only', and being a lady of course you mustn't go in, but when I go in I see about 10 men dressing and undressing. I see one man having his toenails and corns cut. I see clean shirts and socks being handed over a counter, and a sick man ironing men's kilts, to kill (I must whisper) l**e.

Leading off from this room, you can hear splashing going on, and if I peep in, I shall tell you that I see a place very like a stable only whitewashed, and in a lot of baths (old barrels cut in half) a lot of men soaping and washing themselves in hot water, and by Jove they need it. This, my dear, is the Liverpool Scottish Bath.

In a shed outside you will see a lot of old coppers all busy boiling away, fed by anything that will burn, and on a table 5 men scrubbing shirts, for this is the aforesaid regt's Laundry. In the dressing room, an old Grandfather clock strikes 3, on looking at the dial I see the hands point to 4.15, so by a rapid mental calculation I know that it is a quarter to five, and I must get back to my dug-out (in the reserve line) for tea.[18]

So here, while the battle of the Somme raged only a few miles away, Noel was able to write wittily and in detail to a child. His description of the cleansing and recreational facilities that he had set up illustrate how his concern for the men's welfare went far beyond the usual scope of a battalion Medical Officer. As the war went on, this aspect of Noel's interpretation of his role was to become legendary. As the Commanding Officer had apparently remarked: 'This Battalion is here no longer to fight the Germans but to suffer sanitary experiments!'[19]

Private Herd recognized the importance of the Primus stove, remarking that as the war proceeded there was hardly a man without one, and that hours of misery could have been avoided if they had been available right from the beginning.[20] Noel saw to it that there was always paraffin for the stoves. The regimental historian recorded that when the Scottish had to leave this area and move, after a few nights spent here and there, to billets at Ville-sur-Ancre the Doctor was 'intensely annoyed' that the laundry could not go too, though the canteen moved with the men.

This 'dry' canteen had been started up with capital donated by Noel, and was further financed by donations he received from well-wishers back in Liverpool, usually in memory of men or officers who had been killed. In charge of the canteen was Corporal W. Forbes, who used to take the men's orders and endeavour to meet their requests, a service which did much to alleviate the conditions in the line. Later in the year the scheme seems to have lost money, possibly due to theft, much to Noel's distress. In a letter to the Company Quarter-Master Sergeant Scott Macfie, who was on leave at the time, Noel displayed a definite eye to business:

> The canteen flourishes in one of the dug-outs and we sell about 3-500 Fs. per day and we have now got a working basis of 1200Fs., when we went to the Somme we only had 200. So I have got all the lost money back again. Now we hope to pay for cocoa and whist drives out of the profit.[21]

Meanwhile, the battle of the Somme had reached the end of its first disastrous month. Casualty rates were appalling, not least in the 'Pals' battalions, four of which had been raised as part of the King's (Liverpool Regiment). In Liverpool a dark cloud of grief hung over the city as the newspaper columns of the names of the killed and wounded grew ever longer. Such anguish affected the populace that the Lord Mayor had inaugurated a Roll of Honour, a list of the dead, which relatives could see and where families could request the addition of names of their loved ones. The Bishop and Mrs Chavasse at home, wondering if their sons were involved in the 'push' and whether they would be safe, could see for themselves the sad queues of mourners trailing round the Town Hall in Castle Street, waiting to add a name to the Roll.

At the end of July the Liverpool Scottish were moved from Ville-sur-Ancre to bivouacs just outside Meaulte, on the south-eastern outskirts of Albert. Here, they saw other battalions of the King's, including some of the Pals. Noel hoped he might see Bernard, now Medical Officer to the 17th King's (Liverpool Regiment), but was disappointed:

> I am nowhere near Bernard; he is, I should imagine, in a Field Ambulance behind the Push. If he is serving the Pals he has had busy and exciting times because I see they have had a great many casualties.... The Germans are being very hard-pressed now on all fronts. I do think we have turned the corner and are top dogs at last.[22]

However, even Noel found it difficult to remain optimistic when he heard a piece of family news. Second-Lieutenant Louis Edward Joseph Maude of the 11th Battalion, the King's Own Yorkshire Light Infantry, was a cousin on Noel's mother's side, being the son of her brother Joseph. A lively and witty man, Louis, in ebullient mood, had written to Bernard in May:

> By the way, when I was at the Base [Etaples], which I was for six weeks, I found an angel of mercy in May. I went into hospital

for an abscess in my jaw, and there she was. I have written to Aidan who is Wipers way, but he answered me never a word. We are a patriotic family, nicht war?[23]

Now Noel wrote on 23 July:

I have heard that Louis is missing. It will be a terrible blow [to Louis's parents]. There have been some sad losses among our cousins, what a lucky family our own is....
    P.S. I myself was never better and more happy in my life.[24]

Louis was later found to have been killed in action in the vicinity of the Somme villages of Ovillers and La Boiselle. The date of his death was officially recorded as 1 July 1916, but his grave is unknown (though believed to be in Gordon Dump Cemetery). Together with the loss of Arthur in March, this sad event could only add to the apprehension and grief felt by the whole Chavasse family during that terrible year. Bernard, in particular, perhaps the most sensitive of all the brothers, was moved by Louis's loss to think about the impact of war generally:

When you think that this sort of thing is happening every day and many times a day it makes one realise what war means to a country. The streams of wounded whom I tend so hurriedly, the men whom I make special efforts to save — and fail to save, the men who die easily, and the men who die consciously and hardly — these are nothing to me, they are just my work — a part of the ordinary routine. But when you happen to notice a row of medals (which someone must have been proud of) on a tunic folded beside something that has been laid on a stretcher or neatly sewn into a blanket — when you happen to see a bundle of letters from God knows whom taken from a pocket that is very sticky and wet to be forwarded to England with other 'articles of intrinsic or sentimental value' you begin to understand that the presence of 'another dead officer, Sir' in this place means an absence and a gap somewhere at home. Also the fact that Death out here is often very — sometimes astonishingly — handsome, makes it sadder. They are all so damnably youthful.[25]

Noel informed his family that he would be moving three miles nearer the front:

I expect the next few days will be very busy ones. I pray God I do my duty. I have not got such a gay feeling in these sort of do's as I had 18 months ago. I am rather sick at heart of seeing so many men and especially my men go under.[26]

That same day, 30 July, the Scottish were moved to Mansel Copse, just south of the village of Mametz, and on 31 July to bivouacs at Machine Gun Copse. An attack was planned on Guillemont but the Scottish were to be in reserve. They stood-to for many hours, ready to go, but in the event were not needed. For the next few days they did much sterling pioneer work, digging communication trenches, and all the time aware of the terrible fighting that had occurred in places like Bernafay and Trones Wood. The evidence was all around — bodies of horses and men, wrecked transport limbers and wagons, shellholes and all the detritus of war, and in the air the smell of corruption and the sound of billions of buzzing flies.

During the first week in August, Noel was troubled by a tooth:

> I took it to an officer of a neighbouring battalion who used to be a dentist and he smashed it trying to get it out and now I find he has left one fang in.[27]

He was now in constant pain. On 7 August orders were received that an attack was to be made on Guillemont at 4.20am on Wednesday 8 August, by the 164th and 165th Brigades; the 166th Brigade, of which the Liverpool Scottish were part, would be in reserve.

After a heavy bombardment the attack was launched according to plan. The Liverpool Scottish waited, and by the afternoon of the 8th the attack on the right flank had been successful, but the centre and left were more doubtful. Indeed, the Liverpool Irish (164th Brigade) appeared to be cut off in the vicinity of Guillemont railway station. The 166th were ordered in, their attack to begin at 4.20 the following morning, 9 August. The objective of the Liverpool Scottish was to push past Trones Wood and Arrowhead Copse, capture the German front line and go on through Guillemont, consolidating on the eastern boundary of the village.[28]

During the night of the 8th, the Scottish marched up in preparation for the attack. A chapter of errors ensued. No guides turned up to lead them to their jumping-off trenches. Enemy shelling found its mark a few times during the tedious wait for fresh guides to come down the line. When the guides did arrive, they had only the vaguest knowledge of the route, and the men reached the jumping-off trenches with only minutes to spare. The barrage and counter-barrage were deafening, the enemy barrage proving to be particularly accurate on both support trenches and no-man's-land. Fierce machine-gun fire across Death Valley also pinned the attacking troops down.

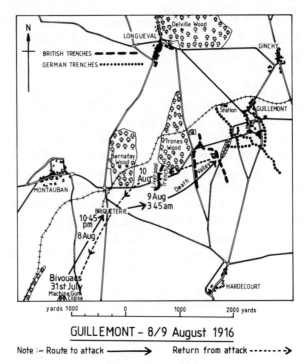

N

BRITISH TRENCHES ■ ■ ■ ■
GERMAN TRENCHES ●●●●●●●●●●●

LONGUEVAL
Delville Wood
GINCHY

Station
GUILLEMONT

Trones
Wood
Bernafay
Wood
Liverpool Trench
Death Valley

MONTAUBAN

10
Aug

9 Aug
3·45 am

BRIQUETERIE

10·45
pm
8 Aug

Bivouacs
31st July
Machine Gun
Copse

HARDECOURT

yards 1000   0   1000   2000 yards

GUILLEMONT – 8/9 August 1916

Note :~ Route to attack ⟶   Return from attack ------⟶

Led by Lieutenant-Colonel Davidson, the Scottish rallied and re-rallied, making four charges in all, but without success. The attack on Guillemont had failed.

Post-mortems have sought explanations for the débâcle. The preliminary bombardment was non-existent; the enemy wire was not cut; the terrain was unfamiliar, and briefing of non-commissioned officers and men had been inadequate. Most of these reasons may be summed up as lack of time: the decision for the 166th to attack was at such short notice that no one could have had time for adequate preparation.

The Liverpool Scottish had gone into the attack with twenty officers and about 600 other ranks, and the casualties were very heavy. Five officers were killed, five were missing and seven were wounded. Of the men, sixty-nine were killed, twenty-seven missing and 167 wounded.[29] Sir Douglas Haig allotted only one sentence to the attack on Guillemont in his despatch describing the battle of the Somme:

> In a subsequent local attack on the 8th. August our troops again entered Guillemont, but were again compelled to fall back owing to the failure of a simultaneous effort against the enemy's trenches on the flanks of the village.[30]

As for Noel, the first his family knew of his involvement was when they received word that he had been wounded. Almost at once, however, they heard from him:

> Don't be in the least upset if you hear that I am wounded. It is absolutely nothing. The merest particle of shell just frisked me. I did not even know about it till I undressed at night.[31]

News of Noel's wound even reached the columns of the *British Medical Journal*[32] and the *Daily Sketch*.[33] He had gone to the dressing station to have the area bathed, and because he was so dirty he had been given an injection of tetanus toxin. This meant that his name had to be entered in the Visitors' Book, and official notification of next-of-kin followed automatically. He was able to send a fuller account of his part in the attack a few days later, and described the three charges he had witnessed which were doomed to failure. The casualties were not as bad as he had feared, but the flies in the air had been frightful, and men lying in the open had wounds full of maggots. He went on:

> In the evening I took up a party of volunteers, and we pretty well cleared No Man's Land. We collected a lot of identification discs and so cut down the tragic missing list.
>
> We found and brought in 3 badly wounded men lying only about 25 yards from the Hun line, but 2 have died since I am sorry to say. Then we started off again, but this time we ran into the Hun trenches and got bombs thrown at us for our pains, but the whole party got in with only one scratch between the lot of it.[34]

He found when he eventually undressed to go to sleep that he had two 'spicules' of shell in his back, hence the visit to the dressing station. He was ordered not to go back into the affray, which annoyed him greatly. He said he did not like sending his men out into danger; he thought it 'cheers the men up if a practical civilian like myself is seen in the trenches'.[35]

As might be expected, the role played by Noel Chavasse in the attack upon Guillemont, though modestly described by himself, was amplified by other witnesses. Frederick Jackson remembered:

> That night, Dr. Chavasse went out into No Man's Land with his devoted stretcher-bearers, looking for wounded men and bringing them in. The amazing thing about this rescue exploit was that he carried and used his electric torch as he walked about

between the trenches, whistling and calling out to wounded men to indicate their whereabouts, and so be brought in. Ignoring the snipers' bullets and any sporadic fusillade, he carried on with his work of succour throughout the hours of darkness.[36]

Sergeant Bromley saw Noel and the stretcher-bearers creeping from shellhole to shellhole in broad daylight, looking for and dressing the wounded. Possibly this was in the evening of 9 August, as daylight would have persisted until quite late.[37]

One who had been closely involved with the Doctor was Private Edmund Herd, who from April 1916 was acting as Noel's orderly as well as being a stretcher-bearer. He recorded in his diary:

[Guillemont was] a busy time for the S.Bs. I was completely exhausted after the severe and ghastly work. I was buried for a short time, but got out. How I escaped the hail of bullets was a miracle.... As soon as darkness fell, which wasn't so dark really on account of the hundreds of Very lights, all available S.Bs. went out to bring in the wounded and dead. There was only one casualty among the S.Bs., that was the Doctor, who got a piece of shrapnel in his thigh.[38]

Three days later Herd was helping the 9th Kings (Liverpool Regiment), for Noel would sometimes volunteer his stretcher-bearers to other units in need of man-power.

The Liverpool Scottish spent a few more days in the area east of Albert, and then moved further back to billets at Meaulte. Here they were addressed on 16 August by Major-General Jeudwine, who commended them on the action at Guillemont. The battalion then went by train to a rest area at Valines, west of Abbeville and only ten miles from the coast.

Noel was given a few days' sick leave and headed at once for Barnt Green, from where he wrote home, on black-edged paper in mourning for Arthur, that he had received the leave very unexpectedly, he had not known where his parents were and so he had come to Gladys's home. Could the family all meet up, perhaps at Rossall (in Lancashire, a popular holiday area with his mother) or Pen Dyffryn or London? Wherever it was to be, he wanted Gladys with him, he wrote, 'because on returning to France I expect to go back into the push again'.[39] While in the Midlands he was going to see a Birmingham dental surgeon; evidently his broken tooth was still troubling him. In the event, he met up with his parents and Marjorie at Rossall. He had intended to write a lot of letters 'but did not as I had something better to do'.[40] Gladys, of course, had been staying at Rossall as well.

All too soon Noel rejoined his battalion. At the end of August they returned to the Somme area, and on 7 September began to dig a new front line at the north end of Delville Wood. Noel wrote home, once again in optimistic mood:

> It is nice to think that our heavy fighting is seeing its end. The Huns are beaten to a frazzle in front of us. We are feeling top dogs. There is nothing like the losses we had at first.[41]

But Delville Wood was no rest area. It had suffered such a tremendous battering that hardly any trees remained standing, the ground had been torn up and was churned into sticky mud by heavy rain, and the dead of both sides lay strewn about, impossible to count or to bury. Noel described one of the nights he spent there with his stretcher-bearers:

> We found an R.E. man. My S.B. Corporal bent over him and found him bleeding badly from one arm and held the main artery, and then we put a tourniquet on with a respirator string. Then I found that the arm was all but off and was only a source of danger. So I cut it off with a pair of scissors and did the stump up. We had to do everything by the light of an electric torch and when we got a stretcher it took us two hours to get him out of the wood....
>
> The mud was fearful. While I and my Corporal were dressing a case we both sank up to our knees in the mud of the trench. Men had to be dug out and some poor wounded of another battalion perished in the mud. We had one sad casualty. A poor fellow was crouching at the bottom of the trench when there was a slip which buried him, and he was dead when he was dug out. Both his brothers have been in the Scottish and have been killed. His mother committed suicide after the death of the 2nd. There is only a sister left.[42]

The men had been singing and Noel was very impressed with their spirit. He felt they often put the officers to shame, yet it was the officers who usually had the best of everything in the way of material comfort.[43]

Meanwhile, a development back in England was soon to raise spirits further. Early in October the Bishop received a letter from Lord Derby:

> I am doing something which is absolutely forbidden by War Office rules and yet I cannot resist the temptation to break the rules. I think I am right in saying it is one of your sons who is

in the RAMC attached to the Liverpool Territorials. If I am correct then I want to congratulate you and him most sincerely on gaining the Victoria Cross. I had the honour yesterday of submitting his name to His Majesty for the bestowal of this magnificent Order and I cannot tell you how pleased I was to do so. [44]

When he received a letter from the Bishop informing him of this recommendation for his actions at Guillemont, Noel's optimism for once deserted him. On 16 October he wrote back:

I fear that honour is not given as easily as all that, and recommending is not getting, so I shall adopt the attitude of a Doubting Thomas and till I see it in print I will not believe. If it will give me a bit of extra leave it will be worth having. [45]

He told no one else in the battalion.

The Liverpool Scottish had now left the Somme and moved once again to Ypres, by way of Pont Remy and Poperinghe. The pattern was one of eight days in the front line and close support, in the Wieltje sector, eight days at the B or C Camp near Brandhoek, and eight days in the Canal Bank dug-outs and Ypres. Ypres was, as one might expect, even more battered and grim than when the battalion had seen it last. The enemy was using a new and more powerful mortar, the *Minenwerfer*, and its shells or 'Minnies' caused a number of casualties amongst the Scottish. Noel's concerns were the usual ones:

We now have Thermos flasks as big as milk cans — a great blessing. We are in dug-outs on a canal bank. The men can get really clean and they fish as well, and catch and eat eels fed on drowned Huns. [46]

News had already reached the battalion of some of the awards following the attack on Guillemont. Of the sixteen stretcher-bearers, two had got the Distinguished Conduct Medal and two the Military Medal. Then, on 26 October, 1916, the *London Gazette* announced that Noel Godfrey Chavasse, MC, RAMC, had indeed been awarded the Victoria Cross. The Liverpool Scottish received the news 'in the field' on 28 October. The entry in Edmund Herd's diary for that day is brief: 'Wet. We celebrated the Doctor's V.C.'

CHAPTER TWELVE

For Valour

Noel Chavasse had been awarded the Victoria Cross 'for the most conspicuous bravery and devotion to duty':

> During an attack he tended the wounded in the open all day, under heavy fire, frequently in view of the enemy. During the ensuing night he searched for wounded on the ground in front of the enemy's lines for four hours. Next day he took one stretcher-bearer to the advanced trenches, and, under heavy fire, carried an urgent case for 500 yards into safety, being wounded in the side by a shell splinter during the journey. The same night he took up a party of trusty volunteers, rescued three wounded men from a shell-hole twenty-five yards from the enemy's trench, buried the bodies of two officers, and collected many identity discs, although fired on by bombs and machine guns. Altogether he saved the lives of some twenty badly wounded men, besides the ordinary cases which passed through his hands. His courage and self-sacrifice were beyond praise.[1]

Thus Guillemont was added to Hooge in the records of heroism kept by the Liverpool Scottish and the Royal Army Medical Corps.

Reaction in Liverpool was ecstatic. The *Liverpool Daily Post & Mercury* reported:

> Few men have inspired such wonderful affection for themselves amongst the ranks of their colleagues. Letters from the Front have constantly told how eager he was, how ready to expose himself to dangers beyond those called for in the discharge of his duties, and how many a wounded soldier has brightened under the radiance of his cheery disposition.... His battalion almost regard him as their mascot.[2]

The newspaper went on to record the description of the action given by a young Canadian machine-gunner, who was by now back in a Blighty hospital:

> I was up in the line that day, and the men were talking a lot about the fine courage of Captain Chavasse. It was absolute hell all day… Hell would have been heaven compared to the place he was in, but he never troubled about it. It's men like him that make one feel that the spirit of old is still alive in our midst.[3]

An anonymous stretcher-bearer was also quoted:

> At times it was absolutely impossible to stand up without being hit… The Captain took no more notice of the enemy's fire than he would of a few raindrops, and even when bullets were whistling all round he didn't get in the least bit flurried in his work. He made us all feel that it was an honour to work with him.[4]

On 27 October, when the Bishop attended a meeting of the Christian Union at Liverpool University, the Chairman, Professor Gonner, said how proud the University was to think of Captain Chavasse as a past member. Gallagher's included Noel in their cigarette card series, 'Victoria Cross Heroes'.[5] But the adulation must surely have reached a pinnacle on 31 October with the publication of a poem by Canon H. D. Rawnsley, Vicar of Crosthwaite, Keswick, but well-known to Bishop Chavasse and in Church of England circles in Liverpool as a whole:

> All day — with foemen full in view —
> He helped the wounded and the dying,
> The fierce shells burst, the bullets flew,
> But he who won the Oxford Blue
> Kept the old flag of courage flying.
>
> Night fell, and in the fiery zone
> Four hours he toiled to save the living,
> God with him as he worked alone
> To staunch the blood, bind broken bone,
> His dauntless hope to brothers giving.
>
> With dawn he sought the trench again.
> Wounded himself, he bore the wounded,
> For what cared he for splinter's pain
> While in his ears — and not in vain —
> The trumpet of compassion sounded?

Again night fell, with volunteers —
The foeman trenches close before them —
He dug two graves that ask no tears,
To three men spake the word that cheers,
And back to heaven from hell he bore them.

For twenty — pleasant shines the sun
Today, and earth is full of beauty,
Because, unscared by crackling gun,
Star-shell and fury of the Hun,
He followed One, whose life was Duty.
Give him Victoria's Cross to wear!
And say, where'er ye tell the story,
That such as he who do and dare
Take as their Captain, Christ, who bare
His Cross of Sacrifice to glory.[6]

Everyone that knew Noel or whose path had ever crossed his, either before or during the war, was anxious to congratulate him and his family. Gladys, who had been forewarned by Marjorie that Noel was to be decorated with the country's highest honour 'for valour', replied in almost hysterical terms:

Marjorie, you Brick!
I am nearly off my head! I knew he'd get the V.C. sometime but
I never thought he'd get it until he was blown in bits [sic] which
seems to be the fasionable [sic] manner!!
Marjorie, isn't it absolutely it!
I can't write,
Yrs
GLADYS.[7]

She was quite right to remark that men who were awarded the Victoria Cross were often killed in the course of winning it, but more lived to fight another day than lost their lives. During the Somme Battle of July to November 1916, fifty-one Victoria Crosses were awarded; of these, sixteen were posthumous, the remaining thirty-five recipients surviving, and, like Noel, many would fight again.[8]

Noel very soon found himself receiving letters by the dozen. He tried to reply to them promptly, but soon fell behind in the task. A letter to Sergeant Quarter-Master Scott Macfie, then on leave in Liverpool, was typical of many that he sent:

I am sorry to be so late in answering your very kind letter, but I have been a bit overwhelmed. Whatever my feelings may be about deserving the decoration, I must say that your letter and several others that I received from some of the members of the old Battalion did do my heart good, and I shall try hard to deserve them.[9]

Another was to Margaret Twemlow, aged sixteen:

Thank you very much for your nice and kind letter. You must excuse me for being so rude and not having answered it before, but really I have been rather swamped and I am still struggling to get through them all. I knock off about ten a day. People have really been kinder to me than I could have thought possible, and I sometimes feel quite ashamed of myself.

I hope to be getting a little leave somewhere about Christmas and I shall certainly come and see you all. I shall never forget the good times we used to have. Do you remember the Circus and the kicking mule and how you laughed till you were nearly sick?

Please give my love to Cecily (if she is not too grown up; if she is, please give her my felicitations), and to George, and my warmest regards to Mr. and Mrs. Twemlow. I am going to answer the other letters as soon as I can. Please thank Mr. Twemlow very much for his very kind letter which I value very much. [10]

In reply to congratulations from the Board of the Royal Southern Hospital he said:

It is a real pleasure to be able to do anything for our soldiers, and I do count myself very fortunate to be able, by reason of age and good health, to serve them out here. At the same time, we realise that those kept at home, by age and other circumstances, are doing just as good and often better work for our soldiers. And certainly our soldiers do deserve all we can do for them. Every day I admire and love them more for their courage and cheery endurance. Your kind message will stimulate me to greater efforts.[11]

If Noel was inundated with letters of congratulation, the Bishop's Palace experienced a similar postal deluge — possibly an even heavier one, because while people may not have known where to write to Noel on the Western Front, they knew very well where his parents lived. As the Bishop told Christopher:

> We are quite sure you would have done the same thing had you been in his place. But remember if you get any distinction of any kind, you must arrange to come home and answer the letters that pour in. I have *hundreds* to deal with. I am sending, in many cases, a printed letter of thanks.[12]

Noel's sister May, still working at the hospital at Etaples, found herself feted by officers. She wrote home:

> They made me drink Noel's health in Champagne to which I did *not* say no. I am not a T.T. out here! But I grew fearfully nervous when they would keep filling my glass up, and when we had chocolates with liquers [sic] in them — rum! cognac! punch! etc![13]

On 28 October, Noel's fellow officers gave him a dinner to celebrate the award. It was held in the chateau at Elverdinghe, a village to the north-west of Ypres, where they were billeted. The menu survives, adorned with pen-and-ink drawings of landmarks in Noel's military career: the cathedral tower at Ypres with the word 'Hooge' surmounting a Military Cross, and the tower at Albert (Somme) bearing the legend 'Guillemont', with the Victoria Cross at its base. A large representation of the badge of the Liverpool Scottish, with its thistles and prancing horse, dominates the menu, the contents of which give an insight into the delicacies available to determined officers behind the lines, from turtle soup, curried prawns and fillets of beef with asparagus to fruit salad and 'Macarrons Au Gratin' [sic], as well as sherry, champagne, port and a choice of liqueurs. And, to mark the occasion, a portrait of Noel in pencil was executed at great speed by one of his colleagues.[14]

Leave was not forthcoming, however, and it was some weeks before Noel was able to meet up with Gladys and his parents again. In the meantime, he had got himself into trouble with his colleagues in the Royal Army Medical Corps. There were two spheres of military medicine of which Noel was highly critical, and he found fault both in his fellow medics and in the RAMC 'top brass'.

The first target for his anger was the RAMC Field Ambulance Service. Noel had seen his efforts on behalf of wounded men frustrated on many occasions because the Field Ambulance failed to arrive when it was most needed, and was often incapable of coping with the large number of casualties. In the autumn of 1916 he submitted a report to his superiors, pointing out deficiencies and suggesting improvements. It was not well received. Noel wrote to his parents in November:

> As a result of the row I had with the Field Ambulance, it was felt there must be misunderstandings between Regimental and Field Ambulance Medical Officers, so for a month I and all other Regt. M.Os. have been sent to Field Ambulances. It was a great shock. At 12 midnight I was woken up by my relief coming. I am afraid I was very cross.
>
> [At the Field Ambulance] they were very kind to me and still are but of course I was amongst men whom I have offended and sometimes it is rather painful. I aim to find out what good fellows they are but there is not enough to do. Today has been rather frosty and I have been dreadfully comfortable and warm, but I cannot help thinking of my poor fellows in the line, and I can do nothing to help them. Today I heard that the place (where the Scottish are) has been shelled and that 20 of them had been knocked out. I did feel bad.[15]

The place in question was still the Wieltje sector where the battalion had been since early October. As ever, Noel's greatest distress was caused by his enforced absence from battalion duties, where he felt he could do most good.

> A Field Ambulance is no place for an active young chap. It should only be for older men with wives and families... Don't worry about me for the next week or two. I am one of the cushy people now, worse luck.[16]

Unpleasantness from other doctors increased steadily, in sharp contrast to the congratulations and good wishes still arriving by every post. Later in November Noel was moved again, but still not, as he would have wished, back to the battalion. He was therefore absent when the battalion went into action on 26 November in a raid on a German trench system, the 'Kaiser Bill Salient' just south of Wieltje, in which the Scottish suffered some casualties. In his letters, an undertone of despair was detectable for the first time:

> I have been moved as relief to a small hospital with 30 beds, and it takes 35 men to look after them. [I am] lonely, and there is not enough to do. I wonder what is to become of me. I wish I was with my boys again.

The officers [of Field Ambulance] were of course very haughty at first. Some of them I think really hate me, but all in this Ambulance have been most kind. Some of them make rotten remarks behind my back and say that I wrote my report to try and glorify myself and all that sort of thing, but it really does not matter, and I have not had the bad time I expected at all, being cast into this den of Daniels.[17]

Noel's second great criticism of the medical services was to do with venereal disease among the troops, which was developing into a veritable epidemic. (So serious was the problem that the official history of the war, in its volumes dealing with medical services, published in 1923, devoted forty-three pages to venereal disease, compared with fourteen pages on typhus fever, nine pages on trenchfoot and seventeen pages on gas gangrene.) Venereal disease was responsible for more than 15,000 soldiers being constantly out of action in England and France during the later stages of the war. The incidence of the disease was closely connected with the proximity of troops to towns, and the ease with which the troops could obtain access to these centres of population. It was asserted after the war that more VD had been imported into France from the United Kingdom than vice versa, but perhaps this evaluation was politically necessary rather than accurate. It seems unlikely that such a conclusion could possibly be statistically proved.

When the British Expeditionary Force embarked for France in the early days of the war, it took with it large numbers of copies of a leaflet by Lord Kitchener which warned the men to remain celibate. Lectures were delivered to the troops by the National Council for Combating Venereal Disease, and there was special instruction on the prevention and treatment of the condition for newly appointed RAMC officers. After the war, most of the blame was laid at the door of women:

Social conditions operated strongly during the war in favour of a high venereal rate. The sexual morality of females was definitely lower than in peace. The excitement of war, the halo of romance surrounding the soldier, and the greater freedom of life which women enjoyed as a natural consequence of [their war work].[18]

One deterrent that was tried was to deprive men of their proficiency pay during any time they spent in hospital as a result of contracting VD. In addition, an officer or soldier would not be eligible for leave for a period of twelve months after leaving hospital. But still the rate of infection was alarming.

In 1915, a scheme that Noel Chavasse condemned made its appearance. It was decided to allow *Maisons de Tolerance* in some towns, Le Havre being the first. Here a street was allowed to be 'within bounds' for troops, the prostitutes plying their trade with impunity provided that they agreed to take the advice on hygiene and prevention given by the British medical authorities. The scheme spread to Rouen and other towns.[19] In the United Kingdom, of course, brothels were illegal.

The results were startling, both in terms of the number of participants and the number of men infected. In fifty-seven weeks 171,000 men visited the street in Le Havre, but only 243 stated that they had been infected with venereal disease there. The statistical objections to figures like these are obvious; which man could say with any certainty where he had been infected? Most men, if asked, would probably rather not admit to the disease at all, until the need for treatment was inescapable. Treatment was, at the very least, embarrassing; it meant a public admission of a kind of behaviour that was greatly frowned upon. The various types of apparatus for self-disinfection that were placed in urinals, relying on irrigation of potentially infected genitalia with a solution of potassium permanganate, for the men's use, were very unpopular; one's fellows could see exactly what one was doing, and the long-lasting and disconcertingly vivid purple hue with which the affected parts were embellished can only have added to the discomfiture. By 1918 soldiers were being supplied with tubes of calomel cream, a far less visible therapy. (In April 1918, *Maisons de Tolerance* were put out of bounds to all troops 'in deference to strong public feeling in the United Kingdom'.)

Nevertheless, by the end of the war there were twenty hospitals in the United Kingdom entirely devoted to the treatment of venereal disease, a total of 11,000 beds. In France, VD beds numbered 9,000.[20]

Noel was convinced that a major factor was a decline in standards of morality, and male morality in particular, and that it was the duty of officers, Medical Officers and padres to try to stem the tide by example and teaching. So when it was being proposed that these officially sanctioned brothels should be opened in towns behind the lines, with medical examination of prostitutes and other prophylactic measures, Noel was violently opposed. Such an idea was entirely alien to his most deeply held beliefs. When he argued with his colleagues and superiors, he was speaking from the very strong position of having proved, through his care of the Liverpool Scottish, that if the will was there the incidence of disease could be reduced. He failed to see why VD should not be tackled in the same forthright way.

Just before Christmas 1916, for example, Noel warned his batman about potential temptations in the world outside the camp; he exhorted him to be teetotal and gave him a book by Jack London to read instead of going out to the *estaminet*. Then Noel insisted he have a hot bath to 'clean him up for Christmas'.[21] Naive the Doctor may have been, but principled as well. So when he was sent on a course on sanitation, a course which was really intended for newly arrived medics — the lecturers actually apologized to Noel because of his wide experience in the field[22] — he did not hesitate to express his views to the weekly conference of doctors (though he could not bring himself to mention the disease in question in a letter that was going to be read by his mother):

> The subject was the cause of minor ailments among the troops. At last, I could bear it no longer, because they never got to the root of the matter at all. So I popped up and told them what I felt to be the real reason. To my surprise I felt everyone was sympathetic, and afterwards when one young chap got up to try and knock down one of my arguments he was squashed, and at the very end a Regimental M.O. arose to say that he hoped the chairman had noticed the approval at the end of my remarks, because it was to show that they all fully agreed.
>
> I had to write a report on what I had said, which report has fallen into the hands of my Divisional General who is very angry and made scathing remarks about it, to be conveyed to me. It may get my leave stopped but everything in my report was in order.[23]

It is not known just what Major-General Sir Hugh Jeudwine found objectionable in Noel's report; it may simply have been an antagonism to a junior officer professing to know better than the senior medical advisers to the British Army.

Courses such as the one Noel had been sent to were six-day affairs, being repeated constantly for the sanitation officers of battalions in France. As the official historian put it in 1923:

> The Battalion M.O. is the sanitary adviser to his C.O., and it is, therefore, essential for all army M.Os. to be well-grounded in the principles and practice of army sanitation. Occasionally during the war the work of disease prevention was hampered by the attitude of certain M.Os. who were untrained in sanitation and apt to minimize its value and importance.[24]

Possibly Noel Chavasse was seen as one of these young upstarts. However, by the winter of 1916, few original 1914 Medical Officers were still with their battalions. Noel was one of the few. He had virtually trained himself, in the field, in the majority of subjects covered by the six-day sanitation course. A typical syllabus included prevention of infestation by insects, water supply, filtering and testing, urinals and latrines, food storage and cooking, bivouacs, camps and billets, infectious and contagious diseases, personal hygiene and bathing. Noel was a past master at all of these subjects. He had written to his parents in the autumn of 1915:

> I could write for hours about our trench latrines and how we baffle the flies. I bet there are no ones so clean anywhere. The man who does them loves them. They are quite a hobby with him.[25]

No wonder the instructors on the course apologized to him. He called it 'a rum show, very casual', but he enjoyed the rest.[26]

On a happier note, Noel was pleased to be asked to take a service for the patients, one of whom was an Old Boy of the Grafton Street Industrial School back in Liverpool.[27] And there were presents to buy and send home. For his mother Noel bought one of the ubiquitous lace cards, and for his sisters lace handkerchiefs. Marjorie had had a bad cold:

> I am sending you a little lace handkerchief for an Xmas present. It is a delicate little act of condolence for your poor dear nose. Can you blow down it yet? This will encourage you to try. What a happy Christmas it would be if you could get a trump out of it. The lace is 'real Cluny lace', made in Belgium in a convent close behind the lines, very precious and costly. Tell your friends this in the best Maude style.
>
> This is my third Xmas out here. It is getting quite a habit with me. I must try and break myself of it.[28]

Dorothea, the eldest Chavasse daughter, married to George Foster-Carter, now had two children. The latest arrival, a girl, had been born during October, and Noel had written one of his jaunty letters to his sister:

> I hope that she will be more reverent towards Aylmer [Dorothea's elder child] than were my younger sisters who have only really been polite since the war started and even then have had regretable [sic] lapses... Mother announced her arrival much as one announces the arrival of a train, and that her name is Lois Marguerite... I am a bit surprised that you did not call her 'tanks', because Mother's letter arrived about the same time as

the other surprise. They both delighted me immensely and I congratulate most warmly the authors.[29]

For Christmas Noel also sent Dorothea a lace handkerchief, accompanied by strict instructions as to its use:

> It is real Cluny lace, quite an heirloom. Aylmer really likes me coming, does he not? It is very gratifying, the single-hearted affection of a little child. I shall have a little cry on your handkerchief presently. Now, don't let Foster beg it for his Communion vessels, and don't give it to the nurse for the baby to puke over. It is not meant for exalted functions like these. It is meant for you to blow your nose on... Kindly blow your nose on something else before using the one I am sending or it might be ruined by one rash blast.[30]

He was hoping to come home soon, 'incognito', perhaps in order to dodge the crowds of well-wishers that had been calling at the Bishop's Palace. However, he did not expect to be home for Christmas, and mused rather wistfully on what the future might hold:

> I wonder if next Christmas my wife and I will come and spend the day with you, or shall I have to go to my wife's home? Anyway, what bedroom shall you give us? When Chris has a wife too there will be a lot of jealousy as to who gets the best spare room. You will probably have to settle it by putting Aunt Mary into it.[31]

Christopher had spent a large part of 1916 in England, and had been pursuing a project dear to his heart: drawing up and having printed and bound a prayer book for the troops. It was to be in simple language, brief and easy to carry. Like Noel, Chris had a naive, almost unworldly view of the importance of religion to the soldier on the Western Front. He had, of course, had most contact with soldiers who were wounded or dying, when the appeal of religion would naturally be more powerful. Most accounts of trench warfare, however, do not indicate that religious observance had as high a profile as Christopher liked to think. Indeed, hymns were likely to be parodied in a most vulgar way, even the soldiers' hymn, 'Abide With Me':

> We've had no beer, we've had no beer today,
> What's the use of living? Tell us, tell us, pray!

175

Nevertheless, there were undoubtedly many men for whom, as Noel had found, the rites and rituals of Church or Chapel were a great support and comfort. But the question must always have been in men's minds: how could a loving God allow such suffering to occur?

The Bishop had no doubts at all. He wrote to Bernard:

> It is certainly an awful war, but it has no more shaken my faith in God than the existence of the sin, disease and terrors which are ever with us. Why God permits the existence of evil we cannot at present fully understand. It is a profound mystery. But I am certain that he overrules all for good, and that, as Tennyson says, 'Oh yet we trust that somehow good will be the final goal of ill...'[32]

Within four months, however, his faith was to be tested to the limit.

Meanwhile Noel was able to spend the Christmas of 1916 with the Liverpool Scottish. The battalion was at 'C' Camp, Brandhoek, having again had the good fortune to be relieved of front-line duty just before Christmas. On 21 December they were inspected by Sir Douglas Haig, the Commander-in-Chief, who was appointed Field-Marshal a week later. Because of the torrential rain the men were allowed to stay in their huts until Haig approached, then fell in outside. Another inspection took place two days later, by General Sir Herbert Plumer who was in command of the Second Army. Both were complimentary about the battalion's turn-out.[33]

On Christmas Eve, Noel helped to organize a dinner for his stretcher-bearers, something he had intended to do ever since Guillemont the previous August. A party of them walked the couple of miles into Poperinghe, where it was possible to buy extra food and, surprisingly, some tinsel and other decorations to make the canteen more festive. Noel had even managed to obtain a barrel of Bass ale from somewhere.[34]

Poperinghe was an attractive little town, sufficiently far behind the line to be safe from all but the longest-range guns. Its railway station was familiar to thousands of troops who had detrained there prior to a tour of duty in the Ypres Salient. The shops still managed to fill their shelves; barber shops and *estaminets* were also a great draw. One of the best known establishments was Talbot House, in the Rue d'Hôpital, which was opened on 11 December, 1915, as a permanent memorial to Gilbert Talbot, killed near Sanctuary Wood in July of that year. When the Liverpool Scottish knew it, the Reverend 'Tubby' Clayton was in charge, the establishment having been the origin of the Toc H movement. Here men of all ranks could relax, in the garden behind the house or in the reading room on the first floor. Religious services were held in the upper room under the roof, and Noel worshipped there whenever he could (his name is noted in the Toc H Book of Remembrance).

Further along the same street was another club, 'Skindles', so called after an establishment of the same name in Maidenhead. 'Skindles' was patronized by officers, and at least two other establishments of the same name sprang up in the Ypres area. The Poperinghe 'Skindles' hosted many a concert party, such as those given by 'The Red Roses', an entertainment troupe formed by members of the 55th (West Lancashire) Division, of which the Liverpool Scottish were part. Noel and his fellow officers were present at many of these diversions.

Altogether, as pleasant a place to spend Christmas as could be found within earshot of the guns on the Western Front. On the day itself there was no work to be done; presents sent to the men of the battalion by the officers' relatives were distributed, and an excellent meal of roast goose, plum-pudding, beer and port was served.[35]

After the festivities Noel returned to his course on sanitation. Then at last he was granted fourteen days' leave, the date for the presentation of his Victoria Cross having been fixed for 5 February, a Monday. He spent some time in Liverpool — where the Bishop said to him, 'You have been known so far as the son of the Bishop of Liverpool; I shall be known henceforth as the father of Captain Chavasse!'[36] — and a few days at Barnt Green with Gladys. Marjorie had bought a three-diamond ring for her, on Noel's behalf, and she was delighted with it.[37] She then accompanied her fiancé to London for the presentation, although, once again, she and the rest of the party had to remain outside the Palace gates. Noel wrote home from the Hotel Folkestone at Boulogne on his way back to the battalion:

> The investiture passed off alright. The King seemed to be quite sincere and was certainly very kind. There were seven of us altogether, 4 being NCOs and men and these had really performed marvels.[38]

This was all he had to say about receiving his Victoria Cross. Gladys described the event in a little more detail, recounting to the family how the King made an enormous impact on Noel. Afterwards, he could only say: 'What a man! I could readily die for him.'[39]

The Bishop wrote to Bernard, obviously having managed to extract more from Marjorie:

> Noel left us last Saturday week, and was decorated by the King on the following Monday. Marjorie, your Aunt Frances, Gladys and Esme waited outside Buckingham Palace for two hours while

177

the function was going on. The cold was severe and Marjorie has caught cold.[40]

This little picture conveys a great deal about the impact of war on families. Here was a man receiving the Victoria Cross, yet there was no male relative to accompany him or the gaggle of ladies to Buckingham Palace. Apart from his father, who was carrying out a very demanding job at home in Liverpool, every male member of the Chavasse family was either in uniform or had already been killed. Christopher had now returned to France, to attend a chaplain's course at St Omer, and remained at the front with his division.[41]

Noel probably did not appreciate at the time that the award of the Victoria Cross to a man below commissioned rank entitled the holder to a pension of £10 per annum, and a further £5 a year for each Bar; for officers who received the Cross there was no financial benefit. From now on he wore the crimson ribbon signifying that he held the VC; the medal itself was taken back to Liverpool by Marjorie to be kept in safety at the Bishop's Palace. A miniature version of it was made, and Noel kept this with him; after his death it was sent to Gladys with other personal items.[42]

For Noel, it was back to join the battalion in the Potijze sector of the salient. Still optimistic, he told Marjorie that he was 'expecting the war to end soon now and I am just trying to keep the chaps fit until it finishes.'[43]

CHAPTER THIRTEEN

The Salient Again

Straightaway Noel was thrust back into the familiar routine of trench warfare. Now in his third year of duty on the Western Front, his sympathy for men who had simply taken as much as they could, showed itself in many ways. One of his compassionate actions nearly got him into serious trouble, as Frederick Jackson described:

> One day, a man from some other unit presented himself at the Doc's first-aid post. He had a nasty wound through the hand. On examination, Dr Chavasse challenged the fellow, suggesting that he had done it himself. Apparently, the flesh was all burned around the bullet-hole, which indicated a self-inflicted wound. The man confessed, and told him that his nerves had gone. What the Doc said to him, I do not know; but I could guess. However, the Doc cut away all the tell-tale burned flesh, dressed the wound and sent the man down to the Field Dressing-station.
>
> Apparently the matter came to light, and there was a Court Martial. I heard that Dr Chavasse had to attend as a witness. I also heard that he got into a spot of trouble, but all was well in the end.[1]

Noel knew that self-inflicted wounds attracted stiff penalties, as did cowardice in the face of the enemy. Lance-Corporal Taylor witnessed an incident when a member of the Scottish shot away his own index finger (this may be simply a different version of Jackson's story). Taylor never found out what penalty was imposed.[2] Recent research has shown that only six men of the King's (Liverpool Regiment) were 'shot at dawn' for desertion or cowardice, and none of these was in the Liverpool Scottish.[3]

In 1915 Noel had come across some cases that were tried by court martial, but he had nothing to do with the outcome. In a letter home he mentioned '13 prisoners (our own men but not of our regiment)':

> Two of these poor fellows were afterwards taken away and sentenced to death for cowardice (they had dropped out on their

way to the trenches with insufficient cause), but it is rumoured that this was commuted to 10 years' penal servitude.[4]

Written with a total disregard for the rigours of censorship, this was extremely sensitive information in the early part of the war. But it does illustrate that while Noel seemed to know no fear himself, he could nevertheless understand men who felt so terrified that they were unable to carry out what he would have regarded as their duty. This compassion was recorded by the regimental historian:

> The Doctor had a genius for picking out those men who were near a breakdown, either in nerve or general health, but not yet so run down as to be hospital cases. Rather than send them into the trenches, where their collapse sooner or later was inevitable, he kept them at his aid post as light-duty men, where in comparative comfort they had a chance to rest and recover. They paid their way handsomely. Did a man from the line come in for his daily foot-rubbing by the stretcher-bearers he found when he put his boots on again that they had been dried and cleaned for him in the meantime. Did he come in from a night's digging, wearied to exhaustion, he found one of the Doctor's invalids in charge of a cocoa urn and got a hot drink that put new life into him.... These and kindred amenities, such as sock and towel laundries, and a regular battalion canteen service, could only be arranged satisfactorily if a unit spent some time in one particular sector.[5]

Noel himself certainly appreciated the relatively static first few months of 1917, when the Liverpool Scottish were able to settle down in the area of Brandhoek and Ypres. However, the winter weather was not kind to kilted battalions and there were many frostbitten knees to deal with in February. But his activities were coming in for a little praise from superior officers, which helped to redress the balance after the criticism he had received the previous autumn:

> You will be pleased to hear that the Corps Commander saw our drying room and sick billet, and said that it was the best thing of its kind that he had seen in the country. Which is a great feather in the cap of the Medical Section.[6]

Another service that he performed for the men was to cash the postal orders that they often received from England. He would then send the postal orders to Marjorie, telling her to use them to pay for items he was requesting for his canteen.[7] Also, he criticized the unthinking orders emanating from above, and complained that his men did not receive enough rest after leaving the trenches:

> It must be a military necessity, but our Higher Commanders are so aloof that I doubt if they and their staff are really in touch with and understand the battalions, and I get the impression myself of a want of organisation and full mastery of details.
>
> Anyway a Doctor's job is rotten — for any attempts on our part to keep them well is so piffling against this constant overstrain (right or wrong). We do all sorts of things to defeat the disease germs and we whitewash cellars and spray dug-outs... but against orders we are powerless.[8]

As spring advanced he began to be aware of nature once again:

> The mornings are splendid just now, and the birds are singing. 'My heart leaps up' whenever I hear a thrush, and there are blackbirds and larks here too, and I hope some nightingales later on. I cannot tell you how very much the singing of birds affects one out here. It is quite uplifting, in the rather mournful surroundings, it gives a feeling of hope. I suppose we must be nearing the end of the war now. I hope so, even if it will be a bloody business. It cannot be any worse than what, in God's mercy, we have already been through. After the war I shall miss the social side very much, but hope to make up for it by holy wedlock.[9]

An aspect of life that he did not find uplifting was the role played by padres. Right through the war he had criticized their smugness, their inability to communicate with the men and their concern with their own comfort — at least, this was how he saw them.

> As professionals, the Medicals and the Parsons have not come out well in this war, with, of course, some notable exceptions.
>
> The Doctor has ceased to be considered the kindly wise man, ever eager to help the sick and alleviate suffering. He is looked upon as a lazy, cushy, windy man, who performs his job most perfunctorily and often is given to strong drink. And we in the know, know of all the jealousies and dirty tricks played by one doctor on another.

As for Parsons, they are no advertisement to the uplifting influence of the grace of God. Most of them seem very idle, and cannot even look after soldiers' graves if they are in any shelled zone.... It is really pathetic how a Padre is received by everyone with open arms, if he merely undergoes some of the everyday perils of the ordinary infantry now. Very few earn this privilege. They stay behind in safety, and take leave regularly every three months which is criminal, as it deprives some poor infantry soldier of leave when he has endured 15-18 months of the trenches. You see, leave is absolutely governed now by the places on the leave boat. Our Rev. friend of the Square [the Reverend J. O. Coop] is a typical example, and even his good addresses do not go down, as the words do not proceed from the mouth of a man.

One does not go to the Medical or Religious professions to look for self-sacrifice. That old fable has been exploded. It's careless living, careless speaking, but wonderfully patient of any of the Rank and File who sacrifice themselves for the sake of their fellows. And it's my own good little S.B. boys, who have at home been religious boys, and have been choir boys, and Bible class boys, who show me out here that God helps those who trust in Him.[10]

A few days later he was concerned about having to play the role of padre himself:

I am rather shy and find it hard to stroll around tents making fatuous remarks, especially when, as has often happened, these remarks are dished up again at a Battalion concert by a Corporal who thinks he can take me off....

I fear me that I have a down on PADRES — I must look to my own life a bit more. I am getting irritable.[11]

And all of this was going home to his father, who had in his charge hundreds of clergyman and who had trained possibly thousands of young ordinands during the previous thirty years. (One of these was the Reverend David Railton, whose idea for the interment of 'The Unknown Soldier' in Westminster Abbey was taken up by the nation in 1920. Railton was ordained by Bishop Chavasse in 1908, having lived at the small seminary for ordinands next door to the Palace. He had even been Chaplain to the Liverpool Scottish from 1910 to 1911, and had met up with Noel[12] in the desolation of Delville Wood in September 1916.) However, it could also be

In fact when I die. I have a recumbent statue, put up to me in some Cathedral. I shall desire in my will that instead of having my feet against a dog a a bible a something of that kind. that they shall rest on a carving of this hot water bottle.

water bottle.

widow prostrated

could not get children into this effecting picture. they go on after the widow for a 100 yds or so.
I am having a rather dull time of it because of my leg.

28. Part of a letter from Noel to Marjorie thanking her for sending him a hot water bottle.

29. "I thought Gladys was a prize far beyond me. I can hardly believe my luck"
(p.148) (*J. C. A. Quinny*).

30. A posthumous portrait in oils of Noel, commissioned by the Chavasse family in time for Bishop Chavasse's 72nd birthday in September, 1918. It first hung in the dining-room of the Palace in Liverpool, but is now on the staircase of St Peter's College, Oxford (p.224) (*J. C. A. Quinny*).

31. "At the head of the grave stood a wooden cross" (p.214). It is now in the chapel of St Peter's College, Oxford (*A. Clayton*).

32. "In February, 1990, this unique set of Great War medals was given to the Imperial War Museum on permanent loan" (p.224) (*Imperial War Museum*).

argued that this background meant that Noel was uniquely placed to pass judgement on padres. None the less, his comments illuminate a less tolerant and more irascible side to his character than was usually apparent.

Similarly trenchant remarks were expressed by Noel after one of George Bernard Shaw's public utterances. Shaw was already well-known for his forthright attitudes; he had written that war should be renounced, that militarism was a disease in Great Britain as well as in Germany, that if the Kaiser was exiled after the war so should be Sir Edward Grey, the British Foreign Secretary, and that in any case, Britain began it and should therefore not blame Germany. When the *Lusitania* was sunk in May 1915 Shaw had remarked that far worse things were happening at the front, and it was no bad idea for civilians to be given a taste of war. In 1916 one of his one-act plays had been based on a satire of the British military mentality. Consequently Shaw was very unpopular, and so Noel Chavasse was doing no more than reflect public opinion when he wrote:

> The so-called stuffy, respectable, homely religion, of family prayers and Sunday observance, with a conscious effort to do one's duty during the week, which has been the butt of all cheap and fatuous swell-headed sceptics like that fool Bernard Shaw, has been more than vindicated in this war of endurance rather than of flashy deeds. Shaw's breed would not have kept the Hun at bay and then begun to push him back, but the religious middle class boys have.[13]

On a happier note, good news arrived about May and her exploits at the hospital in Etaples. In a despatch from Field-Marshal Sir Douglas Haig dated 9 April, 1917, she was 'mentioned' for her services as a 'Lady Helper' to the Voluntary Aid Detachment.[14] The whole family was, of course, delighted.

As the days lengthened, Noel was kept busy helping to organise fun and games for the men of the battalion. The town of Poperinghe acted as a magnet for troops in its vicinity. Noel told his parents:

> One evening, I borrowed a motor lorry and all my medicals went to a neighbouring town, and there we first went to the Divisional Concert Party (The 'Tivolies'), which was very good. Afterwards to the Y.M.C.A. Hut and each man got a very good feed. There was a piano there and our men had a little concert all on their own. At 9 p.m. the lorry took us back to camp.[15]

The Church Army worker in charge of the hut remembered this occasion and described it in a letter to the Bishop after Noel's death:

> Dr. Chavasse called into our Hut and brought some of his men for tea and biscuits.... As our Hut was honoured by the presence of a V.C., I asked him if he would allow me to announce the fact to the others who were present for I felt sure that he would receive a great ovation. One could not but respect the modesty which forbade me to make any mention of his presence.[16]

On 20 June, the Liverpool Scottish were moved by train to Zudausques for a lengthy stay in which they were to prepare for the next offensive. It therefore seemed worthwhile to establish a more permanent recreational centre, and this took the form of a beer garden. Noel wrote home describing 'Rag Sports' for which he had donated 100 francs as prize money; a canteen was selling light beer brewed in the village, and frequent sing-songs and concerts took place in the open air. 'So you see I am deeply implicated in many a Beer Garden — who would have thought it before the war?'[17] Who indeed? This was a far cry from the Chavasse family life of peacetime. However, Noel had always been possessed of a boisterous sense of humour. The posters advertising the Beer Garden, which he helped to draw up, are ample evidence that his wit had not deserted him:

EISTEDDFODD

To be held in the Beer-Garden on

SUNDAY JULY 15, 1917

Distinguished Patronage Eminent Adjudicators

CONTESTS

1. Male Voice Choirs: Marks deducted for 'Sweet and Low' and 'The Soldier's Farewell'.

2. Imitations of Charlie Chaplin: Competitors are given permission to let their hair grow.

3. Whistling Solos: Indents for birdseed should be submitted at once to the Q.M.

4. Recitations: As there is plenty of beer the services of 'Gunga Din' are not required.

5. Original verses.

6. Pianoforte Solos: Operatic excerpts. Competitors should reconnoitre the piano before the attack for silent keys.

7. Female Impersonations: Don't raid the clothes-lines. Costumes will be provided.

8. Mouth Organ Contest: Three Scottish Melodies.

9. Comic Interludes: Anything at all that is really funny.
Warblers, Barn-Stormers, Troubadours, Whistlers, Mounte-
banks, Spring Poets, Contortionists, Wine-Bibbers, Publicans
and Sinners, Now is your chance.[18]

In the early summer the family learned of a change affecting its youngest
member, Aidan. He had served so far with the 11th Battalion of the King's
(Liverpool Regiment), but this was a pioneer battalion and Aidan preferred
a more active life. In April 1917 he therefore sought and obtained a transfer
to the 17th King's, the battalion of which his brother Bernard was Medical
Officer. Marjorie could not understand this at all. She wrote to Bernard in
the middle of June:

> I can't think why Aidan has changed into your Battalion. Very
> nice and flattering for you of course, but a great deal more
> dangerous. I can't think what he was thinking of. I suppose he
> wants to be made a Captain or something. I only hope he gets a
> cushy wound soon. Then we shall all receive shoals of
> sympathising letters and be devoutly thankful all the time.[19]

But such a cushy wound for Aidan was not to be. The 17th King's were now
stationed in the Ypres Salient, a few miles south of the Liverpool Scottish
position in the Wieltje sector, and were soon to see action of the fiercest kind.

Noel, too, had fleeting thoughts of a move. In April 1917, an old friend
and mentor from the Royal Southern Hospital in Liverpool, Mr
Douglas-Crawford, whose houseman Noel had been in 1912 and 1913, came
out to the Base Hospital at Etaples on military duty. He had a proposition
for Noel who, thinking of Gladys and his hopes for the future, wrestled with
the problem of what to do; but really, his decision was a foregone conclusion.
As he put it to his parents:

> I have had a letter which has unsettled me for a bit. It is a very
> kind sympathetic letter from 2 doctors in the Base Hospital where
> Douglas Crawford and Hay are in (two old friends), asking me
> to apply to be sent there as there is a vacancy for a surgeon on
> the staff. It is a great temptation. I could use all I have learnt at
> orthopaedic surgery and rub up my surgery again under Mr.
> Crawford, so that at the end of the war I shall be a skilled surgeon
> instead of having to learn it all again, and of course it would look
> well on future testimonials. But it is too comfortable. Such jobs
> are for the older men, young fellows like myself ought to be with
> the fighting men, and I am by no means done yet, in fact I am

settling down to this mode of living as my life work and don't look now for the end.

And I don't think I could leave the young lads here to fight it out while I luxuriated in a coast town. The infantry lad does not want to get hurt or killed any more than I do. In fact, one of their most popular choruses as they trudge up to the trenches is — 'Oh my, I don't want to die — I want to go 'ome' — yet he has to stick it out. So why should not I, who as it is have a softer time than they. And although, actually, medicine is nil, yet one has numberless chances for helping men, if one wants to. And really the wounded, the sick, and weary, slogging, anxious infantry soldier do make a tremendous appeal to all the best in a man.[20]

A week later he had definitely turned down the offer:

I have written to the base hospital, and said that though I valued the offer very much, I though I had better stay with the lads, and so would not apply. I felt rather depressed about it for about a quarter of an hour.[21].

Noel may have felt frustrated that he was unable to practise as much medicine as he would have wished, but in several areas his medical skills were constantly being stretched and enhanced. For example, the battalion Medical Officer was the only practitioner available to deal with toothache. Noel however, made no pretensions to accomplishments in that connection. When Sergeant Bromley had toothache he visited the dressing station to see the MO. However, this was not to be:

The Sergeant in charge asked me my business, and when I boldly replied that I wanted a tooth out, he replied, 'You're a hero, aren't you? Do you see that chap?' (pointing to a man on a stretcher covered with a blanket and looking very sorry for himself) 'Well, he had a tooth out this morning!' Discretion being the better part of valour, I said 'Good Morning,' about turned, and marched out, resolved to suffer in silence rather than be dragged round the Dressing Station at the end of a pair of forceps.[22]

Throughout the war, Noel regularly received medical literature, the *British Medical Journal* at first, which was 'received with loud cheers!'[23] Certainly the medical press had turned its contents over almost entirely to matters relevant to the war. A typical issue of the BMJ in January 1917 contained articles on:

> The Carriers of Amoebic Dysentery.
> Treatment and Training of Disabled Soldiers.
> Contractures following Gunshot Wounds.
> Diseases of the Male Urethra.
> Nerve Grafting as a Means of Restoring Function
>   in Limbs Paralysed by Gunshot or
>   Other Injuries.
> The Incidence of Tetanus Among Wounded
>   Soldiers.
> Sodium Salicylate in the Treatment of
>   'Trench Feet'.
> The Military Medical Services in 1916.
> Mobilization of the Profession.
> The Changing of Dressings.[24]

There was obviously plenty here to interest a battalion Medical Officer. Noel, however, had changed his preference:

> Please stop sending the B.M.J. as it has got very poor and is not worth 6d. The Librarian of the Medical Institute at Liverpool is going to send me the Lancet every week, it is more in my line.[25]

He was also keen to practise his art on civilians, when he came across them in rest areas. In November 1915 he had treated a civilian's little girl for diphtheria, and he longed to treat crippled children but could not because he would never be able to complete this lengthy treatment.[26] This was at the heart of Noel's medical ambitions — to specialize in orthopaedics.

In 1915, at Alder Hey in Liverpool, Noel's old teacher Robert Jones had set up the first Military Orthopaedic Hospital in the country. Other such hospitals followed, and in 1916 he became Inspector of Military Orthopaedics. An appliance which Jones promoted for all he was worth was the Thomas Splint, invented in 1870 by Hugh Owen Thomas of Liverpool. This device was not well known before the First World War, and Jones was responsible for its widespread adoption on the Western Front in treatment of fractures of the femur.[27] Noel was one of the early pioneers of the Thomas Splint. On the battlefield it had to be applied before the wound was dressed, and the boot had to be left on so that the fracture remained immobilized. The result was that the pain and bleeding were reduced, less shock was experienced, and the injured more often arrived in good shape at the Casualty

Clearing Station. Noel wrote to Robert Jones in June 1917, just after Jones had received a knighthood:

> Every aid post now has Thomas splints in stock. But I have been carrying one about on my medical cart for the last two years. I hope we shall be able to save more fractured thighs.[28]

The Times reported Jones's knighthood in its columns with quite extravagant praise, describing his work as 'exceedingly brilliant' and claiming that he was 'universally acknowledged to be the greatest orthopaedic surgeon in Britain'.[29] Noel hastened to congratulate his old teacher, but his letter ended on a sombre note:

> Our Scotch boys will soon, I think, be severely tested. I do pray God we all play the man and live up to the traditions of our comrades who have fallen. I wonder when it will all be over.[30]

Indeed, the Liverpool Scottish were soon to face possibly the most horrendous of all the trials that had confronted them in the long-drawn-out war of attrition. Field-Marshal Haig had decided, 'It is essential that the Belgian coast shall be cleared this summer.'[31]

At the foot of a slight ridge east of Ypres, running up to a small village on its crown, Noel Chavasse was to 'play the man' for the last time. The name of the village was Passchendaele.

CHAPTER FOURTEEN

Passchendaele

The names of certain places will always epitomize the horror of the First World War, names such as Ypres and Beaumont Hamel, Delville Wood and Hill 60. But the most evocative name of all must surely be that of Passchendaele. From obscurity, this little village was thrust into a limelight of notoriety; men who saw Passchendaele and lived, came back and named their homes after it; for many, Passchendaele *was* the Great War.

Of course, Passchendaele was only the symbol of the campaign to be waged in Flanders during the late summer and autumn of 1917. Sir Douglas Haig planned an attack east of Ypres. The previous two campaigns in the Ypres salient had been defensive; now the Allies were to take the offensive and force the enemy to retreat. This would bring freedom to Belgium; after all, Great Britain had entered the war in the first place to prevent the violation of the 'scrap of paper' which guaranteed Belgium's neutrality. In addition, Germany would be forced to evacuate the important Channel ports from which U-boats were operating. The battle of the Somme in the previous year had had ambiguous results for the British and French; now, in an area where an attack had not been launched (and lost) before, there was a good chance, in the eyes of the decision-makers, that valuable ground could be gained. It was to take place in the summer, when the weather could surely be relied upon.

So the offensive was planned, Cabinet approval having been given some months earlier. Like much previous effort in Flanders, this was part of the war of attrition, the wearing down of the enemy by constant bombardment. On 7 June, 1917, nineteen mines were exploded simultaneously at ten past three in the morning on the Messines − Wytschaete Ridge. The noise was reportedly loud enough to be heard in Downing Street,[1] so it is certain that the Liverpool Scottish heard it in their billets at Vlamertinghe, west of Ypres. Plumer's forces then overran the ridge and all objectives were taken.[2]

Haig then pressed on with the rest of the preparations for the battle that was to become known as 'Third Ypres'. The original date of the proposed major offensive was 25 July; however, the preliminary bombardment was so successful that it forced the enemy to move his guns back, and a postponement of three days was necessary to allow the Allied guns, particularly those of the French to the north, to move forward. Factors such as poor visibility added further delay, and the final date chosen was Tuesday, 31 July.[3]

The Liverpool Scottish, meanwhile, had moved to Zudausques, a village west of St Omer, and received an enthusiastic welcome from the local inhabitants. It was here that the Beer Garden was set up, and sports were held. In a memorable cross-country run, the Doctor came in first and the Adjutant, Captain B. Arkle, second.[4]

Noel's thoughts were constantly turning to Gladys and his future.

> If the war does not get on any quicker, I shall take time by the forelock and get married somewhere about Christmas. What is your candid opinion of it? Gladys wants it very badly, and I think Aunt Frances would like it. I shall like it for a lot of reasons but shall feel rather a fool after the war — a married man without a job.
>
> Still, it's a bit pathetic to have to leave a bronze cross to a nephew or a cousin twice removed. I don't think I really earned it as many have had to do, but deep in me I prize it more than I can say.[5]

Gladys certainly had no intention of waiting until after the war. If Noel was unable to get home leave, and in the lead-up to the next 'push' leave seemed unlikely, she was determined to cross the Channel and marry him in France. By the end of June she was applying for a special licence and planning her departure for France. She would have to observe the etiquette of the day, and could therefore not travel alone, but a chaperone was near at hand in the shape of her sister. Gladys and Esme decided to give up their nursing work at their mother's hospital at Rednal and go to Paris to do voluntary canteen work at the Gare du Nord. As far as is known, Noel was in the dark about the special licence; as his letter indicates, he thought they might marry at Christmas. He had not reckoned with Gladys's energy and determination.

On 30 June the battalion moved again, this time to Esquerdes, a few miles away, and the Liverpool Scottish, as part of the 55th Division, began preparations for their part in the forthcoming attack. The mistakes of Guillemont had apparently been heeded, as the regimental historian recorded:

> The ground allotted to the Division for the assault was the sector it knew so well in front of Wieltje and Potijze, and there was ample time in which to teach every man the main outline of the attack as a whole and his own particular place in it. ... The first

work undertaken was to map out with the aid of aeroplane photographs a facsimile not only of the enemy's front-line system of trenches with all its saps, strong-points, known machine-gun emplacements, etc., but of his defences further back — trenches, fortified buildings and gun positions. The stretch of country on which this full-scale plan was laid out was chosen as far as possible for its resemblance to the actual ground over which the attack would take place, and on it the Royal Engineers marked out with tapes the positions and outlines of the German defences. Then came the digging of the trenches themselves.[6]

On 2 July the trenches were completed, and two days later training began in earnest:

Each platoon was taken slowly over the ground representing its position in the attack and all points were explained to the men by their platoon-commanders.[7]

There followed three dress rehearsals, involving the aeroplanes and the tanks that would be participating in the actual attack. The noise of the barrage was simulated by drum rolls and the gun flashes by Very lights. Leaving nothing to chance, one of these rehearsals took place at dawn, just as the battle plan indicated.

Good news arrived about Noel's twin brother. Christopher had been posted back to the front from Salisbury Plain at the beginning of 1917, and he had been in action at Bullecourt in France, as Marjorie told Bernard:

[Chris] was out collecting wounded, and I am glad to say that he has been recommended for the D.S.O. I daresay he won't get it, but it is very nice to have been recommended, all the same. It shows he is appreciated by the General. After that, I think the family honours might as well cease, as after all it is a little dangerous getting them, and the family luck might go at any time. This is meant as a little warning to you, as I hear that you are out for a decoration yourself. My informant did not put it quite so crudely, that's just my way of putting it.[8]

Official news of Christopher's award was a little longer in arriving. But in the meantime, the Chavasse family luck was indeed running out.

Aidan, Noel's youngest brother, was, like Bernard, in Flanders with the

17th King's, one of the 115 so-called 'Pals' battalions in the New Army. By 1 July, 1917, the 17th King's were holding the front-line trenches at Observatory Ridge, only a mile or so from Hooge and just south of the notorious Menin Road, some five miles from Ypres. They had been involved in the fighting that followed the explosions of mines on the Messines Ridge on 7 June, and now frequently found themselves in trench raids and reconnaissance expeditions into no-man's-land. Aidan's last action was described in the battalion War Diary:

July 4th.
12.15 a.m.
Lieut. A. CHAVASSE and 8 Other Ranks left our trenches to patrol German Front Line, with the object of ascertaining disposition of enemy, obtaining identification and killing occupants. This Patrol, on nearing enemy wire, encountered a German patrol, which opened fire on them — wounding Lt. CHAVASSE. Our patrol withdrew to our lines. Lieut. CHAVASSE was missing and Capt. A. J. DRAPER, Capt. C. E. TORREY, Capt. F. B. CHAVASSE (R.A.M.C.), 2/Lieut. C. A. PETERS, and L/Cpl. H. DIXON (11531) searched No Man's Land for him (sic). During the search, Capt. C. E. TORREY was wounded, and taken in to our trenches. 2/Lt. C. A. PETERS and L/Cpl. DIXON discovered Lieut. CHAVASSE in a shell hole; 2/Lt. PETERS was killed when returning to our lines for assistance to carry the wounded officer in, L/Cpl. DIXON remaining to bandage his wounds. After awaiting the arrival of the necessary assistance, L/Cpl. DIXON returned for Stretcher Bearers to carry Lt. CHAVASSE in, but, on going back, the party were unable to find the Officer, and had to retire on account of the dawn breaking.
July 5th.
Battalion holding Front Line.
L/Cpl. DIXON and 3 men left our trenches to search for Lieut. CHAVASSE. Capt. F. B. CHAVASSE also went across No Man's Land to endeavour to find his brother, but the wounded officer was not discovered. The body of 2/Lt. PETERS was carried to our lines by another party.[9]

According to Marjorie, when Aidan was missing:

a notice was put up: 'Have you got our Officer?' But the beastly Huns would not answer. How I hate them. Aidan was very game.

He bombed the Germans after he was left. I hope he got some of them.[10]

Thus Aidan disappeared. Bernard had been due to depart for home leave that very day, but stayed behind in the hope that his brother might be rescued. Now he set off for home, arriving in Liverpool by 7 July. He found his mother and Marjorie alone at the Palace, his father being in London to attend a sitting of the House of Lords. Word was rushed to the Bishop, and he wrote hastily to Bernard:

> Thank God you have reached home safely. Thank God for all the courage and love you have shown in trying to find your brother. I pray God that his wound may not be serious and that the Germans may have carried him in and are taking care of him. I am calling at the War Office to inquire what steps I had better take to get news of him. If necessary, and if it will be any comfort to your dear mother and to you, I will come home tomorrow afternoon if you will telegraph. Take great care of yourself, my dearest boy, for you have passed through a great ordeal and are bound to feel the strain. You have the satisfaction of knowing that you have done all that man could, to bring dear Aidan in, and that as a result you have every reason to believe that he has been taken in by the Germans. God bless you.[11]

This letter crossed with one from Mrs Chavasse which exhorted the Bishop to pull whatever strings his position allowed, in order to get news. Aidan was her youngest child, on whom she doted. Now she was distraught, but preferred her husband to stay in London where he could make representations to the War Office and elsewhere. They were both adamant that Aidan was still alive, lying wounded in German hands; this is what everyone who enquired was told. It may be that Bernard viewed the situation more realistically, but he tried to keep up their hopes.

The Bishop wrote again the next day, from the House of Lords:

> The letter which your dear mother wrote on Sunday has only just reached me this (Tuesday) morning. I had already gone to the War Office, to Cox's Bureau for the Missing, and to the Red Cross people at 18 Carlton House Terrace. Thank you for all that you did to bring dear Aidan in, you could not have done more. You risked your life on his behalf. I must write to Captain Torrey and to the father of Lieut. Peters.[12]

By this time the newspapers had got hold of the story. The first report in the *Liverpool Daily Post* on 11 July carried the headline 'BISHOP'S SON WOUNDED AND MISSING'. It went on to give a garbled account, stating that Noel had been involved. By the next day's edition, after presumably interviewing Bernard, the paper was able to give a more accurate account, filling in many details. It appeared that Aidan, when wounded, had refused to allow any of his colleagues to stay with him, and during the day he spent in the open had managed to 'bomb away the Germans who had endeavoured to capture him' (this action making it even less likely that he was taken in by the Germans alive). It does seem that no less than five separate rescue attempts were made, although the War Diary concludes its description after only two. The paper assumed like everyone else that Aidan was a prisoner.[13]

Hopes that Aidan was still alive were fuelled by a letter from Aidan's Company Commander in the 17th King's. He told the Bishop that he felt sure Aidan was in German hands 'and I only hope, that with proper attention, he will have a good passage to recovery.'[14]

Soon after this May forwarded a letter from the British Red Cross, which she had received at the Liverpool Merchants' Hospital at Etaples; this recounted the narrative of Lance-Corporal Dixon, who had been present on Observatory Ridge that night:

> Lieut. Chavasse was attached to D. Coy. I went out on patrol with him on 3rd-4th July. We were coming back from the German wire about 3 a.m. when Lieut. Chavasse was hit by a bullet in the right leg between the knee and thigh, I was alone with him, and told him that I could not carry him back myself, and left him lying by a shell hole about 10 yards from the German sap. I went back to him and bandaged him up, and he then told me to leave him as it was fast getting light. I did so, but the same evening as soon as it was dark, I went back with his brother to the place where I had left Lt. Chavasse but there was no sign of him. We searched again... without success.[15]

Noel wrote to Bernard, thanking him for his efforts to save Aidan:

> Just a short letter to tell you how proud we all feel of you. Nobody could have done more to get poor old Aidan back. Your efforts seemed to me to have been almost superhuman. I am sorry you had to go through such a terrible experience. I never heard of such a chapter of horrors for a small fighting patrol. I am very sorry about the officer who lost his life trying to get a stretcher. I should like his people's address.

But everybody here thinks that you did magnificently, and hopes that you get your deserts. A D.S.O. *at the least.* You have, by all accounts, deserved something for a long time, and the way you kept on looking for Aidan is beyond mere praise.[16]

This is the last letter of Noel's that exists.

The reference to the Distinguished Service Order is a reflection of the recommendation that had been made for Chris to receive it for the action at Bullecourt. The Bishop wrote to Noel on 24 July, informing him that Chris had in fact been awarded the Military Cross — so both twins now had an indentical award.[17] But Noel never received the letter, and may never have known about his brother's achievement, although there is always the possibility that Chris wrote to him direct. In the event, Bernard received no award for his actions on Observatory Ridge, although his courage in another action was to be recognized before long.

By now the Liverpool Scottish were well ahead with their special training for the attack on the Passchendaele Ridge. On 20 July they marched to St Omer from their billets at Esquerdes, travelled by train to Poperinghe where they had a short period of rest, and then marched up to the trenches in front of the village of Wieltje, trenches with which they were very familiar from an earlier tour of duty at the end of 1916. A preliminary bombardment was already in progress, and this early shelling had the unfortunate effect of drawing enemy fire down on the roads and communication trenches through which large numbers of troops were moving; eight men and an officer of the Scottish were killed.[18]

In the next few days there were further disasters. A German attack with mustard-gas shells was so effective that two officers and sixty-seven men had to be evacuated to hospital. As the regimental historian described it:

It was impossible to avoid casualties in a heavy concentration of this gas. The box-respirator protected the throat and eyes but the dense fumes which hung about the trenches and shell-holes attacked the skin — especially the softer parts of it — and caused painful sores. In these circumstances the kilt is not an ideal garment.[19]

Further gas and high explosive shell attacks meant that by 24 July the Scottish had lost, as far as the battalion's fighting strength was concerned, four officers and 141 other ranks. That day the battalion was relieved and marched back to 'Derby Camp', between Poperinghe and Ypres, where the next six days were spent in getting battle equipment and ammunition in order. In addition, in common with usual practice, certain battalions in the division were ordered to leave their commanding officers behind; Lieutenant-Colonel Davidson of the Scottish was one of these, and accordingly relinquished his command to his second-in-command, Major J. L. A. Macdonald of the Highland Light Infantry.

The third battle of Ypres was about to begin.

So far as the 55th (West Lancs) Division was concerned, the plan of attack was that at zero hour (the actual time of which was a well-kept secret right up to the last minute) four battalions were to attack the German front system of trenches and then advance to a line (the 'Blue Line') drawn through Cheddar Villa and Bossaert Farm and hold the line there. Orders written on 24 July indicated that details of the artillery barrage were not yet known. However, the shrapnel barrage would creep forward at the rate of 100 yards every four minutes. The barrage map confirms this.[20]

One hour and fifteen minutes later, a further four battalions were to pass over this Blue Line and push onwards to another line (the 'Black Line') east of Canvas Trench, Wine House and Capricorn Support Trench. Three and a half hours after zero, the battalion to the left of the Black Line was to go forward and capture Capital Trench. Finally, six hours and twenty minutes after zero, the brigade in reserve, the 164th, was to advance over the ground already taken and establish itself along the 'Green Line', about three-quarters of a mile further on. The barrage was to cease at zero plus eight hours and twenty minutes.

Instructions were given about the accompanying aeroplanes and tanks. Allied planes would be recognized by the rectangular marking on the 'right lower plane', and by a white dumbbell painted on either side of the body. Planes fulfilling a spotting role would signal to the ground by means of Klaxon horns and white Very lights; troops on the ground would contact planes by lighting white flares and by the use of Watson fans — when open, these would be turned over at intervals of fifty seconds, to show alternate coloured and white sides. As for tanks, the men were warned not to divert from their objective by bunching round them for protection.[21]

Major-General Jeudwine, commanding the 55th Division, sent a letter of encouragement to all ranks; it is noteworthy that the principal incentive put forward to spur the troops on to greater effort was the promise of Military Medals.

> I wish to impress on all ranks how greatly every man can help towards success by trying his utmost to stick to his job, and to go on, no matter at what cost, till the objective is gained and victory won. When two or three resolute men do this it is not only what they achieve individually that is of such value to their side, but it is the example they set to their comrades, and the

influence they exert on those around them, that has such far-reaching effects....

In any case where, during the attack, a soldier, though wounded, goes on to meet the enemy, or remains at his post, the case is to be brought to notice by the Commanding Officer in the form of a recommendation for immediate award. I shall be glad to recommend all such cases for favourable consideration for the award of the Military Medal to those concerned.[22]

On 29 July, a Sunday, all fighting stores and rations were issued, and the battalion, consisting of twenty-five officers and 475 other ranks, set off to march to its assembly positions. The weather, which had been fine during June and July, broke during this march. There was a heavy downpour accompanied by thunder and lightning, the shellholes filled with water and the trackways became muddy and difficult to negotiate. When the rain stopped, temporarily, there was still a high level of humidity, and little drying-out was possible.[23]

All were in place by the small hours of the morning, after a five-hour march, laden down with two full days' rations as well as the usual battle equipment. Battalion Headquarters was established at Wieltje dug-out, described by Sergeant Bromley as

a vast underground excavation containing dozens of passages, nooks and corners, in which a considerable number of troops were quartered. It was exceptionally deep, and although relatively secure from shellfire, I for one would have preferred a less invulnerable shelter and more fresh air.[24]

Private Herd called this dug-out 'a marvel of engineering'.

From the bottom of an ordinary village well saps were run in various directions and at intervals along these saps (about 3½ feet wide) there were good-sized 'rooms' used by the various H.Qs. etc. In one of these rooms there was installed an oil engine which generated an electric dynamo providing electricity and working water pumps. Access to the Dug-Out was made through 4 or 5 gradually sloping tunnels.[25]

Wieltje dug-out was certainly large enough, at the height of the battle, to accommodate several hundred injured men while they waited for transport to carry them down the line.[26]

At 3.30pm on 30 July, the men moved up to their 'jumping-off' trenches,

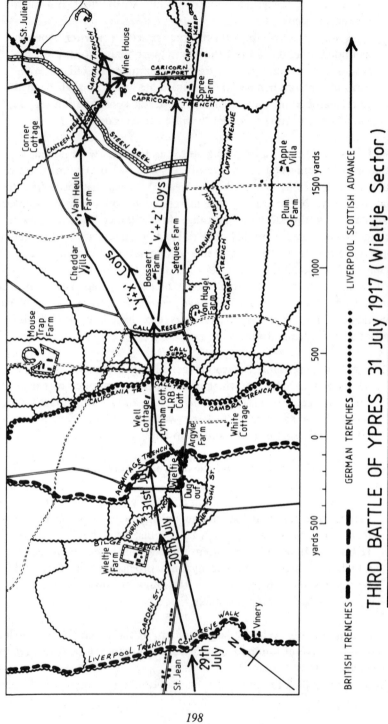

THIRD BATTLE OF YPRES 31 July 1917 (Wieltje Sector)

BRITISH TRENCHES ▬ ▬ ▬ GERMAN TRENCHES ●●●●●●●● LIVERPOOL SCOTTISH ADVANCE →

enemy shells falling around them continuously. Word was received that zero hour was to be 3.50am on 31 July, and when it came the Scottish were already in open ground, ready to move. Under the protective barrage, the Blue Line was reached with minor casualties, and companies pressed on to the Black Line; they did not need the six light bridges which had been carried up to facilitate the crossing of the Steenbeke, a stream which proved not to be a formidable obstacle after all. The land sloped down to the Steenbeke, then rose gently towards Passchendaele Ridge.

As the Liverpool Scottish advanced, the enemy could be seen streaming away up the slope.[27] There was heavy machine-gun fire coming from Capricorn Trench, and, due to a mass of uncut wire, progress was halted. Soon, however, one of the two tanks whose job it was to assist the battalion rumbled into view — by this time, 7.00am, it was daylight — and was immediately sent to break a gap through the wire. Unfortunately, it was disabled by three direct hits from a field gun, but by then its work was done. Capricorn Trench was soon taken. Indeed, by 7.45am all the battalion's objectives had been achieved. Many prisoners had been captured too, and some, being Red Cross men, were particularly useful to the Medical Officer. By 9.00am the whole of the Black Line was occupied by British forces.[28]

As soon as the Blue Line had been taken, battalion headquarters was moved from Wieltje dug-out to Bossaert Farm. It was within yards of this location that Noel established his regimental aid post, in a captured German dug-out at, or adjacent to, Setques Farm.[29] The position was to the north of the road running from Wieltje to the Passchendaele Ridge. The whole area rapidly became what was known as a hot spot and battalion headquarters moved once again, this time to a position on the far side of the Steenbeke. Noel, however, kept his aid post at its original location. There was no need nor expectation for him to establish his post so near to the action, and he could with all justification have remained in safety underground at Wieltje dug-out. But that would not have been in character.

The dug-out where Noel laid out his equipment and tended the wounded had been sparsely furnished by its previous occupants. As had happened so often during this war, the British were again surprised by the fittings found in captured German posts. To enter this dug-out one went through a doorway facing back towards the German lines, to the side of which was a small window, also looking back towards the Passchendaele Ridge, across a rural landscape already devastated by the Allied barrage. The back of the dug-out, facing the advancing Allied troops, was therefore blank, apart from one or two small apertures which enabled observation of the attacking forces and from which snipers could fire in comparative safety. One then descended a flight of steps, cut into the Flanders clay, to a small room which contained a couple of chairs and a small table. There was space for one or two men to lie down but the dug-out could hold, at best, only six or seven men. Once their wounds had been dressed, Noel's patients had to leave the dug-out, if they were at all mobile, and take shelter in 'funk-holes' in the nearby trenches or in shell holes amongst the ruined farm buildings. As always, it was hoped that the RAMC ambulances would get through to take the wounded back, but often the injured had to lie where they were and wait until nightfall for help to come.

Early in the attack on 31 July, while standing up and waving to soldiers to indicate the location of the aid post, Noel was hit by a shell splinter. It may be that his skull was fractured — his brother Christopher certainly believed that to be the case,[30] although Bernard referred to it as 'a scalp wound'.[31] He was, however, well enough to walk back to the dressing station at Wieltje dug-out, where the wound was dressed. He was told, or at least advised, to stay in the dug-out until he could be taken back to the casualty clearing station for proper treatment. But he refused, declaring that there was no one to take his place. So back he went to the aid post on the Passchendaele Road.

There was very little food, a shortage of water, and the constant scream of shells overhead. Again and again the stretcher-bearers went out to fetch the wounded, and as night fell Noel collected his torch from the box of medical supplies brought up by his orderlies and systematically combed the torn-up area that the Germans had fled from only hours earlier. This was not no-man's-land as such, as it was now in the possession of the Allied forces, but it was under continual bombardment, from the guns of the retreating Germans and from Allied artillery, whose shells might fall short at any time.

At about eight in the evening it began to rain. Sergeant Bromley, in the Headquarters trench beyond the Steenbeke, was appalled by the conditions in which men were having to fight:

> The rain continued incessantly throughout the night, and in a very short time our trench became merely a muddy ditch half full of water, and our condition became absolutely filthy . The night brought a certain amount of relief from hostilities, but the climatic conditions became even worse, and we simply stood and shivered until daylight came. What an indescribable scene presented itself as dawn came, and we looked back to our old trenches. Mud and water everywhere, stranded limbers, dead men and mules, damaged tanks, broken trees etc., made a scene of desolation comparable only with the Somme.[32]

Early in the morning of the second day of the attack, Wednesday 1 August, a queue of wounded had formed outside the aid post, having made their way to it as soon as there was enough light to see by. This was a miserably grey scene; the men were standing in inches of muddy water already — indeed, a small torrent of water was pouring down the dug-out steps and collecting in the little room at the bottom. There was no more room inside, so the injured stood patiently in the rain, while Noel and his assistants tried desperately to clean and dress wounds, before pointing out to those who could walk the safest way back to the dressing station at Wieltje. No time now for Noel's famous hot drinks and dry clothing routine.

Helping him were some captured Germans, one of whom was a qualified Medical Officer. A witness reported:

> Chavasse carried on indomitably. He was particularly pleased with his German M.O. assistant, and the way the latter buckled to his job. 'Good fellow, fine fellow', he kept saying.[33]

Here it was that Noel had a narrow escape from death. He was sheltering as best he could in the doorway of the dug-out, calling each man forward for treatment, when a shell flew past him and down the stairs, killing a man who was waiting to be carried away by the Field Ambulance. It may be that Noel received a second injury on this occasion, but if so it was not bad enough to require any treatment other than that which his orderlies could give.

At this point a degree of uncertainty arises about his wounds. Herd, one of his stretcher-bearers, said nothing in his diary about Noel being wounded again after the initial wound to the head.[34] Henry Willink of Liverpool, who was serving in Flanders at the same time (and whose sister Beatrice was to marry Christopher Chavasse), wrote home to say that Noel had been wounded three times before he received the fatal wound. He added that men were saying Noel had won the Victoria Cross four times on this day.[35]

At some point during 1 August, Noel received a wound which would normally have required his removal from the battlefield. The historian of the Liverpool Scottish recorded that he was twice hit in the head, and that he suffered intense pain thereafter, but carried on caring for the wounded.[36] In 1954 a former stretcher-bearer described being sent to bring Noel back after he had been wounded. He found him in his aid post, sitting at a table with his legs in six inches of water and a bandage round his head. The 'Doc' refused to go and told the stretcher-bearers to take another wounded man instead. Within hours, according to this account, Noel was wounded again, this time mortally.[37]

Whether this really occurred or not, there is no doubt that he was wounded for the last time on Thursday, 2 August. His Commanding Officer, who had remained behind at Poperinghe, wrote to the Bishop within hours of the event:

> I am sorry to say that Noel has been badly wounded today. He was hit early in the attack on July 31st., but stuck to the Battalion and carried on his duties. This morning at 3 a.m. he was caught by a shell and hit in several places.[38]

What had happened was that another shell had entered the aid post, this time during the night while Noel was sitting in a chair in the lower room, leaning on the table in an attempt to get some sleep. All the occupants of the dug-out were either killed outright or wounded so seriously that they were immobilized. Herd recorded that a primus stove in use in the dug-out was untouched and still alight, but a man who had been using it was dead, presumably from concussion, and with no visible wound.[39] It is ironic, after all his brave sorties into no-man's-land at Hooge, Guillemont and elsewhere, that Noel should have been felled inside his own aid post.

He had received four or five wounds, the worst being a gaping hole in the abdomen from which he bled profusely. Nevertheless, aware that relief would be a long time in coming, he managed to drag himself up the stairs and out along the remnants of the trench to the road. He stumbled and crawled along this lane in the darkness, in the direction of Wieltje, the filthy mud of Flanders entering and infecting the wound. The thorough preparation for the attack, involving much familiarization with the ground, meant that he knew where he was and which would be the best route to follow in order to obtain help as quickly as possible. He stumbled across a dug-out occupied by Lieutenant Charles Wray of the Loyal North Lancs. Regiment, who later sent an account to his local newspaper telling how Chavasse examined his own wound because the medical personnel went to help his men.[40] They, too, were soon brought down, but as far as is known no one from the aid post survived. His servant, Private C. A. Rudd, was also mortally wounded and was taken to the same hospital.

Colonel Davidson continued:

> Some splinters struck him in the stomach, and these are the only wounds which are dangerous. He was brought down quickly, and was taken to a special hospital for abdominal cases.[41]

This was Casualty Clearing Station No.32, at Brandhoek between

Poperinghe and Ypres, which had only moved from Warlencourt on 8 July, in preparation for the battle.[42] As Noel was brought to the hospital, a startling coincidence took place at Brandhoek crossroads.

> The first medical unit through which he passed on the way to the Casualty Clearing Station, where he died, was the 46th. Field Ambulance, the C.O. of which was Lt.-Col. Martin-Leake, who himself was the first man ever to be awarded the Bar [to the V.C.] in November 1914. He had been awarded the Cross while serving under Lt.-Col. Baden Powell in the South African Constabulary at Vlakfontein in 1902.[43]

To return to Colonel Davidson:

> I saw him about 11 a.m. when he had been operated on. He was still unconscious, but the surgeon said he was doing as well as could be expected, and that his pulse was as strong as it had been before the operation. I have just returned after seeing him again. He seems very weak, but spoke cheerfully. The operation is said to have been successful and as he has been X-rayed the surgeons feel confident that the splinters have all been removed.
>
> They are very guarded in their opinions, but consider he has quite a fair chance of pulling through. He is in very good hands. The O.C. Hospital is an old St. Thomas' man and knows all about Noel. The surgeon who operated is a specialist from Guy's, and although the Hospital is in the line, they have Army sisters.... I will try to get this letter down by special messenger which will probably get it to you sooner than a telegram. I need hardly say that Noel has been magnificent again. Everyone in the Division is speaking of him. I will keep you advised as to his progress.[44]

Colonel Davidson's letter reached the Bishop and Mrs Chavasse on 7 August. The Bishop seems to have had a premonition of tragedy, for he wrote to Bernard two days earlier:

> We feel sure that Noel has been, or is, in the midst of the fighting, and are almost certain that your Battalion has been taking part also. God protect you and make you deliverer and succourer of many.[45]

At the time, Noel's parents and Marjorie had been staying at a country house, Morton Pinkney Manor in Northamptonshire, which had been lent to them for the summer holidays by a Miss Grey of Oxford. On 7 August Marjorie wrote to apprise Bernard of his brother's wound:

> Noel has been knocked out at last and is very badly wounded.... He was taken at once to a special hospital and the bits taken out, and he was afterwards rontgen-rayed.... How rotten everything is. There is no news of Aidan yet, still it might arrive any day now. I believe you have been in the thick of it. I only hope a letter won't be arriving about you tomorrow. We have had enough.[46]

Sadly, a letter did arrive on 8 August from a Lieutenant Marshall of the 17th Battalion to say that Bernard had indeed been in action again and had received injuries to his knee. His mother was devastated to hear that her third son was wounded:

> How it goes to my heart to hear of your being done up, although I trust the wound itself is slight. I can fairly picture what you have been through. Rest, dear son, rest absolutely, until you come round again — and don't try your heart by smoking too much! I hope you will have our letters sent yesterday telling you that Noel was very seriously wounded on August 2. This morning we have another note from the Chaplain [the Reverend Eustace Hill] who saw him next morning, the 3rd. He was very, very ill, but had said to the doctor he meant to fight for life. That is the last we know, and the time seems so long — wires also take as long as letters to come and go.[47]

The Bishop's last letter to Noel, which arrived at the hospital after his death, had crossed with Colonel Davidson's. In it Noel's father had informed him that his fianceé was on the point of leaving for Paris with her sister Esme.[48] In fact Gladys had not left; she had been told of Noel's wound by telephone, and as the Bishop and his wife were making their way back to Liverpool they planned to stop over at Barnt Green and put her in the picture.

Just as they were leaving Morton Pinkney on the morning of 9 August, the telegram arrived. Noel had died peacefully, at one o'clock in the afternoon of 4 August, 1917. It was the third anniversary of the outbreak of war.

CHAPTER FIFTEEN

'This Devoted and Gallant Officer...'

Their feelings as Marjorie drove the car through the summer countryside towards Bromsgrove can be imagined. By lunchtime the wide sweep of the drive off Linthurst Road at Barnt Green was taking them round to the front of The Linthurst Hill. Gathered in the porch at the front door were Gladys, Esme and their mother Aunt Frances, who had for once abandoned her work at the hospital at Rednal in order to greet the Liverpool Chavasses. Gladys surely guessed that the worst had happened as soon as she saw their faces.

From Barnt Green, his faith as certain as ever, the Bishop wrote to Bernard:

> You will have heard by this time that our dearest Noel has been called away....Our hearts are almost broken, for oh! how we loved him. Your dearest mother is pathetic in her grief, so brave and calm notwithstanding. But again and again, we keep praising and thanking God for having given us such a son. We know that he is with Christ, and that one day — perhaps soon — we shall see him again. What should we do in such a sorrow as this, if we could not rest on the character of God, on his love, and wisdom, and righteousness....
>
> We spent last night at Linthurst, both trying to comfort dear Gladys. Our hearts ache for her.[1]

Bernard did know of Noel's death, and had been trying to find out as much as he could about the circumstances. The 17th King's, with Bernard as Medical Officer, had been in action since 31 July just a mile or two south of the Liverpool Scottish. Here it was that Bernard had received his knee wound, and had performed brave acts in saving the wounded that were to be officially rewarded in September. On the day of Noel's fatal injury, the 17th were in trenches along the Hooge road. Relieved on 4 August, they moved to Ouderdom, a village within riding distance of Brandhoek where Noel lay in hospital. Bernard was able to go to No.32 Casualty Clearing Station as soon as the news reached him on 6 August; but, sadly, this was not until after Noel's funeral. Nevertheless, he was able to interview all of the major participants in his brother's last fight, and wrote a detailed account to his parents:

> On the evening of the 6th. I went over to 32nd. CCS Brandhoek (behind Ypres) 2 miles and a half east of Poperinghe. I saw his grave, the Colonel of the Hospital (Sutcliffe), the Sister who attended him, Major Fagge who operated, and the Padre (Eustace Hill) and his orderly [Rudd] — also badly wounded — and others.
>
> On the night of the 2nd, he came down to the dug-out and was sitting on the chair by the little table getting a little sleep. Rudd was there and one or two others — patients and so on, asleep during an interval in the arrival of casualties....While they were resting a shell came in....[Noel] was wounded in five or six places, but the one which mattered was in the abdomen — the 32nd. CCS being a special hospital for such cases where the most splendid treatment is given.
>
> As soon as he was warm and comfortable Major Fagge operated. The fragment was removed and the ileum which was punctured in several places was repaired. But he did not rally and died at 1 p.m. on the 4th. He was not in any pain. He was rather dazed and morphia was given freely. He was conscious throughout. His main idea seemed to have been a quiet determination to pull through if possible. He received the Holy Communion when offered it but without any idea of giving up. For the same reason he did not give any messages, and said he did not feel up to dictating any letters.[2]

This letter gave the greatest comfort to the Bishop and his wife. Indeed, the Bishop had it reprinted and sent it out to all members of the family, distant and near, and in answer to the many letters of sympathy that were soon to start arriving.

It was not the good fortune of the majority of families to have such a detailed account of the last hours of a son who fell in the Great War, but the Chavasses, as has been seen, were especially well-placed for the accumulation of information. Bernard, as an officer and a doctor, had the freedom to go over to Brandhoek to discuss Noel's condition with the doctors there on equal terms. Because the name of Chavasse was so well known, not least because of Noel's Victoria Cross, high-ranking officers who had come across Noel or in whose units he had served, hastened to write to the Palace in Liverpool with their own version of events.

Sister Ida B. Leedam who had nursed Noel during his last hours had, by yet another of the coincidences that punctuate his story, been on the staff of the Royal Southern Hospital in Liverpool during 1913 and early 1914 while Noel was a registrar there. She now wore the uniform of the Queen Alexandra's Imperial Military Nursing Service, but she and Noel instantly recognized each other. Coming from Liverpool, she was determined to tell the Bishop exactly what happened in 32nd CCS:

He was sitting up in bed... delighted at finding a Southern nurse for his night sister. The first night (August 2nd.) he was with us, he passed a very comfortable night, sleeping off and on, talking now and then of the Southern days. The next day (August 3rd.) was also another comfortable day, sleep off and on, worried a little about his men and servant (Rudd) who was very badly wounded (since dead). Saying all the time I must get up tomorrow and go to the boys. I came on at night, receiving a very fair report and a hopeful one....

I asked him how he felt, he answered, very good, I feel very fit, when you have a little time write a letter for me to my girl, I will tell you what to say. So after I had fixed the other officers up, I went and sat down by his bed. He changed his mind and said, 'Wait, later, Sister'. At 11 p.m. he became restless, pulse poor and asked me not to leave him.... At 3 a.m. (August 4th.) pulse much worse, still more restless but cheerful. At 4 a.m. became worse. The M.O. coming in nearly every hour....

These are his last words he ever spoke to me, 'Sister, write that letter for me,' which I did and sent to Miss G. Chavasse. 'Give her my love, tell her Duty called and called me to obey. Take care of Aidan, Sister, if ever he comes to you, try and find him and let Father know all about him.' What about your father, I said. The Colonel will write to him, but when you get leave go round and see him. Give him my love and tell him about everything. It will be better than writing and you live in the same town. Poor dear Father, he loves his boys, and we are causing him a great deal of pain, with all his hard work, but cheer him, Sister, tell him I am quite happy....

At 4.30 a.m. the Chaplain came in and your son asked me what he was doing. I told him, bringing Communion to a sick officer who had asked him. 'Sister, it is up with me. I would like to have the same.' So I went and brought Padre Hill to him and at 5 a.m. he made his last Communion on earth and when it was all over he said 'Do not forget what I have told you.' He became very quiet until 10.00 a.m. and then wandering and restless, his men always in his thoughts, and passed away 1 p.m. the same day. He had very little pain.[3]

There are some obvious differences between Bernard's version and that of Sister Leedam. It appears that Noel did send messages, that he did write a letter to Gladys, and that he did know death was inevitable. What happened to the letter to Gladys is not known. Bernard may well have missed out these details in the hope of sparing his parents further anguish. However, the phrase used in Sister Leedam's account, 'Duty called and called me to obey', became Noel's epitaph in a variety of versions of accounts of his death.

His funeral took place the following day, 5 August. As Bernard put it,

> They decided that he would like best to be laid alongside his brother Tommies (as if he were one of them). No special arrangements were made. But the men of his Battalion were not to be denied. The whole Battalion paraded and all the Medical Officers of the hospital. The mere presence of the Battalion was unprecedented, but when one knows that they were men on their way out of the line after four days of fighting and terrible weather, that probably every man was smothered in mud from head to foot, and ready to drop from sheer exhaustion, one wonders whether any such tribute was paid to any man before.[4]

Strangely, Sister Leedam's account of the funeral makes no mention of the attendance by the Liverpool Scottish:

> He was buried next day, a large number of officers, Sisters, medical men present, near here.... He lies in a large field with a little cross with his name upon it and in time it will be very nicely laid out, when the Huns have given up shelling over the field.[5]

The historian of the Scottish has nothing to say about Noel's funeral. However, the War Diary of the battalion does point out that the men left the trenches in which they had fought since 31 July on 3 August, before Noel's death, and that from there 'they went on the same night to Ypres and entrained for Vlamertinghe where they bivouacked'.[6] The next day they moved to Watou, passing very close to Brandhoek, and they could easily have marched to the cemetery. Herd's diary records that he, for one, attended.[7] They had therefore not come directly out of the trenches to the funeral, but had been out of the line for two days.

Bernard's emotions were, obviously and understandably, running very high. Only a month had passed since he had lost his youngest brother. Aidan was still officially only missing; but Bernard, having seen men horribly wounded and knowing that the vast majority of men posted 'wounded and missing' were subsequently found to have died, must have entertained few illusions about Aidan's fate. Now Noel had gone too. The terrible waste and loss that had disturbed Bernard all through the war was now being experienced with profound intensity by his own family. His own tribute to Noel shows mingled pride and loss:

> With all the sorrow of it, one does feel very proud of him. He was behaving gallantly when already wounded he received his fatal wound, and he never lost his courage during his last hours. This was not the snuffing out of a beloved nonentity, but the death of a man of valour who was also a man of God.[8]

This sentiment was entirely in accord with his parents' views. A reply was quickly despatched from the Palace:

> Your letter was a real comfort. It drew many tears from our eyes — tears of sorrow at the death of such a noble son — tears of thankfulness that he followed his Saviour so closely in his death, and literally laid down his life for his men. Ah, my dearest boy, he was indeed a hero, and as you say justly, he was a man of valour because he was a man of God. Continually, your dear Mother and I thank and glorify God for such a son and for his wonderful and beautiful life spent in helping others, and crowned at last by his noble death, for the sure and certain hope that he is with Christ.
>
> I hope we were of some comfort to your Aunt, Gladys and Esme. When we reached Liverpool and bought an Echo we found the announcement of his death in the Stop Press column.... Letters are pouring in. The grief is widespread, the sympathy wonderful. I am keeping on my work as usual, I should not be worthy of him if I gave up. Your mother's secret grief is intense. At such a time as this, none can tell the comfort of having a wife to share and halve one's sorrow.[9]

The 'Stop Press' notice mentioned by the Bishop appeared in the *Liverpool Echo* on Friday 10 August. It reported:

CAPTAIN CHAVASSE VC
Died from wounds
News reached Liverpool of death from wounds of Capt. Noel

G. Chavasse VC, one of the Bishop's gallant sons. Capt. Chavasse was a well-known and popular athlete, and won several championships at Oxford.

The press was fully to exploit the news during the next few days. Meanwhile, other letters were arriving. One came from King George V at Windsor Castle, signed by the Lord-in-Waiting, Lord Stamfordham:

> The King is grieved to hear of the death from wounds of your son which is all the more pathetic when Captain Chavasse had, by his exceptional gallantry, self-sacrifice and ministering to his wounded comrades in the face of great danger gained the highest distinction of an outward character to which a soldier can aspire. His Majesty remembers with pleasure presenting the Victoria Cross to your son and that he had previously won the Military Cross.
>
> His Majesty sympathises truly with you in your sorrow and feels that the whole Army will mourn the loss of so brave and distinguished a brother.
>
> The King fears from the newspaper reports that you have a further anxiety as another of your sons is stated to be wounded and missing of whom, however, His Majesty earnestly trusts that you may receive reassuring news. [10]

Another letter was from Major-General Jeudwine, commanding the 55th Division:

> His death is a great loss to the Regiment, the Division, and the whole Army. We, his comrades, were proud of the distinction he had already won and of the noble deeds for which it was conferred by the King. His gallantry again on this occasion was magnificent... many men who would probably have perished but for his self-sacrificing efforts were found, brought in and attended to by him before he received other wounds which proved fatal. This work was done in circumstances of great danger and hardship, extending over three days, and his devotion was magnificent. [11]

This reads like a citation; and in a sense it was, but news of Noel's final award was some weeks away. Brigadier-General L. G. Wilkinson, who commanded the 166th Brigade until April 1917, wrote in similarly glowing terms:

I constantly met your son and appreciated his work. He was quite the most gallant and modest man I have ever met, and I should think the best-liked. What he did for his battalion of Liverpool Scottish was wonderful, and his loss to them is irreparable. I do not believe a man of more noble character exists.[12]

By 11 August, the Liverpool press carried detailed obituaries of Noel, such as this one from the *Liverpool Courier*:

It may be said that he fully lived up to that standard of British pluck and bravery of which the great distinction of the Victoria Cross is the symbol.... In the pursuit of his humane and perilous duties he seemed to have a charmed existence. It is not too much to say that a large number of men in the fighting line owe the fact that they are alive today to his magnificent bravery and heroic self-sacrifice....

The deepest sympathy of Liverpool people will go out to Dr. and Mrs. Chavasse in the loss of such a noble and patriotic son, who has given his life in the service of his country. That sympathy will be the greater because of the fact that no news has yet been received of the Bishop's younger son, Lieut. Aidan Chavasse, who over three weeks ago was reported wounded and missing after performing a fine act of bravery.[13]

Canon H. D. Rawnsley once again composed a tribute in verse, as he had done on the occasion of the award of the Victoria Cross to Noel in October 1916; it was printed in the *Liverpool Daily Post and Mercury* on 15 August:

Mourn for the dead we ill could spare,
A man to think and do and dare,
　　Dear Oxford's gallant son,
His is the gain but ours the loss
Who, ere he won Victoria's Cross,
　　Another cross had won.

Pure soul of self-forgetfulness,
Can we not see him in the stress
　　Of battle's fierce attack
Binding up wounds all day, at night
Facing the bombs and rocket light
　　To bear the stricken back?

Can we not see him, tho' he bled,

Lead volunteers through hail of lead
　To rescue men in pain,
And bear them through a storm of shell
To safety from the powers of hell
　And still return again?

Oh, wheresoe'er brave soul you are
Beyond this holocaust of war,
　Know this: we men who mourn
Pray you who won so many a race
May see your Umpire face to face,
　Victor beyond the bourne.

In the days that followed, the papers began to print further tributes sent in by the families of members of the Liverpool Scottish, which often took the form of letters sent home from the Front:

> I don't know how to tell you, but no doubt you already know the terrible news that the doctor has given his life. A life that I am convinced absolutely could not be spared. It is no boast to assert that the loss of him is as great as any the nation has ever suffered, and anybody who thoroughly knew his personality must admit the truth of that.... By a stroke of exceptionally good luck, I was able to pay my last respects to him as he was placed in the grave, but his memory is something that cannot die with me, as with thousands of others.[14]

Obituaries appeared also in the *British Medical Journal*[15] and of course in the *Liverpool Diocesan Gazette*,[16] which contained a long letter from the Bishop based on Bernard's description of Noel's last hours.

In contrast, a second cousin, the Reverend Claude Chavasse, of the Royal Field Artillery, wrote to his mother in the middle of August:

> I am afraid I am rather fazed by all Cousin Frank's sons and their exploits. How do they go? People are always asking me, and I feel so silly when I can't tell them. There is a photo of Noel in the Daily Mail today in a Glengarry. I thought he was RAMC.[17]

Noel's eldest sister, Dorothea, from the vantage point of her home in Birkenhead, was able to observe the sadness of her parents and Marjorie. Writing to a friend she said,

Of course, they are all very brave, but it is a sad house just now. We shall have to move into our new house in a few weeks, and then I shall send my babies over to lighten it for them a little.[18]

As for Christopher, there is little contemporary evidence of his reactions to the death of his twin, but he must have written home in great sorrow, for the Bishop replied with a touching reference to the Chavasse children's 'We Are Seven Amateur Band' of so long ago:

Your letter has just come. We have still twin boys, you have still a twin brother. The lake child who told Wordsworth 'we are seven' can teach us a lesson.[19]

May also wrote to try and console him:

I know what you will be feeling and that you will be broken-hearted because you did not get to Noel in time. I think it nearly broke mine — for even though I telegraphed for news up the line I could get none, and I couldn't find out which CCS he was in. And after all he had gone home before we knew that he was even wounded.... I can't realize the years without him — but he will never be dead, to us.[20]

At the time of Noel's death, as we have seen, Chris was stationed at Bullecourt in France, and had been recommended for the award of the Distinguished Service Order. On 25 August it was announced that he had instead been awarded the Military Cross, with the following citation:

For conspicuous gallantry and devotion to duty. His fearlessness and untiring efforts in attending to the wounded were magnificent. Although continually under fire, he volunteered on every possible occasion to search for and bring in the wounded. No danger appeared to be too great for him to face, and he inspired others to greater effort by his splendid example.[21]

He managed to get home at the end of August for a few days' leave, and his father wrote to Bernard:

The announcement that [Chris] has been awarded the Military Cross...has given genuine satisfaction. It will comfort him also, for he feels dear Noel's death terribly.[22]

Either on his way home, or on his return from leave, Christopher was able to make a detour and visit the cemetery where Noel had been buried. The village of Brandhoek was filled with hospital hutments and cemeteries. The Military Cemetery had been in use since May 1915, but was deemed full just before Third Ypres and was closed in July 1917. The New Military Cemetery, covering 1,370 square metres and containing Noel's grave, was open for only two months, July and August 1917, and here were buried those who died at three nearby Casualty Clearing Stations — the 32nd (where Noel was treated), the 44th and the 3rd Australian. The total number of graves by the end of August when Christopher visited the cemetery was 558, including twenty-eight German prisoners-of-war.

Chris photographed the grave and the prints that survive in his albums show a muddy graveyard, Noel's grave simply a mound of earth upon which a few blades of grass were already beginning to grow.[23] But at the head of the grave stood a wooden cross, ornately fashioned by that same craftsman member of the Liverpool Scottish whose work Noel had so admired. At its foot was the recently acquired badge of the 55th (West Lancashire) Division, a single red rose encircled by the motto 'THEY WIN OR DIE WHO WEAR THE ROSE OF LANCASTER'. These words came from a poem written by Liverpool-born Lieutenant C. Wall (RFA), who had been killed in action in June 1917:

> Now England's blood like water flows,
> Full many a lusty German knows,
> We win or die, who wear the Rose
> of Lancaster.

Next to Noel's grave was that of Second Lieutenant Frederick John Wright, attached to the 1/8th Battalion the King's (the Liverpool Irish). He had only received his commission on 25 January, 1917, at the age of eighteen. At nineteen he was dead. Wounded on 31 July, as the Liverpool Irish charged across no-man's-land only yards behind the Liverpool Scottish, he had been taken to No.32 Casualty Clearing Station at Brandhoek, where he had lingered for four days. Was he the officer who had asked for Holy Communion as Noel lay dying nearby? They were buried on the same day, side by side.

In the same cemetery, a few yards away, is the grave of Private C. A. Rudd, Noel's servant, who died on 10 August.

It is said in the Chavasse family that, with the closeness of twins, Christopher knew the moment that Noel died; he described this feeling in a letter of sympathy to a bereaved friend in 1960:

I think my experience has been rather what I went through when I lost my leg [in 1942]. My loss of my twin was like amputation — I felt half of me had gone, for we were extremely close, so that I knew (I have proof of this) when he died, though he was 80 miles from me on the battle-front, and the news did not reach me till he had been dead a week.... I still mourn my Noel every day of my life, and have done so for 44 years.... I seem still to think over things with Noel, and to feel he might walk into the room any minute. And sometimes I wake in the morning, feeling I have been with him in my sleep — and I believe that our spirits have been together.[24]

Under the stress of his terrible bereavement Chris's health gave way. He succumbed to trench fever in early September, after his return from the saddest home leave of his war; it may be that his resistance was low, both spiritually and physically, when he was normally so strong in both respects.

May came home on leave from Etaples, arriving at Lime Street Station in Liverpool on Tuesday 21 August. She had recently written to Bernard from the Liverpool Merchants' Hospital:

I hoped, how I did hope, that you or Chris had been able to get to Noel — as for me, when I knew he was wounded, I telegraphed and telephoned all over the place, but all to no purpose — and even then it was too late. I am afraid Chris will be heartbroken. Thank God for work in these days — it's the only thing that keeps me going — and I am so submerged with it here at present that I haven't much time to think of anything but other people's problems.[25]

Her health also gave cause for concern, and she looked white and tired. She was found by Dr Macalister to have a kind of blood-poisoning, and was treated with what the Bishop called 'the extra-violet rays on her face'.[26] She was so much under par that her fortnight's leave was extended by a month on Macalister's orders.

At Barnt Green, Gladys was distraught. At the beginning of August she had expected to be married within a few days. Now her fiancé was dead. Soon after the news of Noel's death, his last letter had arrived at The Linthurst Hill, the unfamiliar handwriting of Sister Leedam making its contents almost more heartrending than she could bear. Then, when the Liverpool party had gone on their sad way home, a letter had arrived from Bernard, giving her all the dismal details of Noel's last hours, details which she at first refused to accept but which she could not help devouring avidly.

The newspaper in Bromsgrove printed an obituary, for the community and especially the parish church knew him well from his frequent visits to Barnt Green over the years:

> He was engaged to his cousin, Miss Gladys Chavasse, and the marriage was to have taken place very shortly. Miss Chavasse has done a great deal of work at Bromsgrove in connection with the Women's Volunteer Reserve and other movements during the war, and her many friends here condole with her in her great sorrow.[27]

Like May, Gladys decided to throw herself into work; she saw no reason why she should not take up the Church Army post in Paris as arranged, and it would have the added benefit of getting her away from England. She might feel a little closer to Noel too. Her sister Esme was determined to go as well, and the two girls (Gladys was twenty-four years old, Esme twenty-one) left England for Paris on 14 August.[28] Gladys was therefore not able to be present at Liverpool's tribute to her dead hero.

Within days of Noel's death the idea of a memorial service had been mooted, not just in tribute to Noel, but for all the Liverpool Scottish who had died in those first four days of the battle for Passchendaele, 'for King, Country and Righteousness', as the Memorial Order of Service put it.[29] The War Diary of the battalion showed that in the month of August 1917, and including 31 July, four officers and fifty-one other ranks had been killed or had died of wounds, eight officers and 172 other ranks had been wounded, and six other ranks were missing. This was a severe blow to the city where most of the men's families lived. However, the immediate reason for holding a memorial service now, and not after Hooge or Guillemont, was surely that Noel Chavasse had been one of those who died in this battle.

The Bishop hoped that the service could have been held in the Lady Chapel of the Cathedral; after all, Noel had been present at the laying of the foundation stone in 1904, and had seen the Lady Chapel completed in 1910. But Dr Chavasse was advised that so large would be the numbers of people wishing to attend, the Lady Chapel would not hold them, so the memorial service was held instead in the Parish Church of St Nicholas, close to the Pierhead on the Mersey waterfront.

—— It would have been wonderful if the whole family could have been together that day, to provide each other with much-needed support; but Aidan was 'missing' and Bernard was unable to get leave. The Bishop wrote to him urging him to try, even offering to pay his expenses, but it was not possible.[30] Even so, there was a large family contingent, including Noel's parents, his twin brother and three sisters, as well as other relatives. Also present were the Lord Mayor of Liverpool (Major John Utting), Colonel Forbes Bell of the Liverpool Scottish, and many other representatives of the civic, religious, commercial and social life of the city.

In the Liverpool press the reports of the service, held at three o'clock in the afternoon of 29 August, during a violent storm, were composed in a lofty and often elegiac manner, but uppermost was a sincere sympathy for all who mourned loved ones that day.

> Throughout the service the elements ran riot, but within the building all was tranquillity and peace. Mother Church held her sheltering wings over those who had come to her for consolation and solace, and none were unrequited. ...Widowed wives and bairnless mothers wept silently at times, while stalwart khaki-clad figures were not ashamed of the visible tears that fell as they remembered some dear comrade who had made the great sacrifice. The mourning gathering stood truly for the triumph of life over death, and smiled in chastened comfort at the thought that none can die more happily than he who lays down his life for his country.[31]

The preacher was Canon J. B. Lancelot, Vicar of St James's, Birkdale, Southport, who had known all the Chavasse boys well during their years at Liverpool College, where he had been Head Master until his retirement in July 1917. The choirs of the Lady Chapel and of St Nicholas's sang, and the cathedral organist, Mr Goss-Custard, provided the music. The report went on:

> The Ven. Archdeacon Spooner conducted the Service, and his voice shook with emotion.... The Lesson was read thrillingly by the Rev. J. Hamilton, assistant chaplain to the Regiment.... Canon Lancelot took as his text, 'Rejoice in the Lord alway'.... [He said] there was that in his blood which made the Scot one of the finest fighting men on earth.... Such a man, given an adequate cause, a cause in which he can believe that God himself is interested — would do wonders. They saluted the gallant Battalion, and held all its fallen, both officers and men, in proud and honoured remembrance. Alluding to Captain Noel Chavasse, the preacher said it was no wonder that the King felt the whole Army would mourn the loss of so brave and distinguished a brother, or that his Brigadier declared him to have been the most gallant and modest man he had ever met, or that the Major-General commanding his Division should say that his

devotion was magnificent, or that the whole Battalion, smothered in mud as they were and ready to drop from exhaustion, insisted on parading for his funeral.... He might have been a great surgeon, he might have been a really great clergyman and medical missionary, such was the vision that floated before his mind from boyhood.[32]

The Bishop had obviously allowed Canon Lancelot access to all the letters of sympathy that had been received at the Palace. In a letter to the absent Bernard, Marjorie found the service 'dreadfully trying. The Church was simply packed,'[33] but the Bishop wrote more positively:

> Your Aunt Mary thought it was the most beautiful service of the kind she had attended. We had the two hymns dear Noel chose — 'Just As I Am' and 'Praise to the Holiest'. The congregation took them up and sang them splendidly. The dominant chord in the Service was Praise. There was a triumphant note about it which was very uplifting.[34]

Sad though Bernard must have been at missing the memorial service, he had just heard some good news of his own. He received a signal on 30 August stating that he was to be awarded the Military Cross for his actions along the Hooge road in the first days of the battle of Passchendaele. He had also had the offer of a post at a Casualty Clearing Station, which would take him away from the 17th King's, and away from front-line fighting. He told Marjorie:

> I wasn't far from getting a distinctive decoration — I mean the VC — for which my colonel and my Brigade both put me up (although only the Lord knows why).... These things do not grow like mushrooms and would probably be ruled out on the ground that you could not give 2 VCs to 2 brothers.[35]

His conscience told him to stay with the battalion to the end, but he was wearied by the carnage and greatly distressed by the loss of two brothers in such a short time. Marjorie replied sympathetically:

> It seems to me lately that sorrow is one of the natural things in the world... and that it is not to be shirked, either for ourselves or others. If you feel that your place is at the front, well, you've got to be there, and not even for the sake of your parents ought you to give it up. I think it very noble of you to want to stay

there, and it makes me very proud of you, yes, prouder than if you just got a V.C. It's the deserving that counts. You know Noel could have applied for a base job under D. Crawford if he had liked. He nearly did for Gladys' sake, but he felt he could not leave his men. That he did not, makes the trouble better, not worse.... And I don't believe that anyone who has been, and is, so surrounded by prayer as you boys are, will go unless God absolutely means you to. It is fairly easy to see that Noel has done perhaps more by dying than he could have done if he had lived. Aidan, if he is not alive, is more of a mystery....

My congratulations — I joyously announced the M.C. downstairs, but I haven't mentioned the base offer.[36]

The Bishop sent his congratulations the next day:

We are all delighted to hear that you have gained the Military Cross.... We are very proud of you, and your decoration and that of Chris have come like rays of light in a cloudy dark day. Let us know, when you hear, the account given of the deeds that won so great a prize. God bless you, my dearest boy, and keep you safely under His wings.[37]

On 6 September Bernard made his mind up and moved to Number 11 Casualty Clearing Station at Godeswaersvelde, where he spent the rest of the war. His Military Cross was gazetted on 29 September, although the citation was not published until 9 January, 1918:

For conspicuous gallantry and devotion to duty. During four days of heavy fighting he attended the wounded with untiring energy and exceptional gallantry at very great personal risk. On one occasion, while dressing the wounded in a shell crater under very heavy shellfire, he was hit by bits of shrapnel about the legs and face, but continued to dress each man in his turn and to encourage others who were waiting. On the following day, while dressing the wounded under very heavy shellfire, he was blown over by a shell, but picked himself up and continued his work with the greatest pluck and devotion. He refused medical assistance in both cases, and his indomitable courage was the cause of saving many casualties.[38]

Meanwhile, a breathtaking piece of news had reached the Palace. It began with a letter from Lord Derby:

I signed something last night which gave me the most mixed feelings of deep regret and great pleasure and that was the submission to His Majesty that a Bar should be granted to the Victoria Cross gained by your son. There is no doubt whatever that this will be approved and while it cannot in any way diminish your sorrow, still from the point of view of those who are your friends, it is a great pleasure to think that your son in laying down his life laid it down on behalf of his fellow countrymen, and that it is recognised, not only by those who knew him and served actually with him, but by the King and the Country as a whole. In all the records of Victoria Crosses given I do not think there is one which will appeal to the British Public more than the record for which this Bar is to be given, and as I said at the beginning of my letter, it was a great pleasure to think that this recognition of his services is thus recorded.[39]

Said the Bishop:

The news broke me down for the time and I cannot think of it without tears. Would that it had been God's will that he had lived to receive it! But God cannot make a mistake, and whenever I feel inclined to repine, I praise God for him, and for you all.[40]

Could any family have had a more illustrious and patriotic war record? Two sons killed, two Military Crosses and a Bar to the Victoria Cross in less than two months! Noel's Bar was to be kept confidential until it appeared in the *London Gazette*. In the intervening days, the Bishop received official word in a letter from Colonel Graham, Assistant Secretary for War, who asked whether he would like to go to London to receive the Bar from the King, or whether it should be presented less formally by Lieutenant-General Sir W. Pitcairn Campbell, Western Command. He preferred the latter, but a thought occurred to him, and he inquired of Bernard:

Cannot you and Chris so arrange matters that you receive your Military Crosses the same day? It will be delightful if you can.[41]

This arrangement did not prove possible, however, and the Bar was accepted privately by the Bishop later in the year.

At last, on 14 September, the Bar to the Victoria Cross was announced in the *London Gazette*. The citation read:

Though severely wounded early in the action whilst carrying a wounded soldier to the dressing-station he refused to leave his post, and for two days not only continued to perform his duties but in addition went out repeatedly under heavy fire to search for and attend to the wounded who were lying out. During these searches, although practically without food during this period, worn with fatigue and faint with his wound, he assisted to carry in a number of badly wounded men over heavy and difficult ground. By his extraordinary energy and inspiring example he was instrumental in rescuing many wounded who would have otherwise undoubtedly succumbed under the bad weather conditions. This devoted and gallant officer subsequently died of his wounds.[42]

CHAPTER SIXTEEN

Epilogue

The opening stages of the battle of Passchendaele may have been tragic for the Chavasse family, but it should be remembered that the Army High Command were speaking of the campaign that had begun on 31 July, 1917, as a success. On 3 August, as Noel Chavasse lay dying, Major-General Jeudwine issued the following Special Order of the Day to the 55th Division:

> The attack you made on the 31st is worthy to rank with the great deeds of the British Army in the past, and has added fresh glory to the Record of that Army.
>
> The courage, determination and self-sacrifice shewn by Officers, Warrant-Officers, N.C.Os and men is beyond praise. It is a fine exhibition of true discipline, which comes from the mutual confidence of all ranks in themselves, their comrades, their leaders and those under them. This in its turn is the product of hard training.... You captured every inch of the objectives allotted to you. It was not your fault that you could not hold all you took. You have broken, and now hold, in spite of weather and counter-attacks, a line that the enemy has strengthened and consolidated at his leisure for more than two years. This will, I believe, be the beginning of the end.[1]

Some thirty officers and 600 other ranks had been taken prisoner by the division, and many weapons had been captured. Divisional casualties were 168 officers and 3,384 other ranks, but 'the Division had found itself'.[2]

The campaign was to grind on for more than three months, and the battle for Passchendaele, or the 'Third Battle of Ypres', was technically terminated on 10 November, 1917. Sir Douglas Haig could not claim it as a victory, but was at pains to blame natural obstacles such as the terrain and the weather for the lack of more obvious success.

> This offensive, maintained for three and a half months under the most adverse conditions of weather, had entailed almost superhuman exertions on the part of the troops of all arms and

services. The enemy had done his utmost to hold his ground, and in his endeavours to do so had used up no less than seventy-eight divisions, of which eighteen had been engaged a second or third time in the battle, after being withdrawn to rest and refit. Despite the magnitude of his efforts, it was the immense natural difficulties, accentuated manifold by the abnormally wet weather, rather than the enemy's resistance, which limited our progress and prevented the complete capture of the ridge....

Given a normally fine August, the capture of the whole ridge, within the space of a few weeks, was well within the power of the men who achieved so much.... Time after time the practically beaten enemy was enabled to reorganise and relieve his men and to bring up reinforcements behind the sea of mud which constituted his main protection.[3]

The total British casualties are unknown, possibly around 100,000. The ferocity of the fighting can be judged to some extent from the considerable number of awards for bravery that were made as a result of the battle. Between 31 July and 10 November, 1917, the official dates for 'Third Ypres', sixty Victoria Crosses were confirmed. Of these, thirteen recipients died in the performance of the act of valour; altogether thirteen Victoria Crosses were won on 31 July, and six of these men died.

The cemeteries on the Passchendaele Ridge tell their own story. The largest, Tyne Cot, contains 12,000 graves of British and Commonwealth soldiers, many of then unidentified. The names of 34,000 others, whose last resting place is unknown but who died after the Messines mines had been blown in June 1917, are listed around the curtain walls behind the Cross of Sacrifice. In this cemetery 721 Kingsmen are buried, and many of the graves that bear only the inscription composed by Rudyard Kipling, 'A Soldier of the Great War, Known unto God', must be occupied by sons of Liverpool who died in that terrible campaign.

The Menin Gate, completed in 1927, stands on the spot where the infamous Menin Road emerged from the sheltering walls of Ypres. It commemorates 60,000 dead from Britain and the Commonwealth who have no known graves. High up beneath the arching roof is a list of the names of 955 men and officers of the King's (Liverpool Regiment), and among them is the name of Lieutenant Aidan Chavasse.

Bishop Chavasse explored every possible avenue of inquiry before finally admitting, in February 1918, that Aidan was dead. In March he wrote to Christopher:

About three weeks after Aidan was missing I had a vivid dream about him. I dreamed that he suddenly appeared at home, but he was clad only in shirt and trousers, and said, 'I have escaped. I am free.' Sometimes I wonder now if it was God's intention to say that he was free indeed.[4]

Mrs Chavasse's health never recovered, and each year on the anniversary of Aidan's death she dreamt that he called to her from no-man's-land. On the eve of the tenth anniversary she died.

There was also the task of settling Noel's estate. He had made a will, and wished for his money to go to Christopher — there was about £700 in War Loans and stocks and shares. His wristwatch had been broken when he was wounded, but when it was repaired Chris was to have it. Chris was also to choose whatever he wanted from amongst Noel's athletics cups.[5] Some personal effects and letters were to go to Gladys. His medals were to remain with the family and came via Christopher into the safe-keeping of St Peter's College, Oxford. In February 1990, this unique set of Great War medals was given, in the presence of Her Majesty Queen Elizabeth the Queen Mother, to the Imperial War Museum in London, on permanent loan. They may be seen there in the Victoria Cross Gallery, together with Christopher's. The medals of May and Bernard have also been deposited in the museum by the Chavasse family.

Christopher decided to use Noel's money to provide a permanent memorial to him. This eventually took the form of a portrait which was hung above the fireplace in the dining-room at the Bishop's Palace — the same room in which that last family dinner took place, before the younger Chavasses went their different ways in a world at war. The Bishop saw the face of Noel looking down at him when he returned to Liverpool after a holiday in October 1918, and was greatly touched by this gift for his seventy-second birthday.

> It is very beautiful, and the sight of it greatly affected me. The likeness is excellent and the surroundings are striking.... If the picture reminds us of what we have lost, as it does, it will quicken the hope of reunion and prove a means of grace to urge us to follow in his footsteps that we may be partakers with him of God's Heavenly Kingdom.[6]

The portrait now hangs on the staircase of St. Peter's College, Oxford.

The award of the Victoria Cross *twice* was unprecedented in the Great War. Lieutenant-Colonel Arthur Martin-Leake, RAMC, through whose Field Ambulance Noel had passed on his way to the hospital at Brandhoek, had won his Bar in 1914, but his original Victoria Cross dated from the Boer

War. Noel's achievement was unique in 1917, and remained so. Captain Charles Hazlitt Upham, of the New Zealand Infantry (Canterbury Regiment), was the third and last man to be awarded the Cross and Bar — both in the Second World War, in Crete and in the Western Desert. Amazingly, he too is linked with Noel Chavasse; Captain Upham's aunt-by-marriage was the wife of a second cousin of Noel's.[7] Coincidentally, two of the Upham's children are twins.

Naturally, every establishment associated with Noel Chavasse wished to honour his memory. His first school, Magdalen College School in Oxford, named one of its houses after him and his name appears on a Memorial Board. Liverpool College also has a Chavasse House, and a board bearing the names of Noel and Aidan amongst the 125 Old Boys who lost their lives now graces a wall in the Lower School; in addition, in 1934 a chapel was opened, whose altar was given by Bernard Chavasse in memory of Noel. Bernard also donated a cross of modern design, placed on the exterior end wall of the new chapel, to the memory of Aidan and all the other Old Lerpoolians who died in the Great War and have no known graves. The school's 1980s library extension contains, in pride of place, a tablet dedicated to Noel.

Others hastened to remember Noel in a variety of ways. The British Medical Association announced that its Council had resolved to award him the Association's Gold Medal.[8] Being the son of a 'Lord Bishop', he is commemorated on the House of Lords War Memorial and in Oxford the memorial boards in St. Peter's College Chapel (the former church of St. Peter-le-Bailey) and in the Library of Trinity College bear his name. A brass tablet was placed on a wall in the Royal Southern Hospital's main corridor, engraved with the words (which Bishop Chavasse had approved):

In Memory of Noel Godfrey Chavasse, M.B.(Oxon),
V.C. and Bar, M.C.
Who gave his life for his Country while attending
to the Wounded on the Battlefield in Flanders,
August 4th, 1917.
House Surgeon at this Hospital 1912-1914.

Sadly, this tablet was removed during air-raid precautions in 1939, and has disappeared. The hospital was demolished in 1979. His name also appears on the memorials of Liverpool University and of the Liverpool Medical Institution.

The City of Liverpool was proud of Noel Chavasse and of the Liverpool Scottish; indeed, it was proud of all its citizens who had made the supreme sacrifice in the Great War, and a Memorial Hall was constructed in the Town

Hall, where the names of 13,245 Liverpool men who died are listed. Noel's name is included; unaccountably, Aidan's is not, even though the Bishop was present at its unveiling by the Prince of Wales on 2 July, 1921.

Both the Royal Army Medical Corps and the Liverpool Scottish were able to claim Noel Chavasse as their own. In Liverpool, the RAMC renamed their Wellington Barracks in tribute to him, and in 1988 a new centre was built called Chavasse House. Noel's dress sword and a portrait repose here in the Officers' Mess. The Liverpool Scottish, during their annual Hooge Day Service in 1979, unveiled a tablet at their new barracks at Forbes House, Childwall, Liverpool, the inscription of which concludes with the words: 'Courage is the Quality which Guarantees All Others'. In the same year, Pipe Sergeant T. G. Pritchard composed a Slow Air entitled 'Captain N. G. Chavasse'.

In Liverpool Cathedral's War Memorial Chapel, a huge illuminated book contains Noel's name and citations, alongside those of 35,000 other men of the Liverpool Diocese who fell in the Great War.

In the 1990s, the City of Liverpool plans to develop a 'Chavasse Park' on the banks of the River Mersey, and a recently refurbished office block in the city has been named Chavasse Court. The Liverpool Moat House Hotel has a Chavasse Suite, the Liverpool Cricket Club has a Chavasse Room, and Wavertree British Legion Club takes great pride in its Chavasse Bar.

But what of those who knew Noel best, his family?

Bishop Chavasse retired from the See of Liverpool in 1923, just a year before his great new Cathedral was consecrated. He took his wife back to Oxford, where they lived close to St Peter-le-Bailey for some years. While they were staying at Garsington Rectory just outside Oxford, Noel's mother, now seventy-six, died peacefully in her sleep during the night of 3 July, 1927. Her husband followed her the next year at the age of eighty-one. They were both buried in Founders' Plot at Liverpool Cathedral — the only burials ever to have taken place there. Around their gravestone are simple memorials to Noel and Aidan 'who lie in Flanders'.

Christopher, after the Armistice in 1918, had gone with the Army of Occupation to Euskirchen, near Cologne, and finally resumed civilian life early in 1919. That year he married Beatrice ('Itza') Willink of Liverpool, and began a steady rise through the hierarchy of the Church of England. In 1928 he established St Peter's Hall in Oxford in memory of his father, with the familiar church of St Peter-le-Bailey as its chapel. In 1961 St Peter's became a full college, and the chapel became something of a memorial to the Chavasse family. The original cross from Noel's grave in Flanders is there, and there are memorials to his father, mother and brothers. Christopher went on in 1942 to become Bishop of Rochester; he died in 1962. His eldest son, called Noel after his uncle, served with Field-Marshal Montgomery in the Second World War, and was awarded the Military Cross.

Bernard became a renowned ophthalmic specialist, with consulting rooms in Rodney Street, Liverpool's medical quarter; he lectured at the University, and was the author of authoritative texts on squint. He died in a car accident in 1941.[9] In 1937 the Liverpool Scottish left the King's, becoming the 2nd Battalion the Queen's Own Cameron Highlanders in 1939.[10] Bernard's son Edgar served with this unit during the Second World War.

Dorothea faithfully carried out the duties of a vicar's wife in several parishes, until her early death in 1938, leaving a husband and three children. Marjorie, after the deaths of her parents, took up work for Dr Barnardo's, applying enormous energy and enthusiasm to helping innumerable children and contributing vigorously to the charity's work. Her twin sister May finally got her wish and qualified as a nurse, serving in the Second World War as a member of the Queen Alexandra's Imperial Military Nursing Service. They celebrated their hundredth birthday in August 1986, and were the excited recipients of a rare 'double' telegram from Her Majesty the Queen, in the midst of a huge family birthday party. Marjorie died at Windsor in 1987, and so only May remained, the last of her generation. The end came peacefully for her at Gerrards Cross in February 1989.

And Gladys — who had known Noel as well as anyone, except for Christopher. After the Armistice, she continued her voluntary work with the Church Army, and went with her canteen to Euskirchen, the same location in the Rhineland as Christopher. Here she met a padre, the Reverend James Ferguson Colquhoun ('Pud'), and married him at Bromsgrove in December 1919. Christopher was one of the officiating clergy. 'Pud's' career in the Army Chaplain's Department took them abroad almost permanently, but he was a kind and generous man who looked after her devotedly until his death in 1937. They had no children.

When the Second World War broke out in 1939, Gladys once again set off to run a canteen for the troops; she was evacuated from Dunkirk in 1940 and was 'Mentioned in Despatches' as a civilian for 'gallant and distinguished services in Italy' (at Monte Cassino) in 1945.[11] She was a much-loved cousin and aunt of all the younger Chavasses, but grew profoundly deaf, and on holiday in France in 1962 she crossed a road without hearing an oncoming car and was killed instantly. She was buried in the family vault at Bromsgrove.

When the New Military Cemetery at Brandhoek was laid out by the Imperial War Graves Commission, Noel's headstone was inscribed with the representation of a single Victoria Cross. However, in 1959 the Commonwealth War Graves Commission received information from its Belgian office that a Distinguished Service Order should be credited to

Captain Chavasse. When the headstone was replaced in 1975, the DSO was included, but the mistake was soon challenged by visitors to the grave. In 1979 the letters DSO were blotted out by a stone-filling technique, and a complete re-design of the stone was begun. A design with two small VC emblems was approved and was erected over the grave on 28 April, 1981. The inscription in the white stone, chosen by Noel's father, has always been the same: 'Greater love hath no man than this, that a man lay down his life for his friends'.[12]

Opinions vary as to whether Gladys ever visited Noel's grave; it has been said that she could not find it.[13] As there are three military cemeteries at Brandhoek, ambiguity about the grave's location is quite possible, and still confuses visitors. Christopher used to tell how Noel's little dog Jell, abandoned in the Brandhoek area after his master's death, led her to the grave.[14] Members of the family certainly recall her visits to Bruges, where she stayed at a convent while visiting Flanders.[15] The weight of evidence suggests, in fact, that she was a regular visitor to the grave.

Gladys also marked the anniversary of Noel's death each year with an 'In Memoriam' notice in *The Times*, and she treasured a photograph of him, his 'Officer's Advance Book', his writing case and his miniature Victoria Cross until the end of her life.

Liverpool Scottish (1/10 KLR) MOVEMENTS 1914-19

(Source: A. M. McGilchrist, *The Liverpool Scottish 1900-1919*, H. Young & Sons, Liverpool 1930.)

1914

FRANCE

November	3	Le Havre
	4	Abbeville
	5	St Omer to Blendecques
	20	Hazebrouck
	21	Bailleul

BELGIUM: 9th BRIGADE, 3rd DIVISION

	25	Westoutre
	27	Kemmel sector (until March 1915)

1915

March	2	Ouderdom
	10	Ypres
	11	Hill 60/Zillebeke
April	4	Dickebusch/St Eloi sector/Scottish Wood. Battalion HQ at Voormezeele
May	26	Dickebusch
	28	Vlamertinghe
June	2	Armagh Wood, east of Zillebeke
	6	Vlamertinghe
	10	Busseboom
	16	Attack on Hooge
	17	Busseboom
July	14	St Eloi trenches
	29	Gordon Farm
	31	Ouderdom

August	1	Potijze/Kaaie salient
	13	Ouderdom
	19	White Chateau, Kruisstraat
September	3	Zillebeke Lake dug-outs
	24	White Chateau, Kruisstraat/Sanctuary Wood trenches
	28	Ramparts, Ypres/Maple Copse
October	12	Sanctuary Wood
	19	Ouderdom
	23	Godewaersvelde
November	4	Winnezeele
	21	Reninghelst
	22	St Eloi trenches
	29	Reninghelst
December	6	St Eloi trenches
	13	Reninghelst/Dickebusch

JOINED 166th BRIGADE, 55th WEST LANCASHIRE DIVISION

1916

FRANCE

January	9	Heucourt, near Abbeville
February	6	Prouville
	10	Doullens to Amplier
	11	Berle-au-Bois, Rivière sector trenches, south of Arras. Rest periods at Sauty/Bellacourt
July	11	Simoncourt
	13	Agny trenches, near Rivière
	18	Simoncourt
	19	Sombrin
	20	Bouquemaison
	21	Bernaville
	25	Ville-sur-Ancre, south-west of Albert
	27	Meaulte
	30	Mansel Copse, near Mametz
	31	Machine Gun Copse, north of Maricourt
August	6	Mansel Copse
	9	Attack on Guillemont
	12	Meaulte
	19	Valines, west of Abbeville
	28	Moyenville
	30	Maricourt

	31	Meaulte
September	7	Delville Wood
	11	Ribemont, south-west of Albert
	16	near Albert
	18	Pommier Redoubt/Flers
	28	Ribemont
	30	Pont Remy

BELGIUM

October	3	Poperinghe
	4	Ypres, Canal Bank dug-outs
	5	Wieltje sector/Brandhoek/Elverdinghe/Ypres
November	28	Raid on Kaiser Bill salient
December	2	Wieltje trenches
	18	Brandhoek
	27	Ypres, Canal Bank
	28	Wieltje trenches

1917

| January | 13 | Brandhoek |

FRANCE

| | 14 | Bollezeele, north of St Omer |

BELGIUM

February	3	Mouton Farm, Elverdinghe
	9	Brandhoek
March		Potijze sector trenches/Brandhoek/Ypres convent, school and prison
June	2	Vlamertinghe
	11	Railway Wood trenches
	14	Vlamertinghe

FRANCE

| | 20 | Zudauques, west of St Omer |
| | 30 | Esquerdes |

BELGIUM

July	21	Wieltje trenches
	31	Advance towards Passchendaele as part of Third Ypres
August	2	NGC mortally wounded
	3	Vlamertinghe
	4	NGC dies in hospital at Brandhoek
	4	Watou, west of Poperinghe

	7	Zouafques, north-west of St Omer
September	13	Goldfish Chateau, near Vlamertinghe
	14	Wieltje trenches
	18	L4 Post, near Ypres
	19	in British line across Wieltje–Gravenstafel road
	23	Goldfish Chateau, then to Watou

FRANCE

	27	Beaulencourt, south-west of Bapaume
	29	Villers-Faucon, south of Epéhy
	30	Epéhy trenches
October	13	Villers-Faucon
	23	Epéhy trenches
December	2	Tincourt, east of Péronne
	6	Flamincourt
	8	Aubigny/Izel-les-Hameaux, north-west of Arras
	14	Beaumetz-les-Aires, north-west of St Pol

1918

February	9	Westrehem, west of Béthune
	10	Lapugnoy, west of Béthune
	12	Verquin, south of Béthune
	14	Le Preol, near the Aire–la Bassée canal
	25	Givenchy trenches
March	4	Gorre, near Béthune
	12	trenches south of Festubert
	17	Le Hamel, north-west of Festubert
	26	Cambrin trenches, south-east of la Bassée
April	7	Le Quesnoy, east of Béthune
	8	Le Hamel
	9	Attack on Givenchy
	16	Raimbert, west of Béthune
	20	Verquin
	21	Gorre trenches, east of Béthune
	27	Labourse, south-east of Béthune
	29	Vaudricourt, south of Béthune
	30	COMBINED WITH 2/10 KLR
May	2	Festubert sector/Vaudricourt/Drouvin
September	23	Béthune
October	3	Advance to la Bassée–Fromelles line
	4	Hocron, north-east of la Bassée
	17	Allennes, south-west of Lille

	18	Séclin, south of Lille
	19	Grande Ennetières
	20	Bourghelles, south-west of Tournai
BELGIUM		
	21	Froidmont
November	9	Gaurain-Ramecroix, east of Tournai
	10	Villers-Notre-Dame, south-west of Ath
	11	ARMISTICE
		Attre, south-east of Ath
	15	Ath
December	18	St Job, Brussels

1919

March	7	Antwerp
November	7	Cologne
	9	Calais
	11	London
	12	Liverpool

SELECT BIBLIOGRAPHY

Coop, J. O. *The Story of the 55th Division, 1916-19*, Liverpool Daily Post Printers, 1919

Fussell, P. *The Great War and Modern Memory*, Oxford University Press, 1975

Gliddon, G. *When the Barrage Lifts: A Topographical History and Commentary on the Battle of the Somme, 1916*, Gliddon Books, 1987

Graves, R. *Goodbye To All That*, Cape, 1929

Gummer, S. *The Chavasse Twins*, Hodder & Stoughton, 1963

Hayward, J. D. *The Liverpool Merchants' Mobile Hospital in France*, Hayward, Liverpool 1919

Lancelot, J. B. *Francis James Chavasse, Bishop of Liverpool*, Blackwell, Oxford 1929

Macalister, C. J. *The History of the Liverpool Royal Southern Hospital*, W. B. Jones, Liverpool 1936

MacDonald, L. *They Called It Passchendaele*, Michael Joseph, 1978

McGilchrist, A. M. *The Liverpool Scottish, 1900-1919*, H. Young, Liverpool 1930

McLaughlin, R. *The Royal Army Medical Corps*, Leo Cooper, 1972

Macpherson, W. G., et al. *Official History of the Great War: The Medical Services*, HMSO, 1928-31

Maddocks, G. *The Liverpool Pals*, Leo Cooper, 1991

Simkins, P. *Kitchener's Army*, Manchester University Press, 1988

Wainwright, D. *Liverpool Gentlemen*, Faber & Faber, 1960

Westlake, R. *The Territorial Battalions*, Spellmount, 1986

Wilkinson, A. *The Church of England and the First World War*, SPCK, 1978

Wilson, T. *The Myriad Faces of War: Britain and the Great War, 1914-1918*, Blackwell/Polity Press, 1986

Winter, D. *Death's Men: Soldiers of the Great War*, Allen Lane, 1978

Wolff, L. *In Flanders Fields: The 1917 Campaign*, Longman Green, 1958

Wyrall, E. *The History of the King's Regiment (Liverpool), 1914-1919*, 3 vols, Edward Arnold, 1928-35

SOURCES
Newspapers, Journals, Directories and Registers

Birmingham Post
Bromsgrove, Droitwich & Redditch Weekly Messenger
Daily Mirror
Daily Sketch
Daily Telegraph
Hansard
Liverpool Courier
Liverpool Daily Post & Mercury
Liverpool Echo
London Gazette
The Times
Western Mail

Army Medical Services Magazine
British Medical Journal
General Medical Council Register
Lancet
Orthopaedics Illustrated

Liverpolitan
Liverpool Diocesan Review
Quiver (Cassell, London)

Grafton Street Industrial School Record (Liverpool)
Harrow School Scroll of Fame
Isis
The Lily (Magdalen College School magazine)
Liverpool College Upper School Magazine
Liverpool University Roll of Service (Liverpool University Press, 1922)
Oxford University Roll of Service (OUP, 1920)
Rugby School Memorial Book

Army List
Commonwealth War Graves Commission, Memorial and Cemetery Registers
Officers Died in the Great War (HMSO, 1919)
Soldiers Died in the Great War (HMSO, 1921)
Liverpool Scottish Regimental Gazette
Liverpool Scottish Roll of Honour
Liverpool's Scroll of Fame (G. Thompson, Quills, Liverpool, 1920)

Gore's Liverpool Directories
Kelly's Oxford Directories

Unpublished Sources

Chavasse Papers, Bodleian Library (and some papers still in family's possession)

Sam Moulton's Diary, Bryden McKinnell's Diary, 'Recollections' of W. G. Bromley and 'Reminiscences' of H. S. Taylor, Liverpool Scottish Regimental Museum

Edmund Herd's Diary, Department of Regional History, Liverpool City Museums

Liverpool Royal Southern Hospital records at Liverpool Local Record Office

Medical and Veterinary Students' Address Books, and Minutes of Medical Faculty 1912, in University of Liverpool Archives

Royal Army Medical Corps, File RAMC 801/16, Contemporary Medical Archives Centre, Wellcome Institute for the History of Medicine, London

Battalion War Diaries: 1/8 Bn (Liverpool Irish) and 1/17 Bn (1st City; 'Pals') King's (Liverpool Regiment), 1914-18, Department of Regional History, Liverpool City Museums; 1/10 Bn (Liverpool Scottish) King's (Liverpool Regiment), Liverpool Scottish Regimental Museum

Miscellaneous papers in Liverpool Medical Institution and in 208 (Merseyside) General Hospital RAMC (V)

Parish Registers, Bromsgrove Parish Church

Miscellaneous papers in Liddle Collection, University of Leeds

---

Key to References

BL	Bodleian Library, Oxford
BMJ	*British Medical Journal*
IWM	Imperial War Museum
KLR	King's (Liverpool Regiment)
LC	*Liverpool Courier*
LCM	*Liverpool College Magazine*
LDPM	*Liverpool Daily Post & Mercury*
LE	*Liverpool Echo*
LRO	Liverpool Record Office
RAMC	Royal Army Medical Corps
RSHL	Royal Southern Hospital, Liverpool
WTHM	Wellcome Trust for the History of Medicine

Family References

CMC	Christopher Chavasse
DC	Dorothea Foster-Carter (née Chavasse)
EJC	Edith Jane Chavasse
EMC	Marjorie Chavasse
FBC	Bernard Chavasse
FGRC	Gladys Chavasse
FJC	Francis James Chavasse
MLC	May Chavasse
MFM	Mary Fawler Maude
NGC	Noel Chavasse

REFERENCES

1. Beginnings

1. FJC, *Liverpool Diocesan Gazette*, Vol. XV, No. 177, September 1917, p.97
2. Ibid.
3. Lancelot pp.3-7, 45, 65-6.
4. Congregation of St Peter-le-Bailey to FJC, n.d. (circa May 1880), BL 1/3-4.
5. Lancelot p.8
6. Lancelot p.53.
7. Lancelot p.64
8. Lancelot p.97.
9. *Kelly's Oxford Directory* 1905, p.224.
10. Gummer pp.21-5; family papers courtesy E. F. J. Chavasse.
11. *Kelly's Oxford Directory* 1905, p.111.
12. E. H. Bickersteth, Bishop of Exeter, to FJC, 26.10.1890, BL 1/19-23.
13. Marquess of Salisbury to FJC, 21.11.1891, BL 1/28-9.
14. BL 5/37-8.
15. NGC to MFM, n.d., BL 5/31-2.
16. Gummer p.21.
17. NGC to MFM 28.12.1891, BL 5/7-8.
18. NGC to MFM 27.2.1892, BL 5/9-12.
19. NGC to EJC, n.d., BL 5/39-40.
20. NGC to EJC n.d., BL 5/41.
21. Gummer p.20.
22. Miss L. Foster-Carter to the author.
23. EMC typescript, n.d., at Liverpool Cathedral, p.1.
24. Salisbury to FJC 3.3.1900, BL 1/47-8.
25. Quoted in Lancelot p.20.
26. FJC to Salisbury 7.3.1900, BL 1/49.
27. EMC loc.cit.
28. *Liverpool College Upper School Magazine*, No. 84, July 1919, pp.16-17.
29. Gummer p.33.

2. Liverpool

1. *Quiver,* 1888, p.31.
2. A. R. Allan, *The Building of Abercromby Square,* University of Liverpool, 1986, pp.14-16.
3. Ibid p.16.
4. Ibid p.19.
5. Thomas Chavasse to FJC 19.4.1900, BL 1/81-2.
6. LDPM 4.6.1900.
7. EMC typescript, n.d., at Liverpool Cathedral, p.2.
8. LDPM 1.6.1900.
9. Miss L. Foster-Carter to the author.
10. Wainwright, p.203.
11. LCM New Series, No. 28, 1900, p.13.
12. LCM New Series, No. 35, 1903, p.15.
13. Liverpool College Prize Day Programmes, 1901 and 1902.
14. LCM New Series, No. 31, 1901, p.15.
15. LCM New Series, No. 33, 1902, p.23.
16. LCM New Series, No. 38, 1904, p.19.
17. NGC to DC 13.2.1904, BL 5/56.
18. Wainwright p.284.
19. LCM New Series, No. 30, July 1901.
20. CMC to FJC 8.10.1917, BL 5/30.
21. *Gore's Liverpool Directory* 1904.
22. Gummer pp.29-30.
23. Lancelot p.169.
24. Miss L. Foster-Carter to the author; family papers courtesy Mr. E. F. J. Chavasse.
25. Mrs F. Albu to the author.
26. Courtesy Mr E. F. J. Chavasse.
27. NGC to MFM 27/8/1901, BL 5/53-4.
28. EMC op. cit. p.4.
29. Quoted in J. Riley, *Today's Cathedral,* SPCK, London 1978, p.22.
30. Riley op. cit. p.24.
31. LDPM 19.7.1904.
32. Riley op. cit. p.25.
33. NGC to FJC 31.5.1908, BL 5/213.
34. Miss L. Foster-Carter to the author.

3. Return to Oxford

1. NGC to EJC 24.10.1904, BL 5/59-60.
2. NGC to EJC 7.6.1915, BL 6/84.

3. NGC to EJC 12.11.1904, BL 5/64.
4. NGC to FJC 12.11.1905, BL 5/107-8.
5. NGC to EJC 12.11.1904, BL 5/63.
6. NGC to FJC 10.3.1905, BL 5/83.
7. NGC to FJC 7.5.1905, BL 5/90.
8. NGC to FJC 29.4.1906, BL 5/133.
9. NGC to FJC 16.3.1905, BL 5/84.
10. NGC to DC 6.2.1905, BL 5/76.
11. NGC to DC 15.11.1904, BL 5.66.
12. NGC to FJC 26.4.1905, BL 5/85.
13. NGC to EJC 18.6.1905, BL 5/98.
14. NGC to FJC 14.3.1906, BL 5/131.
15. FJC to NGC and CMC 10.11.1905, BL 12/30.
16. NGC to FJC 29.4.1906, BL 5/133-4.
17. EJC to NGC 23.11.1906, BL 5/152b.
18. NGC to EJC 5.12.1906, BL 5/156.
19. NGC to FJC 10.6.1906, BL 5/141-2.
20. NGC to EJC 16.6.1906, BL 5/143.
21. LDPM 18.7.1906; C. Harris, *The Building of the New Liverpool Cathedral*, 1911, pp.46 and 52.
22. NGC to EJC 4.11.1906, BL 5/151b.
23. NGC to EJC 22.5.1907, BL 5/173.
24. NGC to EJC 5.12.1906, BL 5/156.
25. Medical and Veterinary Students' Address Books, Liverpool University archive.
26. NGC to EJC 17.6.1907, BL 5/177.
27. NGC to FJC 5.12.1907, BL 5/199.
28. NGC to FJC 28.10.1906, BL 5/150.
29. NGC to FJC 13.5.1907, BL 5/170.
30. NGC to FJC 3.6.1907, BL 5/174.
31. NGC to FBC 25.11.1906, courtesy Mr E. F. J. Chavasse.
32. LCM New Series, No. 45, 1906, p.7.
33. *Isis*, No. CCCXLVII, 2.11.1907.
34. NGC to EJC 6.11.1907, BL 5/189.
35. CMC to Major-General R. E. Barnsley 4.4.1957, WTHM.
36. NGC to FJC 8.3.1907, BL 5/163.
37. NGC to EJC 22.5.1907, BL 5/173.
38. Quoted in Gummer p.36.
39. NGC to EJC 8.8.1907, BL 5/182.
40. NGC to EJC 24.1.1908, BL 5/200.
41. NGC to EJC 20.10.1907, BL 5/184.
42. NGC to FJC 28.10.1907, BL 5/187.

43. NGC to FJC 10.11.1907, BL 5/190.
44. NGC to FJC 5.12.1907, BL 5/199.
45. NGC to FJC 10.11.1907, BL 5/190.
46. Ibid.
47. NGC to EJC 16.3.1908 and 22.3.1908, BL 5/211.
48. NGC to FJC 31.5.1908, BL 5/213.
49. NGC to FJC 28.7.1908, BL 5/220.
50. NGC to DC 3.8.1908, BL 5/217.
51. NGC to FJC 14.11.1908, BL 5/228.
52. NGC to FJC 31.5.1908, BL 5/213.
53. P. L. Fisher to CMC and NGC 1.6.1908, courtesy Mr J. C. Chavasse.
54. *The Times*, 13.,18.7.1908.
55. *The Times*, 22.7.1908; and CMC to Major-General R. E. Barnsley 4.4.1957, WTHM.
56. W. Ramsden and N. G. Chavasse, 'Ueber Proteinsole stetig variierenden Dispersitatsgrades' in *Zeitschrift fur Chemie und Industrie de Kolloide* (Dresden 1913), xii, 250-52.
57. NGC to FJC 30.1.1909, BL 5/231.
58. Ibid.
59. NGC to FJC 23.5.1909, BL 5/240.
60. LDPM 7.10.1908.
61. EMC typescript, n.d., at Liverpool Cathedral, p.3.
62. Westlake pp.33-4.
63. *Oxford University Roll of Service*, OUP 1920, p.3.
64. NGC to EJC 24.1.1909, BL 5/229.
65. NGC to FJC 30.1.1909, BL 5/231.
66. FJC to FBC 14.2.1909, courtesy Mr E. F. J. Chavasse.
67. NGC to FJC 23.5.1909, BL 5/241-2.
68. NGC to EJC 13.6.1909, BL 5/243.
69. NGC to EJC 10.5.1909, BL 5/237.
70. NGC to EJC 20.11.1907, BL 5/194.
71. *Grafton Street Industrial School Record*, July-August 1909, Chavasse Album, BL.
72. Report to Chairman and Committee, *Grafton Street Industrial School Record*, 4.12.1909, Chavasse Album, BL.

4. Dr Chavasse

1. FJC to FBC 14.11.1909; courtesy Mr E. F. J. Chavasse.
2. EMC to NGC 11.5.1910, Mr J. C. Chavasse.
3. LDPM 30.6.1910.
4. FJC to FBC 14.2.1909, courtesy Mr E. F. J. Chavasse.

5. NGC to FJC 21.8.1910, BL 5/247.
6. NGC to EJC 3.7.1911, BL 5/251.
7. NGC to EJC 20.8.1911, BL 5/253-4.
8. Gummer pp.41-2.
9. FJC to FBC 25.1.1912, courtesy Mr E. F. J. Chavasse.
10. Liverpool University Archives, Minutes of Medical Faculty, 15.3.1912.
11. F. Jackson, *The Life of Sir Robert Jones*, Hodder & Stoughton 1934, p.155.
12. General Medical Council Register, 1912. Noel's certificate was No. 45151.
13. NGC to EJC 9.6.1912 and 10.6.1912, BL 5/255 and 257.
14. RSHL Residents' Leave Book 1912, LRO.
15. RSHL Rules No. 28, LRO.
16. RSHL General Committee Minutes 1912, LRO.
17. Mr R. Eager in conversation with the author.
18. NGC to EJC 9.6.1912, BL 5/255.
19. *Western Mail* 18.2.1913; *Birmingham Post* 19.2.1913.
20. BMJ 14.12.1914, p.373.
21. NGC to EJC 2.6.1913, BL 5/261.
22. Macalister p.163.
23. LE 2.4.1913.
24. *Liverpool Scottish Regimental Gazette* No. XXVII, December 1912, p.9.
25. Ibid p.11.
26. Ibid pp.14-15.
27. Ibid p.49.
28. Liverpool Scottish Recruiting Appeal, *Regimental Gazette* No. XXVIII, December 1912.
29. NGC to FJC 13.8.1913, BL 5/263.
30. NGC to FJC 20.8.1913, BL 5/266.
31. NGC to FJC 20.8.1913, BL 5/265.
32. *Liverpool Scottish Regimental Gazette*, Vol. 2, No. II, January 1914.
33. *Liverpool Scottish Regimental Gazette*, Vol. 2, No. VI, May 1914, p.2.

5. For King and Country

1. LDPM 5.8.1914.
2. LDPM 11.8.1914.
3. McGilchrist p.9.
4. LDPM 22.8.1914.
5. MLC to EMC 6.8.1914, courtesy Mr J. C. Chavasse.
6. Sam Moulton's Diary 8.8.1914.
7. McGilchrist p.13.

8. NGC to EJC 12.8.1914, BL 6/1.
9. NGC to EJC 14.8.1914, BL 6/3.
10. NGC to EJC 14.8.1914, BL 6/3-4.
11. NGC to FJC 18.8.1914, BL 6/5.
12. NGC to FJC 5.9.1914, BL 6/8.
13. NGC to FJC 18.8.1914, BL 6/5.
14. FJC to EMC 15.8.1914, courtesy Mr J. C. Chavasse.
15. NGC to EJC 20.8.1914, BL 6/7.
16. NGC to Robert Jones 20.8.1914, courtesy Liverpool Medical Institution.
17. NGC to FJC 5.9.1914, BL 6/8.
18. J. J. Bagley, *The Earls of Derby 1485-1985*, Sidgwick & Jackson 1985, pp.220-21; and G. Maddocks, *The Liverpool Pals*, Leo Cooper 1991, p.23.
19. Ministry of Pensions, *Location of Hospitals and Casualty Clearing Stations, BEF, 1914-19*, 1923, p.16.
20. NGC to FJC 4.10.1914, BL 6/11.
21. NGC to FJC 5.9.1914, BL 6/8.
22. NGC to EJC 27.9.1914, BL 6/9.
23. NGC to FJC 4.10.1914, BL 6/11.
24. McGilchrist p.14.
25. NGC to FJC 4.10.1914, BL 6/10.
26. NGC to EJC 25.10.1914, BL 6/13.
27. NGC to EJC 25.10.1914, BL 6/14.
28. Ibid.
29. Sam Moulton's Diary, 27.10.1914.
30. McGilchrist p.16.
31. NGC to FJC 31.10.1914, BL 6/15-16.

6. Marching Away to War

1. NGC to DC 31.10.1914, BL 6/17.
2. NGC to FJC 2.11.1914, BL 6/19.
3. NGC to FJC 5.11.1914, BL 6/20.
4. NGC to FJC 5.11.1914, BL 6/21; and McGilchrist p.17.
5. Bryden McKinnell's Diary, 5.11.1914.
6. NGC to FJC 5.11.1914, BL 6/20.
7. Bryden McKinnell's Diary, 6.11.1914.
8. NGC to FJC 17.11.1914, BL 6/23.
9. Bryden McKinnell's Diary, 18.11.1914.
10. Ibid, 10.11.1914.
11. Ibid, 13.11.1914.
12. NGC to FJC 17.11.1914, BL 6/23.

13. Ibid.
14. Bryden McKinnell's Diary, 17.11.1914.
15. NGC to FJC 17.11.1914, BL 6/24.
16. NGC to CMC 2.1.1915, BL 6/40.
17. Bryden McKinnell's Diary, 13.11.1914.
18. NGC to FJC 22.11.1914, BL 6/25.
19. Bryden McKinnell's Diary, 19.11.1914.
20. NGC to FJC 22.11.1914, BL 6/25.
21. Bryden McKinnell's Diary, 17.11.1914.
22. NGC to FJC 22.11.1914, BL 6/25.
23. NGC to FJC 23.11.1914, BL 6/26.
24. NGC to DC 26.11.1914, BL 6/28.
25. NGC to FJC 22.11.1914, BL 6/25.
26. General R. E. Barnsley to Sir Arthur Gemmell, 7.5.1956, WTHM.
27. Bryden McKinnell's Diary, 24.11.1914.
28. NGC to FJC 26.11.1914, BL 6/27.
29. McGilchrist p.20.
30. NGC to FJC 26.11.1914, BL 6/27.
31. Bryden McKinnell's Diary, 26.11.1914.
32. Ibid, 27.11.1914.
33. NGC to FJC 5.12.1914, BL 6/29.
34. Ibid.

7. From Kemmel to Ypres

1. NGC to FJC 11.12.1914, BL 6/33.
2. Bryden McKinnell's Diary, 30.11.1914.
3. Ibid, 24.12.1914.
4. NGC to FJC 11.12.1914, BL 6/33.
5. Bryden McKinnell's Diary, 8-9.12.1914.
6. *Lancet* 11.12.1914, p.1304.
7. Macpherson et al, *Official History: Medical Services: Surgery of the War*, Vol. I, p.170.
8. BMJ 27.1.1917.
9. NGC to FJC 16.12.1914, BL 6/34.
10. NGC to FJC 29.12.1914, BL 6/36.
11. Sam Moulton's Diary, 21.12.1914.
12. Liverpool Scottish Archive.
13. Sam Moulton's Diary, 3.2.1915.
14. Bryden McKinnell's Diary, 23.12.1914.
15. W. G. Bromley, 'Recollections', in *Liverpool Scottish Regimental Gazette*, September 1931.

16. Sam Moulton's Diary, 1.12.1914.
17. W. G. Bromley loc.cit.
18. NGC to FJC 29.12.1914, BL 6/38.
19. Bryden McKinnell's Diary, 29.12.1914.
20. Sam Moulton's Diary, 30.12.1914.
21. Bryden McKinnell's Diary, 1.1.1915.
22. NGC to DC 12.1.1915, BL 6/42.
23. NGC to FJC 9.7.1915, BL 6/94.
24. Bryden McKinnell's Diary, 14.12.1914.
25. NGC to FJC 28.1.1915, BL 6/51.
26. NGC to FJC 21.2.1915, BL 6/56.
27. NGC to FJC 13.1.1915, BL 6/46.
28. Bryden McKinnell's Diary, 28.2.1915.
29. NGC to FJC 1.3.1915, BL 6/59.
30. LCM No. 70, December 1914, p.1.
31. LCM No. 71, March 1915, p.1.
32. Robert Eager, in conversation with the author.
33. Bryden McKinnell's Diary, 5.2.1915.
34. NGC to FJC 1.3.1915 and 17.3.1915, BL 6/59-64.
35. McGilchrist p.32.

8. In the Salient

1. McGilchrist p.33.
2. Bryden McKinnell's Diary, 1.4.1915.
3. NGC to FJC 21.2.1915, BL 6/56.
4. Information courtesy Mr J. C. A. Quinney.
5. NGC to FJC 27.3.1915, BL 6/68-9.
6. *Lancet*, 19.2.1916, p.422.
7. P. Lovegrove, *A Short History of the RAMC*, Aldershot, 1951, p.42.
8. LE 12.6.1916.
9. Bryden McKinnell's Diary, 12.3.1915.
10. Sam Moulton's Diary, 13.3.1915.
11. NGC to FJC n.d. (c. March 1915), BL 6/67.
12. NGC to FJC 27.3.1915, BL 6/69.
13. Ibid.
14. Gummer p.55.
15. Bryden McKinnell's Diary, 11.3.1915.
16. E. J. Finlay to Major-General R. E. Barnsley, 11.6.1961, WTHM.
17. NGC to FJC 19.4.1915, BL 6/72.
18. NGC to Mrs Jones 25.3.1917, Liverpool Scottish Archive.
19. *Daily Sketch* 21.12.1915.

20. Bryden McKinnell's Diary, 23.3.1915.
21. Ibid, 24.3.1915.
22. F. Jackson, 'Captain N. G. Chavasse', in *Army Medical Services Magazine*, Vol. XXIV, No. 3, 1970, p.2.
23. Bryden McKinnell's Diary, 7.4.1915.
24. NGC to FJC 2.5.1915, BL 6/75.
25. NGC to FJC 2.5.1915, BL 6/76.
26. NGC to FJC 16.5.1915, BL 6/78.
27. NGC to FJC 14.6.1915, BL 6/86.
28. Ministry of Pensions, *Location of Hospitals and Casualty Clearing Stations, BEF, 1914-19*, HMSO 1923, p.12.
29. IV Corps Administrative Orders, in CMC war scrapbook, courtesy Mr J. C. Chavasse.
30. NGC to FJC 16.5.1915, BL 6/78.
31. Hayward, *Liverpool Merchants' Mobile Hospital*, pp.17-29.
32. NGC to Lady Frances Chavasse, 5.5.1915, courtesy Mr J. C. A. Quinney.

9. Hooge

1. Bryden McKinnell's Diary, 28.4.1915
2. NGC to Lady Frances Chavasse, 5.5.1915, courtesy Mr J. C. A. Quinney.
3. McGilchrist, p.40.
4. Sam Moulton's Diary, 6.5.1915.
5. NGC to FJC 23.5.1915, BL 6/81.
6. NGC to FJC 19.4.1915, BL 6/74.
7. NGC to FJC 31.5.1915, BL 6/82.
8. NGC to FJC 24.9.1915, BL 6/118.
9. A. Babington, *For the Sake of Example*, Leo Cooper 1983, p.83.
10. Ibid p.39.
11. Bryden McKinnell's Diary, 17.5.1915.
12. Sam Moulton's Diary, 1.6.1915.
13. NGC to Madeleine Twemlow, 5.6.1915, Liddle Collection.
14. NGC to FJC 14.6.1915, BL 6/86.
15. McGilchrist pp.42-3.
16. Bryden McKinnell's Diary, 14.6.1915.
17. NGC to FJC 20.6.1915, courtesy Mr J. C. Chavasse.
18. NGC to Margaret Twemlow, 24.6.1915, WTHM.
19. McGilchrist pp.48.
20. A. Glendinning to his father, 17.6.1915, Liverpool Scottish Archive.
21. Edmund Herd's Diary, 16.6.1915, KLR Archive.

22. W. G. Bromley, 'Recollections', in *Liverpool Scottish Regimental Gazette*, September 1932.
23. Sam Moulton's Diary, 18.6.1915.
24. McGilchrist p.48.
25. Ibid p.49.
26. Edmund Herd's Diary, 27.6.1915.
27. E. J. Finlay to Sir John Lomax, 22.5.1961, WTHM.
28. *London Gazette* 1916, Vol I, 14.1.1916, p.577.
29. McGilchrist p.49.
30. Ibid p.51.
31. NGC to Cecily Twemlow, 23.7.1915, WTHM.
32. NGC to FJC 18.7.1915, BL 6/95.
33. NGC to FJC 6.8.1915, BL 6/102-3.
34. NGC to FJC 25.7.1915, BL 6/98.
35. W. E. Pennington Album, Liverpool Scottish Archive.
36. NGC to parents, 22.8.1915, BL 6/108.
37. NGC to FJC 1.8.1915, BL 6/101.
38. NGC to FJC 22.8.1915, BL 6/101.
39. NGC to FJC 18.7.1915, BL 6/96.
40. NGC to FJC 16.11.1915, BL 6/126.
41. NGC to FJC 30.8.1915, BL 6/110.
42. Gummer p.53.
43. NGC to FJC 22.10.1916, BL 6/219-20.
44. NGC to parents, 22.8.1915, BL 6/108.

10. A Family Affair

1. Edmund Herd's Diary 30.8.1915.
2. NGC to parents, 17.12.1915, BL 6/136.
3. NGC to parents, 19.9.1915, BL 6/114-15.
4. NGC to parents, 24.9.1915, BL 6/118.
5. NGC to parents, 5.10.1915, BL 6/119.
6. McGilchrist p.60.
7. *Lancet*, 11.12.1915, p.1304.
8. NGC to FJC 28.9.1915; printed copy in Liverpool Scottish Archive.
9. NGC to parents, 5.10.1915, BL 6/119.
10. NGC to parents, 19.10.1915, BL 6/121.
11. *London Gazette, Supplement*, 1.1.1916, p.68.
12. McGilchrist p.59.
13. W. G. Bromley, 'Recollections', in *Liverpool Scottish Regimental Gazette*, September 1931 to April 1939.
14. NGC to parents, 4.12.1915, BL 6/128.

15. F. Jackson, 'Captain N. G. Chavasse', in *Army Medical Services Magazine,* Vol. XXIV, No. 3, 1970.
16. NGC to parents, 26.12.1915, BL 6/143.
17. NGC to DC 17.12,1915, BL 6/140.
18. NGC to EMC 13.11.1915 and 4.12.1915; BL 6/122 and 132.
19. Edmund Herd's Diary, 10.11.1915.
20. NGC to parents, 4.1.1916, BL 6/149; also Edmund Herd's Diary, 1.1.1916.
21. LE 23.10.1979.
22. McGilchrist p.62.
23. NGC to parents, 16.1.1916, BL 6/152.
24. Rugby School Memorial Book, n.d.
25. NGC to Twemlows circa 21.1.1916, Liddle Collection.
26. NGC to EMC circa end February 1916; courtesy Mr J. C. Chavasse.
27. NGC to EMC 10.3.1916; courtesy Mr J. C. Chavasse.
28. Harrow School Scroll of Fame, n.d.
29. NGC to parents, 12.3.1916, BL 6/158.
30. NGC to parents, 28.3.1916, BL 6/162-3.
31. CMC war scrapbook; courtesy Mr J. C. Chavasse.
32. NGC to CMC 27.3.1916, BL 6/164.

11. The Road to Guillemont

1. NGC to parents, 8.4.1916, BL 6/165.
2. NGC to parents, 23.4.1916, BL 6/169.
3. NGC to parents, 3.5.1916, BL 6/173.
4. NGC to parents, 19.5.1916, BL 6/177.
5. NGC to parents, 6.6.1916, BL 6/179.
6. NGC to parents, 11.6.1916, BL 6/181.
7. Lt-Colonel Davidson's Diary, 16.6.1916, Liverpool Scottish Archive.
8. McGilchrist p.68.
9. H. S. Taylor, 'Reminiscences of the Great Year' (unpublished typescript, n.d.) p.5, Liverpool Scottish Archive.
10. NGC to parents, 6.2.1917, BL 6/247.
11. Taylor p.6.
12. McGilchrist p.69.
13. F. Jackson, loc.cit.
14. General R. E. Barnsley to Sir A. Gemmell, 7.5.1956, WTHM.
15. NGC to EMC 13.2.1917, courtesy Mr J. C. Chavasse.
16. Sir Douglas Haig's Despatch of 23.12.1916, *London Gazette, Supplement,* 29.12.1916.
17. NGC to FJC 1.7.1916, BL 6/186.

18. NGC to Cecily Twemlow, 7.7.1916, WTHM.
19. NGC to FJC 16.8.1915, BL 6/106.
20. Edmund Herd's 'Addendum' to his Diary, dated 1939, KLR Archive.
21. NGC to QMS Scott-Macfie, 6.11.1916, IWM.
22. NGC to parents, 12.7.1916, BL 6/187.
23. Louis Maude to FBC 8.5.1916, courtesy Mr E. F. J. Chavasse.
24. NGC to parents, 23.7.1916, BL 6/190.
25. FBC to FJC 3.8.1916, BL 2/141.
26. NGC to parents, 30.7.1916, BL 6/191.
27. NGC to parents, 7.8.1916, BL 6/194.
28. McGilchrist pp.75-6.
29. Ibid pp.77-80.
30. Sir Douglas Haig's Despatch of 23.12.1916, *London Gazette, Supplement,* 29.12.1916.
31. NGC to parents, 11.8.1916, BL 6/197.
32. BMJ Vol. II 1916, 26.8.1916, p.304.
33. *Daily Sketch* 22.9.1916.
34. NGC to parents, 14.8.1916, BL 6/198.
35. Ibid.
36. F. Jackson, loc.cit.
37. W. G. Bromley, 'Recollections', p.51.
38. Edmund Herd's Diary, 9.8.1916.
39. NGC to parents, 20.8.1916, BL 6/201-2.
40. NGC to parents, 28.8.1916, BL 6/203.
41. NGC to parents, 7.9.1916, BL 6/204.
42. NGC to parents, 26.9.1916, BL 6/211.
43. NGC to parents, 19.9.1916, BL 6/207.
44. Lord Derby to FJC 4.10.1916, BL 2/61.
45. NGC to parents, 16.10.1916, BL 6/213.
46. Ibid.

12. For Valour

1. *London Gazette,* 26.10.1916, p.10394.
2. LDPM 27.10.1916.
3. Ibid.
4. Ibid.
5. Gallagher Ltd, 7th series of 25, No. 159, 1917.
6. LDPM 31.10.1916.
7. FGRC to EMC 6.10.1916, courtesy Mr J. C. Chavasse.
8. *Register of the Victoria Cross*, This England Books, 1988.
9. NGC to QMS Scott-Macfie, 6.11.1916, IWM.

10. NGC to Margaret Twemlow, 23.11.1916, WTHM.
11. NGC to T. Woodsend, President of RSHL, Minutes of General Committee Meeting, 5.1.1917, LRO.
12. FJC to CMC, quoted in Gummer p.58.
13. MLC to parents, quoted in Gummer p.58.
14. In the possession of Mr J. C. A. Quinney; shown on dust-jacket of this book.
15. NGC to parents, 15.11.1916, BL 6/224.
16. Ibid.
17. NGC to parents, 28.11.1916, BL 6/228-30.
18. *Official History, Medical Services: Diseases of the War*, Vol. II, p.119.
19. Graves, p.103-4.
20. *Official History*, op. cit. pp.123-30.
21. NGC to parents, 19.12.1916, BL 6/239.
22. Ibid.
23. NGC to parents, 10.1.1917, BL 6/243.
24. *Official History, Medical Services, Hygiene of the War*, Vol. I (1923) p.312.
25. NGC to parents, 19.9.1915, BL 6/116.
26. NGC to parents, 19.12.1916, BL 6/239.
27. NGC to parents, 28.11.1916, BL 6/231.
28. NGC to parents, 12.12.1916, courtesy Mr J. C. Chavasse.
29. NGC to DC 25.10.1916, BL 6/222-3.
30. NGC to DC 12.12.1916, BL 6/234.
31. NGC to parents, 19.12.1916, BL 6/239-40.
32. FJC to FBC 6.4.1917; courtesy Mr E. F. J. Chavasse.
33. McGilchrist pp.103-4.
34. Edmund Herd's Diary, 24.12.1916.
35. McGilchrist p.104.
36. Quoted in Lancelot p.199.
37. NGC to EMC 11.10.1916, courtesy Mr J. C. Chavasse.
38. NGC to parents, 6.2.1917, BL 6/247.
39. Quoted in Gummer p.59.
40. FJC to FBC 16.2.1917, courtesy Mr E. F. J. Chavasse.
41. CMC war scrapbook, courtesy Mr J. C. Chavasse.
42. Information courtesy Mr J. C. A. Quinney.
43. NGC to EMC 13.2.1917; courtesy Mr J. C. Chavasse.

13. The Salient Again

1. F. Jackson, op, cit. p.4.
2. H. S. Taylor, Liverpool Scottish, in a letter to the author, May 1990.

3. J. Putkowski and J. Sykes, *Shot At Dawn*, Wharncliffe 1989; revised edition Leo Cooper 1992, p.287.
4. NGC to FJC 13.1.1915, BL 6/46.
5. McGilchrist p.103.
6. NGC to parents, 25.2.1917, BL 6/250.
7. NGC to EMC 7.5.1917, courtesy Mr J. C. Chavasse.
8. NGC to parents, 14.3.1917, BL 6/252.
9. NGC to parents, 27.3.1917, BL 6/258 and 260.
10. NGC to parents, 30.5.1917, BL 6/273-5.
11. NGC to parents, 3.6.1917, BL 6/280-81.
12. NGC to parents, 7.9.1916, BL 6/204.
13. NGC to parents, 30.5.1917, BL 6/276.
14. *London Gazette*, Vol. II 1917, p.5323.
15. NGC to parents, 20.5.1917, BL 6/271.
16. The Revd Mathieson Forson to FJC, 11.8.1917, BL 7/12.
17. NGC to parents, 25.6.1917, BL 6/285.
18. Original poster is in Liverpool Scottish Archive.
19. EMC to FBC 18.6.1917, courtesy E. F. J. Chavasse.
20. NGC to parents, 15.6.1917, BL 6/283-4.
21. NGC to parents, 25.6.1917, BL 6/289.
22. W. G. Bromley, 'Recollections', op. cit. p.26.
23. NGC to FJC 28.1.1915, BL 6/51.
24. BMJ 27.1.1917.
25. NGC to parents, 6.6.1916, BL 6/179.
26. NGC to parents, 16.11.1915, BL 6/126.
27. T. H. Bickerton, *The Medical History of Liverpool*, John Murray 1920, p.261.
28. Quoted in Watson, op.cit. p.157.
29. *The Times* 4.6.1917.
30. NGC to Robert Jones, quoted in *Orthopaedic Illustrated*, Spring 1964, p.4.
31. J. Terraine, *Douglas Haig, the Educated Soldier*, Leo Cooper 1990, p.256.

14. Passchendaele

1. Wilson p.462.
2. G. Powell, *Plumer, the Soldier's General*, Leo Cooper 1990, p.191.
3. Field-Marshal Sir Douglas Haig's Despatch of 25.12.1917, *London Gazette, Supplement*, 4.1.1918.
4. H. S. Taylor, Liverpool Scottish 1915-19, letter to the author 25.4.1990.
5. NGC to parents, 25.6.1917, BL 6/288-9.
6. McGilchrist p.112.

8. EMC to FBC 18.6.1917, courtesy Mr E. F. J. Chavasse.
9. 17/KLR War Diary, KLR Archive.
10. EMC to CMC 9.7.1917, BL 13/1-2.
11. FJC to FBC 9.7.1917, courtesy Mr E. F. J. Chavasse.
12. FJC to FBC 10.7.1917, courtesy Mr E. F. J. Chavasse.
13. LDPM 12.7.1917.
14. A. J. Draper to FJC, 7.7.1917, courtesy Mr. E. F. J. Chavasse.
15. British Red Cross to LMC, n.d., courtesy Mr E. F. J. Chavasse.
16. NGC to FBC 16.7.1917, courtesy Mr E. F. J. Chavasse.
17. FJC to NGC 24.7.1917, BL 6/293.
18. McGilchrist p.117.
19. Ibid.
20. KLR Archive.
21. War Diary 1/8 KLR (Liverpool Irish), 24.7.1917.
22. H. S. Jeudwine to All Ranks, quoted in War Diary 1/8 KLR, 28.7.1917.
23. Coop pp.48-9.
24. W. G. Bromley, 'Recollections', p.69.
25. Herd, 'Addendum' to Diary, dated 1939, KLR Archive.
26. W. G. Bromley, 'Recollections', p.73.
27. Ibid p.71.
28. Coop p.50.
29. The Revd H. Maddox to FJC, 25.5.1922, BL 7/24; and H. S. Taylor, letter to the author, 25.4.1990.
30. CMC sermon reported in *Birmingham Post*, 1.7.1935.
31. FBC to FJC 8.8.1917, courtesy Mr E. F. J. Chavasse.
32. W. G. Bromley, 'Recollections', p.72.
33. *The Englishman*, Calcutta, 2.12.1929.
34. Edmund Herd's Diary, 1.8.1917.
35. H. Willink to his mother, August 1917; quoted in Gummer p.63.
36. McGilchrist p.128.
37. LDPM 10.8.1954.
38. Colonel J. R. Davidson to FJC 2.8.1917, courtesy Mr E. F. J. Chavasse.
39. Edmund Herd, 'Addendum' to Diary, dated 1939.
40. Bishop's letter, *Liverpool Diocesan Gazette* Vol. XV, No. 177 September 1917, pp.97-8; and undated press cutting, courtesy Mr J. C. A. Quinney.
41. Davidson, loc.cit.
42. Ministry of Pensions, *Location of Hospitals and Casualty Clearing Stations, BEF 1914-19*, pp.4 and 18.
43. Major-General R. E. Barnsley, letter to the Editor, *Daily Telegraph*, 11.9.1958.
44. Davidson to FJC, loc.cit.

44. Davidson to FJC, loc.cit.
45. FJC to FBC 5.8.1917, courtesy Mr E. F. J. Chavasse.
46. EMC to FBC 7.8.1917, courtesy Mr E. F. J. Chavasse.
47. EJC to FBC 8.8.1917, courtesy Mr E. F. J. Chavasse.
48. FJC to NGC 3.8.1917, BL 6/294.

15. 'This Devoted and Gallant Officer...'

1. FJC to FBC 10.8.1917, courtesy Mr E. F. J. Chavasse.
2. FBC to FJC 8.8.1917, courtesy Mr E. F. J. Chavasse.
3. I. B. Leedam to FJC, n.d. BL 7/21.
4. FBC to FJC, loc.cit.
5. I. B. Leedam, loc.cit.
6. McGilchrist p.126.
7. Edmund Herd's Diary, 6.8.1917.
8. FBC to FJC, loc.cit.
9. FJC to FBC 16.8.1917, courtesy Mr E. F. J. Chavasse.
10. King George V to FJC 11.8.1917, BL 7/6-7.
11. Major-General H. S. Jeudwine to FJC 9.8.1917, BL 7/4-5.
12. Brigadier-General L. G. Wilkinson to FJC 11.8.1917, BL 7/11.
13. *Liverpool Courier*, 11.8.1917.
14. LDPM 16.8.1917.
15. BMJ 18.8.1917.
16. *Liverpool Diocesan Gazette*, September 1917.
17. Claude Chavasse to his mother, 15.8.1917, courtesy Mrs G. McCrachan.
18. Dorothea Foster-Carter to Mrs. Francis, 23.8.1917, courtesy Miss L. Foster-Carter.
19. FJC to CMC 14.8.1917, BL 12/232.
20. MLC to CMC 13.8.1917, BL 13/6.
21. *London Gazette* 1917, Vol. III, 25.3.1917, p.8807.
22. FJC to FBC 27.8.1917, courtesy Mr E. F. J. Chavasse.
23. CMC photograph albums, courtesy Mr J. C. Chavasse.
24. Quoted in Gummer p.64.
25. MLC to FBC 19.8.1917, courtesy Mr E. F. J. Chavasse.
26. FJC to FBC 27.8.1917, courtesy Mr E. F. J. Chavasse.
27. *Bromsgrove, Droitwich & Redditch Weekly Messenger*, 18.8.1917.
28. This date appears on Esme's passport; courtesy Mr J. C. A. Quinney.
29. Order of Service, courtesy Mr E. F. J. Chavasse.
30. FJC to FBC 27.8.1917, courtesy Mr E. F. J. Chavasse.
31. LDPM 30.8.1917.
32. Ibid.
33. EMC to FBC 31.8.1917, courtesy Mr E. F. J. Chavasse.

35. FBC to EMC 26.8.1917, courtesy Mr J. C. Chavasse.
36. EMC to FBC 31.8.1917, courtesy Mr E. F. J. Chavasse.
37. FJC to FBC 1.9.1917, courtesy Mr E. F. J. Chavasse.
38. *London Gazette, Supplement,* 9.1.1918, p.594.
39. Lord Derby to FJC 5.9,1917, BL 7/20.
40. FJC to FBC 9.9.1917, courtesy Mr E. F. J. Chavasse.
41. FJC to FBC 13.9.1917, courtesy Mr E. F. J. Chavasse.
42. *London Gazette,* 14.9.1917, p.953.

16. Epilogue

1. 1/8 Bn KLR War Diary, Liverpool Museum Archive.
2. Coop pp.54-5.
3. Field-Marshal Sir Douglas Haig's Despatch of 12.12.1917, *London Gazette, Supplement,* 8.1.1918.
4. FJC to CMC 9.3.1918, BL 12/237.
5. Gummer p.66.
6. Quoted in Gummer p.66.
7. Mrs Molly Upham to the author, 16.7.1990.
8. Supplement to BMJ, 25.1.1919.
9. BMJ 26.7.1941, p.141; and *Lancet* 4.8.1941, p.174.
10. Westlake p.212.
11. *London Gazette* 1945 Vol. I, 11.1.1945, p.3341.
12. John, chapter 15, verse 13.
13. E. Gibson and G. K. Ward, *Courage Remembered: The Commonwealth War Graves Commission 1914-1918, 1939-1945,* HMSO 1989, p.176.
14. Canon S. Gummer to the author, July 1990.
15. Mrs M. Knight to the author, February 1990.

INDEX

258